Existentia Africana

Existentia Africana

Understanding Africana Existential Thought

Lewis R. Gordon

Routledge
New York and London

Published in 2000 by

Routledge
270 Madison Ave,
New York NY 10016

Published in Great Britain by

Routledge
2 Park Square, Milton Park,
Abingdon, Oxon, OX14 4RN

Transferred to Digital Printing 2009

Library of Congress Cataloging-in-Publication Data
Gordon, Lewis R. (Lewis Ricardo), 1962–
    Existentia Africana : understanding Africana
    existential thought / Lewis R. Gordon.
       p.   cm. — (Africana thought)
    Includes bibliographical references and index.
    ISBN 0-415-92643-2 (hardcover : alk. paper)
    ISBN 0-415-92644-0 (pbk. : alk. paper)
      1. Afro-American philosophy.   2. Existentialism.
    I. Title.   II. Series.
    B944.A37 G67   2000
    142'.78'08996—DC21   99-047909

Publisher's Note
The publisher has gone to great lengths to ensure the quality of this
reprint but points out that some imperfections in the original may be apparent.

To William R. Jones

Contents

What indeed could be more grotesque than an educated man, a man with a diploma, having in consequence understood a good many things, among others that "it was unfortunate to be a Negro," proclaiming that his skin was beautiful and that the "*big black hole*" was a source of truth. Neither the mulattoes nor the Negroes understood this delirium. The mulattoes because they had escaped from the night, the Negroes because they aspired to get away from it. Two centuries of white truth proved this man to be wrong. He must be mad, for it was unthinkable that he could be right.

—Frantz Fanon, "West Indians and Africans"

Because it is a systematic negation of the other person and a furious determination to deny the other person attributes of humanity, colonialism forces the people it dominates to ask themselves the question constantly: "In reality, who am I?"

—Frantz Fanon, *The Wretched of the Earth*

Your own Truth Commission. Lights. Cameras. Notoriety. Days upon days of probing our insides. We show our insides gladly. All we ask is that you not eat them.

—Monifa Love, *Freedom in the Dismal*

Preface, with Acknowledgments

This book is dedicated to William R. Jones, professor emeritus of African American Studies and Religious Studies at Florida State University at Tallahassee. Prior to his work at Florida State, Jones taught philosophy of religion at the Yale Divinity School. It was during that period that the first edition of his classic work in Africana religious thought, *Is God a White Racist? A Preamble to Black Theology*, appeared. The work challenged black liberation thinkers to take seriously the possibility that the signs and symbols of the Western religions upon which they depended may harbor the seeds of their destruction. Instead, Jones counseled, a liberation project stands a good chance of meeting its goals through an appreciation of human agency in the formation of radical, historical change. Old-time religion may have helped black people survive; liberation, however, requires a more radical path.

Jones took his own counsel seriously. For him, there was, and continues to be, no point in intellectual work if there is no commitment to the values it represents. It is the intellectual's task to take on the struggle over ideas. The importance of that task is evident whenever we realize the revolutionary impact of ideas. Ideas are part of the creative movement of social change. Without new ideas, we would continue to effect more of the same; we would continue simply to change players without changing games.

Bill Jones earned his doctorate in the philosophy of religion with a Brown University thesis on Jean-Paul Sartre's critical methodology. This work was written in the 1960s during the Black Power movement and the Vietnam War. At the heart of Jones's analysis was the conviction that oppression must be overcome, but no such overcoming can emerge without a critical understanding of human reality. Jones emerged, in other words, as an existential revolutionary. He took very seriously the existential insight that struggle involves negotiating the relationship between institutions and situated human beings. In 1974, this commitment took the form of "Crisis in Philosophy: The Black Presence," his urgent call for the development of a black professional philosophical community, which was published by The Proceedings and Addresses of the American Philosophical Association. His efforts motivated the young Lucius Outlaw, Leonard Harris, and several scholars of philosophy in the Mid-Atlantic region to organize discussion groups, thus leading eventually to the founding of the American Philosophical Association Committee on the Status of Blacks in Philosophy. That committee has since had a great influence on the path from black philosophy to Afro-American philosophy to African American philosophy. In addition, through dialogue with international scholars with similar concerns, African philosophy made its way into the American and European curricula, and dialogue with the Caribbean led to contemporary discussions of and in Africana philosophy.

In the meantime, Jones continued his institutional work. He organized special fellowships to increase the number of graduate students of color in the American academy; he continued his research on oppression and developing effective means of combating it; and he worked tenaciously in the antiapartheid struggle. For him, apartheid anywhere was a threat to humanity everywhere. That he lives with this conviction in the United States means that such struggle continues.

Jones is the living embodiment of the convergence of effective radical politics with existential humanistic commitments. Liberation, he argues, makes no sense without the understanding and recognition of the humanity in those who are to be liberated. As well, we should recognize the failure of such realization in ourselves and others.

I came across Jones's work when I was a graduate student at Yale University in the early 1990s. In his work, I found a kindred spirit. Some years later, when I had organized a conference in honor of Frantz Fanon, perhaps the greatest Africana existential thinker, Jones contacted me to see if he could participate. The modesty of this giant is an aspect of the man that never ceases to surprise his admirers. I had not realized how much I admired the man until I found myself talking to him on the phone and clearly overwhelmed with joy at his request. Jones came to the conference as the keynote speaker, and Purdue University awarded this great man the African American Studies and Research Center Award for Outstanding Contribution to Philosophy and the African American Community. I have been fortunate enough to see Bill on several occasions since then, including his retirement celebration, which went from seven in the evening till one the next morning. So many people came to celebrate this wonderful man—including state, municipal, and federal officials, by way of declaring a William Jones Day and a William Jones Week—that it was clear to me that the love and respect I have for Bill was shared, indeed, by a large community of people in and out of the academy.

Bill always had faith in the importance of Africana thought. It is with that continued love and respect in mind that this volume is dedicated to him.

Several of the essays in this volume are expansions of essays that have previously appeared elsewhere. Chapter 1 is based on the introduction to Existence in Black (1997). Chapter 2 is based on an article I wrote for Small Axe (1998). Chapter 3 is based on my contribution to Frederick Douglass: A Critical Reader, edited by Frank Kirkland and Bill Lawson (1999). Chapter 4, is an expansion of an article on Du Bois that appeared in The Annals of the American Academy of

Social and Political Science (2000) and chapter 5 is an expansion of an article that appeared in *Sophia: A Journal of Philosophy* (1996), which is published in the Philippines. Chapter 6 appeared in *Men's Bodies, Men's Gods: Images of Masculinity in a (Post-) Christian Culture*, edited by Björn Krondorfer (1995) and chapter 7 is based on an article that appeared in the *Journal of Religious Ethics* (1999), entitled "Pan-Africanism and African-American Liberation in a Postmodern World."

That said, I would like to thank Paget Henry for his encouragement and friendship over the years, and I would like to thank my wonderful graduate students for reading through various stages of this project: Guy Foster, Renea Henry, Brian Locke, Laurie Mengel, Claudia Milian, Zachary Morgan, Rowan Ricardo Phillips, Renee Levant, Neil Roberts, Shahara Drew, and Stefan Wheelock. Marilyn Nissim-Sabat deserves special thanks for the detailed critical commentary she provided on an early draft of this work; Anthony Bogues deserves thanks, as well, for his critical evaluation of an early version. And, of course, thanks are here extended to Jane Comaroff Gordon, Mathieu Gordon, Jenny Gordon, and 'Sula Comaroff Gordon for their love and, simply, for being here.

one

Africana Philosophy of Existence

The intellectual history of the last quarter of the twentieth century has been marked by, among many developments, a growing influence of Africana thought in the U.S. academy. *Africana thought*, as I will be using it in this book, refers to an area of thought that focuses on theoretical questions raised by struggles over ideas in African cultures and their hybrid and creolized forms in Europe, North America, Central and South America, and the Caribbean. Africana thought also refers to the set of questions raised by the historical project of conquest and colonization that has emerged since 1492 and the subsequent struggles for emancipation that continue to this day. These latter questions and struggles have been characterized by Enrique Dussel, the Latin American philosopher, historian, and theologian, as those that reflect modernity's "underside." They are marked by the contrast between how the modern is often characterized in the Western academy— through, say, philosophical treatment of *ideas*, from René Descartes to Immanuel Kant, or perhaps Michel Foucault's locating of modernity in nineteenth-century European *thought*—and how it has been lived by those on its periphery. The periphery, what Dussel means by *underside* and what Gayatri Spivak has called the "subaltern," regard Western modernity more as a march of sword and Bible than reason and moral persuasion. C. L. R. James, in his classic, award-winning *The Black Jacobins*, summed up this perspective well when he wrote:

> Christopher Columbus landed first in the New World at the island of San Salvador, and after praising God enquired urgently for gold. The natives, Red Indians, were peaceable and friendly and directed him to Haiti, a large island (nearly as large as Ireland), rich, they said, in the yellow metal. He sailed to Haiti. One of his ships being wrecked, the Haitian Indians helped him so willingly that very little was lost and of the articles which they brought on shore not one was stolen.
>
> The Spaniards, the most advanced Europeans of their day, annexed the island, called it Hispaniola, and took the backward natives under their protection. They introduced Christianity, forced labour in mines, murder, rape, bloodhounds, strange diseases, and artificial famine (by the destruction of cultivation to starve the rebellious). These and other requirements of the higher civilization reduced the native population from an estimated half-a-million, perhaps a million, to 60,000 in 15 years (pp. 3–4).

James's narrative then examines the kidnapping of Africans, the development of the slave trade in the Caribbean, and the Haitian revolution, which ironically included French Enlightenment appeals to rights and fraternity in addition to West African humanism. Although works by thinkers like James exemplify a highly critical position on Western modernity, their exemplification is ironic. This is because they face the lived, existential reality of the day-to-day situation of their denied humanity and the historical irony of their emergence in a world that denied their historicity. For example, G. W. F. Hegel denied that black people had (or were capable of having) any historical significance, but subsequently black theorists (including James) addressed both the historical transformation of Africans into blacks and the dialectical struggle to transform the historical moment of global conquest into a period of freedom in Hegelian and Marxist terms. Such thinkers find themselves in a situation akin to Caliban's struggle with Prospero's colonization of his island in William Shakespeare's *Tempest*. Thinking through the periphery, the underside, the subaltern could as well be characterized as "Caliban studies," if we will, where the focus is study through which Prospero's language can be decentered.

Africana thought, as a form of Caliban studies, raises ironic self-reflective, metatheoretical questions. Think, for example, of the importance of writing as a form of intellectual production. Because of the emancipatory aims of Africana thought (as a form of Caliban studies), the activity of writing ascends here to the level of praxis. Although many of the major contributors to Africana thought are gifted orators who emerge from strong, so-called oral traditions (think, for example, of David Walker, Maria Stewart, Frederick Douglass, Alexander Crummell, Edward Blyden, Anna Julia Cooper, Marcus Garvey, Aimé Césaire, Martin Luther King Jr., Malcolm X, Kwame Ture, Angela Y. Davis, bell hooks, Cornel West), the theoretical explorations that dominate today's formulations emerge through engagement with writing, including orations brought to inscription. Yet, like Caliban, modern Africana thinkers' use of Prospero's language is infused with forces of magic: They represent disruptions and rupture. We could imagine an alternative reading of Caliban as a being who had his mother's knowledge, which he could fuse with Prospero's knowledge. This fusion could offer what James has characterized as "creative universality," that which, because it always raises *possibility*, constitutes freedom. Writing is one among many activities with creative universal potential, and it is the theorist's work not only to articulate this in the body of literature left behind by prior theorists, but also to draw out creative dimensions for subsequent generations, the effect of which, in each stage, is the complex symbiosis of epistemological, historical, and ontological possibilities. As Sylvia Wynter, echoing Africana and other Caliban theorists who have preceded her, has articulated this project in her wonderful essay "Is 'Development' a Purely Empirical Concept or also Teleological?," it's the liberation writer's effort to contribute to the construction of new forms of life.

We have, then, a symbiotic dualism. On the one hand, there is the identity question. *Who*, in a word, are Africana peoples? And then there is the teleological question: For *what* ought such people be striving? This latter concern often takes a liberatory form: *How* might the peoplehood of dehumanized people be affirmed? There are also metatheoretical identity and teleological concerns: What is Africana thought and what should be its methodology? All these questions have been struggled with throughout the nineteenth, and most of the twentieth, centuries. In the nineteenth century, they were perhaps best articulated by W. E. B. Du Bois, whose ideas in "Conservation of the Races" and "The Study of the Negro Problems" forcefully reemerge at the dawn of the twentieth century in *The Souls of Black Folk*, which examined these trajectories through race (identity), policy (emancipation), and a humanistic sociology. A humanistic sociology, in Du Boisian terms, meant a way of studying oppressed people without denying their humanity. Africana philosophical thought has struggled through Du Bois's concerns throughout the rest of this century. Alain Locke, for example, queried the possibilities of a "New Negro" while he tried to develop a pluralistic axiology that could address the lived reality of values. The lived reality of values was needed to position the centrality of an "inner life" of black folk. This concern was also taken up by Frantz Fanon, whose search for a "postcolonial," "postracist" society led to his articulation of the lived experience of blacks in the face of sociogenic sedimentations of their identity and political possibilities. For Fanon, blacks are locked in a situation that demands a struggle with social structures that make ethical demands on transformation futile, if not irrelevant and silly. The black (Caliban) raises too many anxieties over the goodness of the modern systems he occupies. As Du Bois argued that the U.S. black faces both the justice and injustice of American society through the two souls the black exemplifies—being an American and being America's uniquely *American racial outsider*—Fanon realized that the more he asserted his membership in Western civilization the more he was pathologized, for the system's affirmation depends on its denial of ever having illegitimately excluded him; he is, as in theodicy, a reminder of injustice in a system that is supposed to have been wholly good.

Africana philosophy, especially in its African American variety, has continued Du Bois's, Locke's, Fanon's, and James's legacy through works that are beginning to have an impact outside of Africana philosophy. Du Bois, James, and Fanon, for example, are not only taught in Africana studies courses. Fanon's writings are now taught in literature, cultural studies, political science, anthropology, and sociology programs and departments, and his influence on the development of postcolonial studies and philosophies of liberation and liberation theology is without question. Edward Said's *Orientalism* and Paulo Freire's *Pedagogy of the Oppressed* owe an extraordinary debt to his ideas. There are, in addition, contemporary voices with field-transcending influence. Cornel West and bell hooks, for instance, are two Africana thinkers with extraordinary influence in the contemporary U.S. academy. West's and hooks's writings are rooted squarely in the Africana humanistic traditions. West in the 1980s, as is well known, had taken up identity and teleological questions through an effort to synthesize pragmatism, Christianity, and Marxism with African American humanism to present a prophetic appeal to "deliverance" (emancipation). In his later writings he has moved away from the Marxist element of his trinity toward a form of radical democratic liberalism, primarily because of his position on the identity question—that it is *American* society that he is attempting to transform, which requires an explication of what is supposedly the best of its tradition. For hooks, it has been a project of postmodern oppositional politics rooted in a pedagogy of liberation (drawn from her mentor, Paulo Freire, and, hence, from Fanon). It is, however, in cultural studies that West and hooks have had more influence than in any other area outside of Africana studies. There, the methodological question of how Caliban should be conducting Calibanistic thought comes to the fore.

Africana existential philosophy is a branch of Africana philosophy and black philosophies of existence. By *black philosophy* what is meant is the philosophical currents that emerged from the question of blackness. I distinguish Africana philosophy and black philosophies because the latter relate to a terrain that is broader than Africana communities. Not all black people are of African descent: indigenous Australians, whose lived reality is that of being a black people, are an example. Similarly, problems of blackness are but a part of Africana philosophy. The divide is not only philosophical—where black philosophy's normative and descriptive concerns may be narrower than Africana philosophy's—but also cultural: although there are Africana cultures, it is not clear what "black culture" is. There are black communities whose cultural formations show a convergence of many cultural formations—from Africa, Europe, Asia, Australia, and the Americas—but there the focus may be Africana, or on something more than race. That being so, the turn to Africana carries a similar divide. In Africana philosophy, there is focus on the unique features of Africana cultural experience on the one hand, and the reality that Africana people are a black people and hence are impacted by the significance of race and racism on the other.

What is Africana existential philosophy? Perhaps its features will best be understood through an anecdote about my putting together a project some years ago. In 1994, I issued a call for papers on black existential philosophy. Responses ranged from discussions of the African roots of black existential philosophy to the liberating struggles of blacks in a racially hostile world. There were, however, a few mysterious abstracts. There is no black existential philosophy, these argued, since existentialism is a European phenomenon addressing European experience. Looking for thought, from Søren Kierkegaard to Simone de Beauvoir, one would find more bourgeois *Angst* than material conditions of black misery. To this criticism, I wrote letters with the following retort: The body of literature that constitutes European existentialism is but one continent's response to a set of problems that date from the moment human beings faced problems of anguish and despair. That conflicts over responsibility and anxiety, over life affirmation and suicidal nihilism, preceded Kierkegaardian formulations of fear and trembling raised questions beyond Eurocentric attachment to a narrow body of literature. Existential philosophy addresses problems of freedom, anguish, dread, responsibility, embodied agency, sociality, and liberation; it addresses these problems through a focus on the human condition.

The human condition occasions many questions, but two recurring ones are: "What are we?" and "What shall we do?" These are also questions of identity and moral action. They are questions, further, of ontological and, as we earlier observed, teleological significance, for the former addresses being and the latter addresses what to become—in a word, *purpose*. Such questions can be further radicalized through reflection on their preconditions: how are such questions, in a word, possible?

In my replies to the skeptics, I asked them if slaves did not wonder about freedom; suffer anguish; notice paradoxes of responsibility; have concerns of agency, tremors of broken sociality, or a burning desire for liberation. Do we not find struggles with these matters in the traditional West African proverbs and folktales that the slaves brought with them to the New World? And more, even if we do not turn to the historical experiences of slaves of African descent and the body of cultural resources indigenous to the African continent, there are also the various dialogical encounters between twentieth-century Africana theorists and European and Euro-American theorists.

Problems of existence address the human confrontation with freedom and degradation. In the nineteenth century, these concerns took similar and different forms on both sides of the Atlantic. In Europe, there were both anxiety over the future and boredom over passions that were dying. In North America, there were other concerns. For white America there was a present and a future to conquer. There wasn't much room for boredom, and since it was self-assured, there seemed little room for anxiety. To find anxiety and dread, one needed to look beyond white America, and since North America wasn't populated solely by white people, finding these sources of concern wasn't difficult. As Anna Julia Cooper's *A Voice from the South*, W. E. B. Du Bois's *Souls of Black Folk*, Ralph Ellison's

Going into the Territory, Frantz Fanon's Black Skin, White Masks, and Toni Morrison's Playing in the Dark have shown us, anxiety, dread, and despair were on the modern world's underside, in the blackness that it often sought to hide in its theoretical and aesthetic moments of self-representation. Few topics have brought on New World anxiety more than these questions of color. Such questions continue to forge the divide in modern loyalties. Who knows how many interracial friendships have fallen prey to those moments of candor?

So, racial problems serve a dominating role. In Africana existential philosophy, this reality has meant detailed explorations of this dominating factor in the lived experience of Africana people. It has meant an exploration of their lived experience of blackness.

The racial problematic for Africana people is twofold. On the one hand, it is the question of exclusion in the face of an ethos of assimilation. On the other hand, there is the complex confrontation with the fact of such exclusion in a world that portends commitment to rational resolutions of evil. With regard to this latter concern, we could paraphrase Du Bois, from The Souls of Black Folk and Darkwater: What does it mean to be a problem, and what is to be understood by black suffering?

These questions of problematic existence and suffering animate the theoretical dimensions of black intellectual existential productions. It is what signals the question of liberation on one level and the critique of traditional (read: European) ontological claims on another. Together they inaugurate Africana liberation thought and Africana critical race theory. The former finds its fountainhead most poignantly in Frederick Douglass. His answer, in 1857, was straightforward: "The whole history of the progress of human liberty shows that all concessions yet made to her august claims, have been born of earnest struggle. This struggle may be a moral one, or it may be a physical one, and it may be both moral and physical, but it must be a struggle. Power concedes nothing without demand. It never did and it never will."

The latter ontological question was examined by many philosophers and social critics of African descent in the nineteenth century, including such well-known and diverse figures as Martin

Delany, Maria Stewart, Anna Julia Cooper, and (early) Du Bois. It was not until the 1940s, however, that a self-avowed existential examination of these issues emerged, ironically through the work of a European philosopher—namely, Jean-Paul Sartre.

Sartre stands as an unusual catalyst in the history of black existential philosophy. He serves as a link between Richard Wright and Frantz Fanon (undoubtedly the twentieth century's two most influential Africana existentialist "men of letters") and the historical forces that came into play for the ascendence of European philosophy of existence in the American academy. These forces provided a context for the academic work of Africana philosophers such as William R. Jones (who wrote his dissertation on Sartre), Noel Manganyi (who produced two books heavily influenced by Sartre's existential phenomenology of the body), Angela Y. Davis (who studied French existential thought as an undergraduate), and Anthony Bogues (whose path from theology to existential Marxism emerged from engagements with the writings of Sartre). Other black academic philosophers who have been influenced by Sartre's work, by way of either Sartre himself or philosophers like Frantz Fanon or Maurice Merleau-Ponty, also include Robert Birt, Bernard Boxill, Tommy Lott, Thomas Slaughter, Percy Mabogo More, Naomi Zack, and the present author.[1]

It would, however, be an error to construct Africana academic existential philosophy as a fundamentally Sartrean or European-based phenomenon. For although there are Africana philosophers who have been influenced by both Sartre and European thought, it would nevertheless be fallacious to assume that that influence functions as the cause instead of the opportunity. Africana philosophers already have a reason to raise existential questions of liberation and questions of identity, as we've already argued, by virtue of racial oppression—oppression manifested most vividly in the Atlantic and East Indian slave trades and the European colonization of the African continent. What those events brought about was not only a period of intense suffering for black peoples, but also the hegemonic symbolic order of Western civilization itself, a symbolic order whose "place" for "the black," if we will, has been fundamentally negative since the Middle Ages and antiquity. There is much debate on this issue, especially in light of postmodern scholarship that locates the genesis of such phenomena in the modern era. The problem is that there are texts from the Middle Ages and antiquity that refer not only to blacks, but also to blacks in very negative terms, as argued by Eulalio Baltazar in *The Dark Center*. Africana philosophers' choice of European thinkers through whom to consider these questions is, therefore, already existentially situated. To place European thinkers as cause would be to place the proverbial cart before the horse.

There is, however, a distinction that can here be borne in mind. I regard *existentialism*—the popularly named ideological movement— as a fundamentally European historical phenomenon. It is, in effect, the history of European literature that bears that name. On the other hand, we can regard *philosophies of existence*—the specialized term that I sometimes call *existential philosophies*—as philosophical questions premised upon concerns of freedom, anguish, responsibility, embodied agency, sociality, and liberation. Philosophies of existence are marked by a centering of what is often known as the *situation* of questioning or inquiry itself. Another term for situation is the lived context of concern. Implicit in the existential demand for recognizing the situation or lived context of Africana peoples' being-in-the-world is the question of value raised by the people who live that situation. A slave's situation can only be understood, for instance, through recognizing the fact that a slave experiences it; it is to regard the slave as a perspective in the world.

Given our conception of philosophy of existence, it is clear that the history of Africana philosophy—at least from David Walker's *Appeal to All Colored Citizens of the World* to Cornel West's Kierkegaardian call for keeping faith and Toni Morrison's tragic questions of identity and ethical paradox in the Present Age (in both her *Playing in the Dark* and *Beloved*)—has its own unique set of existential questions. The same applies to the African and Afro-Caribbean wings of Africana thought, as we see in Kwame Gyekye's discussion of Akan humanism in his *Essay on African Philosophy*; Tsenay Serequeberhan's call for an existential hermeneutics of Africana historico-political reality in his *Hermeneutics of African Philosophy*; and Paget Henry's search for Africana concerns with agency in African conceptions of predestiny and the Caribbean poetic and phenomenological tradition in his *Caliban's Reason*. We find a constant posing of the teleological question of black liberation, the ontological question of agency, and the question of black identity in the midst of an antiblack world. The irony is that, as Fanon has shown in *Black Skin, White Masks*, one cannot in critical good faith raise the question of the black without raising these accompanying existential questions.

This is not to say that Africana philosophy is existential in the sense of reducing it to a philosophy of existence. It is, instead, to say that the impetus of Africana philosophy, when the question of the black or the situation of black people is raised, has an existential impetus. That Africana philosophy cannot, and should not, be reduced to existential philosophy is paradoxically because of a central dimension of the philosophy of existence itself: the question of existence, in itself, is empty. Philosophy of existence is therefore always a conjunctive affair; it must, in other words, be situated. This is because—for complex reasons that will become evident later on—the sine qua non of an existential philosophical anthropology is the paradoxical incompleteness of existential questions. Consider the famous existential credo of existence preceding essence. If essence is read also as conceptualization, then the theoretical or conceptual domain is always situated on what can be called the reflective level. The reflective dimension of situated life always brings in an element of concrete embodiment of relevance. What this means, then, is that theory—any theory—gains its sustenance from that which it offers for the lived reality of those who are expected to formulate it. Africana philosophy's history of traditional Africana Christian, Marxist, feminist, pragmatic, analytical, and phenomenological thought, then, has been a matter of what specific dimensions each of these approaches had to offer the existential realities of theorizing blackness. For Marxism, for instance, it was not so much its notion of "science" over all other forms of socialist theory, nor its promise of a world to win, that may have struck a resonating chord in the hearts of black Marxists.

It was, instead, Marx's and Engels's famous encomium of the proletarians having nothing to lose but their chains. Such a call has obvious affinity for a people who have been so strongly identified with chattel slavery.

Academic Africana existential philosophy has oscillated from time to time on the issue of liberation. In the contemporary academy, for instance, one will find priority placed on the identity question. The concern has taken many euphemisms, particularly in terms of questions of culture and ethnicity, but in the end, it usually amounts to the ever infamous "race question." This consequence is a function of a historical fact: race has emerged, throughout its history, as the question fundamentally of "the blacks" as it has for no other group. It is not that other groups have not been "racialized." It is that their racialization, if we will, has been conditioned in terms of a chain of being from the European human to the subhuman on a symbolic scale from light to dark. As we have already observed, it is not that Africana philosophy has been the only situated reality of blackness, but instead that it has been the only situated reality that is fundamentally conditioned by the question of blackness. The link between Africana philosophy of existence and the question of race is strengthened by the critical race theoretical problem of human designation. What Africana critical race theory has shown is that the situation of blacks cannot be resolved by any philosophical anthropology that makes the human a consequence of essential properties of valuative determination. Race issues are, in other words, not simply issues of chromosomal makeup or morphological appearance, but also, as Alain Locke has shown through several essays on values and identity in The Philosophy of Alain Locke, issues of the values placed upon what has been interpreted as "given." Thus, in spite of biophysical evidence against the notion of races (to which we will later return), all of world history, beyond black struggles for significance, questions the humanity of black peoples. As Fanon has so provocatively put it in his 1956 resignation letter, included in Toward the African Revolution, black defiance to black dehumanization has been historically constituted as madness or social deviance. Blackness and, in specific form, *the black* thus function as the breakdown of reason, which situates black existence, ultimately, in a seemingly nonrational category of faith. It is the plight of, in other words, *the wretched of the earth*. In the face of unreason, nihilism gnaws at black existence. The black stands as an existential enigma. Eyed with suspicion, the subtext is best exemplified by the question, "Why do they go on?"

One can readily see why such European existentialists as Jean-Paul Sartre and Simone de Beauvoir were particularly interested in the existential situation of blacks in such works as Sartre's *Nausea*, *Notebook for an Ethics*, "Return from the United States," and "Black Orpheus," among many others, as well as de Beauvoir's reflections on Richard Wright and Frantz Fanon in her autobiographies. Their philosophies of existence, premised upon a critical encounter with bad faith and reconciliation with responsibility, require an understanding not only of bourgeois or ruling-class self-delusions of *Angst*, but also the force of their circumstances (as de Beauvoir might put it) as social realities of those upon whose labor their society drew its luxuries.

"Why do they go on?" placed in the context of the black, is easily reformulated, simply, as, "Why go on?"

It is, as Albert Camus has so well noted in *The Myth of Sisyphus*, *the* question. If there are readers who may be suspicious of this peculiar invocation of the question of suicide on questions of race, they need only consider that the question of whether blacks commit suicide was treated with such seriousness by psychiatrists in the first half of the century that Fanon had to address the question in *Black Skin, White Masks* in the midst of a *philosophical* argument. Blacks, it was believed, were incapable of committing suicide because, supposedly, like the rest of the animal kingdom they didn't possess enough apperception or intelligence to understand the ramifications of their situation. This reasoning was based on the supposition of what a "true" human being would do if treated as blacks are treated. The following anecdote from the preface of Josiah Ulysses Young's *No Difference in the Fare* illustrates this point well:

Their way of "having church" was very much different from my parish's—an aging, rapidly diminishing, white United Methodist congregation. . . . A United Methodist myself, I had been hired as the assistant pastor to "integrate" the church. . . . My tenure at that church, however, was nearly always an occasion for insult and humiliation. One occasion looms above all others. . . . Two white parishioners, a married pair, and the congregation's wealthiest, invited me and my wife to dinner. At the table, the wife informed us that she had been adopted and had, at first, turned down her husband's proposal for marriage. Her past was an enigma: She said to us—without batting an eye—that she thought she might have been "colored" and have given birth to a black baby. On the heels of this confession came another revelation of the tyrannical "I." A relative had been injured in a car accident and needed a blood transfusion. Her options were the blood of a white man with syphilis, or that of a black man without the dreaded disease. Our host made it clear that the right decision was made in rejecting the "black" blood (pp. 11–12).

Could living positively as a black people make sense to such a person? This question of continuing to live on is connected to a controversial theme of all existential thought. It goes like this: There is a sense in which none of us has ever chosen to be born into this world and possibly any possible world. Yet, in our decision to live on, we live a choice that requires our having been born—in a word, our existence. In the context of blacks, the implication is obvious. No one chooses to have been born under racial designations, but the choice to go on living, and especially choices that involve recognizing one's racial situation, has implications on the meaning of one's birth. Applied to groups, it is the question of whether certain groups "should" have existed. The racist sentiment on this issue is summarized well by Henry Ward Beecher, as quoted by Anna Julia Cooper in A Voice from the South, when he remarks, "Were the Africans to sink to-morrow, how much poorer would the world be? A little less gold and ivory, a little less coffee, a considerable ripple, perhaps, where the Atlantic and Indian Oceans would come together—that is all; not a poem, not an invention, not a piece of art would be missed from the world" (p. 228).[2]

Antiblack racism espouses a world that will ultimately be better off without blacks. Blacks, from such a standpoint, must provide justification for their continued presence.

"Why go on?"

Well, the first thing to bear in mind is the illegitimacy of such demands for existential justification. What could blacks offer when it is their blackness that is called into question? The demand is loaded; failure emerges from the project of providing a suitable response. Symmetry abounds in the performance of the question, since the questioner's existence is treated as prejustified. If the questioner's existence alone is sufficient, why not the existence of the questioned?

"Why go on?"

There is, however, another dimension to this question. One, in the end, goes on because one wants to, and in so doing seeks grounds for *having to* go on. The wanting, however, signifies an intentional framework that has already militated against nihilism, for self-value also emerges from valuing one's desire to bring meaning to one's existence.

In the course of any effort to describe a philosophical position there will always be people who, in the tradition of old, demand names. Who, in other words, are Africana existential philosophers? The problem is made particularly acute by virtue of there being both Africana existential philosophies and Africana philosophers of existence, the first category of which is broader than the second. Although there are many philosophers who have contributed to Africana existential philosophy, not all are Africana nor black existential philosophers, as is clear not only by virtue of Sartre's contribution to the the area of thought, but also other nonblack philosophers such as David Theo Goldberg, Linda Bell, Joseph Catalano, Stuart Charmé, Patricia Huntington, and Martin Matuštík, all of whom have written on antiblack racism, problems of agency in black context, black invisibility, and intersections of race and feminism. Among Africana thinkers, not all who have contributed to Africana existential thought are, or ever were, existentialists, as can be seen by the work of Frank Kirkland, Charles W. Mills, Katie Cannon, Josiah Young, Dwight Hopkins, or Jacquelyn Grant.

Further, the problem of identifying Africana existentialists and contributors to Africana existential thought is exacerbated by the conjunctive dimension of existential philosophy, which makes suspect any unequivocal assertion of individuals being black existentialists. There are, for example, black existential Jews, Christians, and Muslims, black existential Marxists, black existential nationalists. Thus, Cedric Robinson's characterization, in his *Black Marxism*, of Richard Wright as living a journey from communism to existentialism to black nationalism is inaccurate, for example, because of black nationalism's being a concrete instantiation of a form of existential positioning—approaching the world through the situation of black people. Black power demands, among its values, first and foremost the recognition and valuing of black people as sources of value. That said, we can consider black existential thinkers in two ways.

First, there are theorists whose positions have an existential dimension *among other dimensions*, and who may not have formally defined themselves as existentialists. These individuals fall under the designation *philosophers of existence*, and they are existentialists in the way that Europeans like Søren Kierkegaard, Fyodor Dostoyevsky, Martin Heidegger, Franz Kafka, and Martin Buber are studied as existentialists in spite of their never having claimed to be existentialists and, in some cases (for instance, Heidegger's "Letter on Humanism") they have even outright declared that they are *not* existentialists. Given our considerations of what is involved in raising both the question of black suffering and the classical encounter with nihilism—that is, the struggle involved in deciding to live on—black existential thinkers of this type include such diverse figures as Frederick Douglass, Anna Julia Cooper, W. E. B. Du Bois, Alain Locke, Aimé Césaire, Angela Y. Davis, Toni Morrison, Cornel West, bell hooks, Joy Ann James, and many of the central figures in black liberation and black feminist theology (by virtue of their point of focus in biblical interpretation being similar to many black Marxists' points of focus in Marxian interpretation).

We find examples of existential dimensions in Douglass's thought throughout his published work, but especially in his conception of struggle and his interpretation and various efforts to develop a theory behind the significance of his fight with the slave breaker Edward Covey, which I will discuss in the next chapter. For Cooper, an excellent example is her provocative essay "What Are We Worth?" which can also be interpreted as her articulation of the conditions of responding to "Why go on?" in her classic volume, *A Voice from the South*. There she addresses head-on the implications of demanding a race of people to justify their right to exist—in a word, their "worth."

The Du Boisian story is a complex one that is articulated through the course of many volumes and essays, but it is especially noteworthy to see how he recounts, in his last autobiography, *Soliloquy on Viewing My Life From the Last Decade of Its First Century*, his articulation of "the race problem" in *The Souls of Black Folk*, where he presents a portrait of the turning point of his political consciousness. We have already touched upon his famous essay, "Conservation of the Races." That essay has received much recent discussion since Kwame Anthony Appiah labeled Du Bois a racist in his essay "The Illusion of Race" in his book *In My Father's House*. My interpretation of Du Bois's essay, besides being concerned by some of its rather confused catalog of races, is that Du Bois was dealing there, at the end of the nineteenth century, with an important anxiety and justified fear of North American black folk, that it was not only the case that if white Americans had their way they would eliminate black folks from the face of the earth, but also that there were very powerful white individuals—from Jefferson through to Lincoln and onward—devising such a plan. This plan was certainly the case for indigenous Americans, who, according to Russell Thornton, in *American Indian Holocaust and Survival*, were reduced to 4 percent by 1900. Du Bois needed an argument to justify why black people should not be condemned to the fate of the dodo and the last Tasmanian. That is why his first and second concluding recommendations are most significant, stating that "(1) We believe that the Negro people, as a race, have a contribution to make to civilization and humanity, which no other race can make; (2) We believe it the duty of the Americans of Negro descent, as a body, to maintain their race identity until this mission of the Negro people is accomplished, and the ideal of human brotherhood has become a practical possibility." Du Bois's remark, "which no other race can make," had to be made because he knew that if other races could make such contributions, the national response would have been, "Why, then, should we continue to tolerate the presence of Negroes?" Du Bois, I contend, knew that, without a Judaic notion of election, there was no "Negro mission," so his call for Negro identity until the achievement of such a mission was, in effect, a call for Negroes not to be exterminated. In other words, the essay was in spite of its provocative explorations of consciousness and Herderian appeals to linguistic and cultural genius, a policy essay with existential significance. As Du Bois queried earlier in that work, "Is this right? Is it rational? Is it good policy? Have we in America a distinct mission as a race—a distinct sphere of action and an opportunity for race development, or is self-obliteration the highest end to which Negro blood dare aspire?" (emphasis mine).

Nine decades later, Ralph Ellison and Audre Lorde echo Du Bois's concerns. In his essay "What America Would Be Like without Blacks," Ellison laments, "The fantasy of an America free of blacks is at least as old as the dream of creating a truly democratic society. . . . Yet, despite its absurdity, the fantasy of a blackless America continues to turn up. It is a fantasy born not merely of racism but of petulance, of exasperation, of moral fatigue. It is like a boil bursting forth from impurities in the bloodstream of democracy" (p. 105). Lorde, too, is typically succinct and poignant as she declares, in Sister Outsider, that "to survive in the mouth of this dragon we call america, we have had to learn this first and most vital lesson—that we were never meant to survive."

For Alain Locke, most noteworthy is his essay "Values and Imperatives," in which he defends, among several highly phenomenological theses, the view of values as "lived"—that is, valuing. Aimé Césaire is well known for his posing questions of black existence through the lens of what he coined négritude. I have already mentioned Angela Y. Davis; I will return to her now and then in the course of this work, but the reader could consult a developed representation and discussion of her work in the *Angela Y. Davis Reader* edited by Joy Ann James. Similarly, I have already mentioned both Toni Morrison and Cornel West. Morrison's work probes not only problems of black consciousness and the constructions of blacks in American society, but also the complexity of asserting agency in oppressive environments. Her first novel, *The Bluest Eye*, is a masterpiece of black existential expression. It could easily be read along with Richard Wright's *The Outsider* and Frantz Fanon's *Black Skin, White Masks* (which, by the way, prefigures many of the themes in Morrison's *Playing in the Dark*). Cornel West engaged Kierkegaard's writings and the thought of black humanists like Ralph Ellison and James Baldwin as early as his *Prophesy, Deliverance!* but most obviously so in his essay "Black Nihilism."

bell hooks' existential positions are most influenced by the work of Paulo Freire, as she attests in many of her works, especially *Black Looks* and *Teaching to Transgress*, but one can argue that her centering of the liberation and identity questions are already rooted in black existential philosophy. Her affinity with Freire's work is, in other words, animated by the same concerns as black liberation theologians with certain sections of the Bible and black Marxists with certain sections of Marx's works. Most of hooks's writings substantiate this claim. In addition, that Freire's *Pedagogy of the Oppressed* is clearly rooted in Sartre's and Fanon's philosophies of liberation instantiates the existential legacy here.

Joy James is represented by her books *Transcending the Talented Tenth*, *Resisting State Violence*, and *Shadowboxing*, as well as her award-winning anthology *Spirit, Space, and Survival*. These works challenge reductive readings of black feminism and defend models of agency and resistance in a world marked by what she describes, in her essay "Black Feminism," as "existence in gray."

We can also consider black existential philosophers and social critics among those who have taken an openly admitted existential identity as philosophers of existence—those who were or are, in other words, "out-of-the-closet existentialists," including Richard Wright, Léopold Senghor, Frantz Fanon, Ralph Ellison, James Baldwin, William R. Jones, Lucius Outlaw, Naomi Zack, Tsenay Serequeberhan, and this author. Wright's importance is Promethean. His investigations of existential paradoxes through such novels as *Native Son* and *The Outsider*, and his classic essays against simple-minded, reductive readings of the existential condition of black folk still call for careful existential analyses. His insight that even blacks who commit crimes suffer from a gnawing feeling of innocence raises the question of black existence beyond problems of inclusion. How can one have agency in a world of meaningless guilt? Fanon has provided perhaps the strongest *theoretical* statements in Africana existential thought. Senghor's role in the *négritude* movement is a well-known example of the Kierkegaardian and Heideggerian links. Ellison's existential thought is well established, particularly in terms of his classic *Invisible Man* and his collections of essays on literature, politics, and culture, *Shadow and Act* and *Going into the Territory*. There are numerous instances in Baldwin's writings, but a primary example is *The Fire Next Time*.

For William R. Jones's philosophy, there is his classic critique of black theology, *Is God a White Racist?* and his ongoing work on oppression. Lucius T. Outlaw has defended the place in American academic philosophy for not only Africana philosophy and critical theory, but also existential phenomenology. Through several important articles he has issued what is ultimately an *existential* critique of the social-constructivist critical race theorists and Appiah's accusation of Du Boisian race theory as racist—that they fail to articulate the most relevant dimensions of the lived realities of race and racism. In *On Race and Philosophy*, Outlaw, like Du Bois, urges us to take seriously the meaning of a future without black people. Naomi Zack's positions can be found in her influential book *Race and Mixed Race*, which raises questions regarding the existential reality of mixed-race people, and her anthology *American Mixed Race*. Her most explicitly existential essay is her "Race, Life, Death, Identity, Tragedy and Good Faith," where her response to the Du Boisian question of black suffering and identity is, in stream with Appiah, for blacks to give up race and black identity. And for Serequeberhan, whose existential hermeneutical approach to African philosophy stands on the shoulders of Fanon, Almicar Cabral, and Hans-Georg Gadamer, *The*

Hermeneutics of African Philosophy stands as his most systematic statement to date.

This list is not, I should stress, an exhaustive list, and it is not necessarily the case that each of these thinkers converge on the same set of values. For instance, although all ultimately "humanist," middle-period Wright's, Baldwin's, and Zack's works take a more individualistic turn, whereas early and later Wright's, Fanon's, Jones's, Serequeberhan's, and my own work—represented, for example, by my *Bad Faith and Antiblack Racism; Fanon and the Crisis of European Man;* and *Her Majesty's Other Children*—are situated in what may be called black radical existential thought.

I should also like to stress that not all contributors to Africana existential philosophy are black existentialists in any sense. Some of the individuals who have something to say of value on that subject may also be those who are most critical of it, or at least suspicious of an existential philosophy premised upon what Fanon calls "the lived-experience of the black." That being the case, let us press on to an effort to probe such problems through examination of a problem of experience raised by the study of Africana thought: the problem of biography.

two

A Problem of Biography in Africana Thought

Self-criticism has been much talked about of late, but few people realize that it is an African institution.

—Frantz Fanon, *The Wretched of the Earth*

The fallacy of intentionality in the history of ideas is well known: Do not confuse the intentions of an author with the object of his or her production, for it is often the case that the author has a problem of interpretation similar to that of the reader or other interpreter. Although at times intent may offer insight—for instance, into why the project "failed"—the independence of the text has been a rule of thumb in the art of interpretation. This rule, however, has been violated in peculiar ways when it comes to the work of black theorists. For them, a different rule, an insidious rule, continues to reign: the fallacy of reductionistic "experience."

Recall W. E. B. Du Bois's critical observation from *The Souls of Black Folk*: Blacks are often studied as problems instead of as people who face problems in their lives. Du Bois was pointing out that "blackness" often afforded theorists a problematic moment. That problematic moment focused on black people over and against what they may live. The consequence is that their historicity is robbed of its contingency and collapsed into necessity or a form of essentialism. Here, however, we find irony. For although there is at first an anonymity that affords immediate "universality," where any black counts for all blacks, the reality is that such epistemic closure (that is, knowledge of their being black brings knowledge claims to a close) is locked outside of the historical and, hence, exists neither as the universal nor the particular.[3] Consider G. W. F. Hegel's introductory remarks in his *Philosophy of History*, that history took a path from Asia to Europe and made only a shuddering glance at the northeast tip of Africa where, to this day, supposedly Semitic and Asiatic peoples constitute its only sources of culture. Standing neither on the level of history nor on the dialectical level of a particular negation that moves history forward, the black is left as nonbeing, non-Other, nothing. A project emerged, then, of articulating at least a point of universal subjectivity from such an abyss.

It is no wonder that the autobiographical medium has dominated black modes of written expression. The autobiographical moment afforded a contradiction in racist reason: How could the black, who by definition was not fully human and hence without a point of view, produce a portrait of his or her point of view? The black autobiography announced a special form of biography, a text that was read for insight into blackness, which meant that paradoxically some of the problems of epistemic closure continued through an engagement that admitted epistemic possibility. The interest in black autobiography carried expectation and curiosity. One could see the further titillation that emerged from the addendum to several nineteenth-century narratives, including that of Frederick Douglass, "*as written by himself.*" A black man who could write? For Douglass, however, there was, as we will see in chapter 3, further irony: his first autobiography, stated as "written by himself" to stress the absence of amanuensic interventions, was penned by one who was considered property by the laws of the United States. As such Douglass had to present lectures on his book in England to avoid being recaptured under the fugitive slave laws. His work, property produced by his life, mental reflection, and hands, was, ironically, protected by the Library of Congress under copyright laws. The logic of slavery and property should have deemed his work immediate public domain, but instead, his work had more rights in the United States than he had. A textualist dream was in this case a human being's nightmare.

The autobiographical moment need not collapse into essence or epistemic closure. Its history is a complex one, as autobiographical writings have emerged in antiquity with purposes of varied kind. Quite a number of biblical texts are autobiographical while ironically pointing beyond the authors through the uniqueness of biblical textual intent. As Paul Ricoeur has pointed out in "Biblical Hermeneutics," chapter 4 of From Text to Action, however biblical texts were written, they are read for believers as moments of divine intervention: God appears through such encounters. St. Augustine's Confessions served a similar purpose, but it also exemplified engagements that transcended their time as portraits of Faith and Reason. St. Augustine was, in other words, among those North Africans who managed subsequently to pierce through Hegel's schema, in spite of the latter's suspicions of the philosophical richness of medieval thought. Still, for St. Augustine, the autobiographical moment was not meant to portray him in his uniqueness; it was to continue, to some extent, the practice of biblical testimony of God's presence in and above the world. Pagan autobiographical writings—or at least autobiographical voices—served a similar purpose. Apuleius, for instance, used such a voice in his fictional Golden Ass.[4] It is in the modern moment, however, that a unique subject of autobiographical reflections emerged: autobiography as portrait of the man.

The man as being who appears in the autobiographical moment manifested himself among modern philosophers such as David

Hume and Jean-Jacques Rousseau, the latter more known for his autobiographical ruminations than the former.[5] The modern moment afforded such reflection because the turn to theory of knowledge, epistemology-centered philosophy, as *Philosophia Prima* led to a focus on the inner life of "man" and suspicion toward the world that these men shared. Think of René Descartes's egological turn in his *Meditations on First Philosophy*, where the Cogito is the focus, and the proliferation of modern texts that followed with the adjective *human* in their title, the two most famous no doubt being John Locke's *Essay on Human Understanding* and Hume's *A Treatise of Human Nature*. That sociality itself was called into question in these texts led to pure reason or experience—often distinguished as the rationalistic and empirical moments—as foundations of truth. There was, however, narcissism in the autobiographical turn by some of these men, for since they were men who had already written ideas that were being engaged by a community of readers (or at least, readers whom they considered relevant), what more could their autobiographies afford than presentations of themselves *as they would have liked to have been known or remembered?* That one's legacy is a function of the memory of others leaves one's existence at the mercy of the social world, a world in which the past haunts the present through memory and belief. Such a world is highly susceptible to deceit.

Narcissism promises self-deception in that the narcissist, as Frantz Fanon argued in *Black Skin, White Masks* and Jean Baudrillard subsequently argued in *Seduction*, asks his mirror to be *his* truth, which is a false truth, and the mirror promises the narcissist to be such a mirror. In Baudrillard's words, "'*I'll be your mirror*' does not signify 'I'll be your reflection' but 'I'll be your deception.' *To seduce is to die as reality and reconstitute oneself as illusion.* . . . Narcissus too loses himself in his own illusory image; that is why he turns from his truth, and by his example turns others from their truth" (p. 69).

The autobiographical text, in this moment—the modern moment—is, then, the self-created mirror of deception which, by virtue of its publicity (the social world), enforces itself in the "objective" community of readers (audience). In characteristic sarcasm and irony, Friedrich Nietzsche signaled the folly of this medium through his play on the death-of-God motif. The title of his auto-biography, echoing Pontius Pilate's offering of Jesus to the crowd, is *Ecce Homo!* (Behold—the Man!). In the world of fiction, Mary Shelley had already brought out this perversity through the use of the autobiographical voice in her classic *Frankenstein*; the hubristic Doctor Frankenstein's mirror did not reveal that he was God but instead—through a yellow, opened eye—a monster.

The Racial (that is, "abnormal") Autobiography posed a prob-lem for the White (that is, "normal") Autobiography. If the autobi-ography of a person of color revealed itself simply *as autobiography*, then the gap between colored and noncolored, between subhuman and human, would at least have been bridged on the level of inner life. That autobiographies by black authors have continued to be *black autobiographies* to this day has relieved some of these fears, but they have done so by virtue of the transformation of the meaning of biography in these texts. Biography in black contexts hardly stands as optional modus operandi. Whereas the old European may sit down to write memoirs, in the black experience, the moment of self-reflection begins even with youth: there are black authors who produce autobiographical reflections even in their early teenage years, and many black theorists write in this voice from their first publications onward.[6] It's as if living blackness by itself counts as experience. That black voices are already locked in the biographical and autobiographical moment transforms the biographical status of those moments from the contingent to the necessary.

My aim here is not to discount the use of autobiography nor bi-ography in the study of black intellectuals or black intellectual pro-duction. As some of the chapters of this work will attest, it is a practice that on occasion I consider worthwhile. What I would like to raise here is the question of *relevance*. In the world of theory, *where relevant*, nearly all interpretations and methodologies are permitted. My concern is with the implications of the ongoing practice of locking black intellectuals and their productions in the biographi-cal moment. This point can be illustrated through the emergence of two recent phenomena in the history of ideas: the black literary theorist and the black philosopher.

Both the black literary theorist and the black philosopher signify unique anomalies. Although black theorists have been around
since the advent of modern theorizing, it is with the black literary
theorist that the question of theory achieved metatheoretical
significance by virtue of the question of textual independence, especially from the late 1970s through to the present. Unfortunately,
this insight fell to the wayside by virtue of the foci of several influential members of this turn. Such thinkers devoted their energy
to the black autobiographical text. Less concern focused on *what*
previous black writers were saying and more on *which* black writers
were writing or saying these things. Not only were the 1980s and
early 1990s marked by race, gender, and class reductionism, but
also by epistemic reductionism. As, for instance, "the black
woman" emerged as autobiographical moments through, say, an
Oxford University Press book series that reprinted mid- through
late-nineteenth-century autobiographical texts, to what extent have
the arguments of these texts been engaged beyond the fact that
they managed to be produced by black women in such times?[7]
Even though African American literary production began with
Phillis Wheatley, more needs to be said beyond that fact; what, for
instance, did Wheatley write? That she wrote poetry isn't enough.
What did her poems *say*? What can we learn from them today?

Although social and political theorists have struggled with various arguments in the history of black theoretical production—
primarily with concerns of assimilation versus separatism, political
configurations of liberalism, conservatism, and progressive radicalism—there the other extreme often manifested itself: the ideas of
the black theorist were often absent and, instead, his or her
biography became text for political interpretation. Concern was
with where Martin Delany, Frederick Douglass, Anna Julia Cooper,
W. E. B. Du Bois, or Marcus Garvey lived and whom they knew, not
what they argued. Yet there were groups of social and political theorists who laid foundations for the elevation of such questions to
the level of theoretical reflection, and in doing so, they set black social and political philosophical thought in motion. This is not to say
that black philosophical thought did not precede mid-twentieth-

century reflections: one could easily find a set of themes that emerge from black philosophical reflections in the nineteenth century. Whether abolitionists, anticolonialists, or international liberationists, black writers have, by virtue of the historical specificity of modern racism and slavery, reflected seriously on the question of "man" in the modern era. Such reflection makes sense since these thinkers were from communities whose humanity was constantly denied by an oppressing or colonizing community and system of laws. The nature of oppression is such that it challenges oppressed groups to ask, constantly, as Fanon observed in the penultimate chapter of *Wretched of the Earth*, "In reality, what am I?" If one is nearly everywhere told that one is not fully a human being, but one finds oneself struggling constantly with human responsibilities—over life and death, freedom and lack thereof, virtue and vice—the moment of theoretical reflection demands engagement with such idiosyncracy. Whereas scientific anthropology was the Western moment of distinguishing *European man* as Man through study of so-called lesser men, philosophical anthropology became the Africana moment of critically engaging the human being through so-called lesser human beings' struggle for their humanity. Such a struggle took many forms, as we have seen, including engagements with ontological questions of being—for example, essence, necessity, contingency, and possibility—and teleological questions of where humanity should be going—for example, liberation, humanization, revolution, and freedom. Although its history stood richly outside of academic corridors, with at best excursions into universities (by way of, for example, W. E. B. Du Bois, Anna Julia Cooper, Alain Locke, and C. L. R. James), it was not until the 1970s that academic reflections on these matters emerged through a cadre of black academic philosophers and social theorists whose focus was the world of black theorists and their *ideas*.

Now we have another anomaly: the "black theorist" demands our taking seriously the notion of Reason speaking through black bodies. For some theorists, such as Léopold Senghor, this is a hopeless project, although they may not outrightly say so.[8] Although many instances could be advanced, let us consider the way these concerns have manifested themselves in one of the "hottest" recent developments in black intellectual history: Fanon studies.

Henry Louis Gates Jr.'s "Critical Fanonism," and D. A. Masolo's "Sartre Fifty Years Later" have both argued that Fanon is at best an interesting biographical figure, one locked hopelessly in the past, whose retrieval in the name of postcolonial theory would be a mistaken effort at global theoretical aspirations. The text that is favored here is Fanon's highly autobiographical *Black Skin, White Masks*, wherein he is often cited by critics as the source of his own historical entrapment by his introductory announcement of not coming "with timeless truths." Some authors, such as Cedric Robinson in "The Appropriation of Frantz Fanon," have responded by attacking Gates and other literary and cultural studies folks for engaging the so-called "petit-bourgeois" *Black Skin, White Masks*, instead of the historical and supposedly more revolutionary *The Wretched of the Earth*. Responding to both, I have argued against privileging either text, and against the coherence of the "early" versus "late" Fanon (he wrote his first book at the age of 25, and *The Wretched of the Earth* at the age of 35). Moreover, I have argued in *Fanon and the Crisis of European Man* that both approaches represent a form of "theoretical decadence," where the literary theorist (Gates) criticizes thought for not being literary or textual and the political scientist (Robinson) criticizes the literary or textual theorist for not being social scientific and Marxist.[9] Instead, Fanon's *ideas* need to be assessed, in the end, by how useful they are to our various theoretical projects without centering those theoretical projects as *the only* theoretical concern. Here, the biographical moment needs to be assessed as a mode of criticism, for to collapse Fanon into his biography is a way of locking him into those sorts of interests that have dominated the way Douglass, Cooper, Du Bois, Locke, Garvey, Alexander Crummell, Edward Blyden, and many other black intellectuals have been read.

The biographical is almost mandatory fare in the order of blackness. The implication—insidious, patronizing, and yet so familiar and presumed—has achieved the force of an axiom: *White intellectuals provide theory; black intellectuals provide experience.* The status of experience is such, however, that it becomes temporally bound, entrapped in historical specificity. Fanon's becomes a biographical text because his blackness is such that few of his critics can imagine otherwise. In spite of the persistence of Fanon's ideas—his effect on generations from the 1950s through to the present—and in spite of the growing realization of the complexity of his thought, more continues to be written about *Fanon* than his ideas. Compare Fanon to Michel Foucault, who, similarly, raised questions of historical specificity and who drew upon Nietzsche's genealogical method to articulate his brand of poststructural analysis of knowledge régimes. Foucault's thought is studied in the 1990s, though it was inspired by the 1950s through 1970s, and Foucault was comfortable utilizing Nietzsche's nineteenth-century ideas but not Karl Marx's, which he dismissed in *The Order of Things* as—like fish in water—hopelessly locked in their time, unable to "breathe" anywhere else. Moreover, how is it that Foucault could use and reuse Nietzsche without being Nietzschean and out of date, but Fanon, by contrast, is constantly subordinated or dismissed as hopelessly a product of the 1950s and of influence in the 1960s—as though either decade was not part of the twentieth century?[10] I have often wondered, in concert with Ato Sekyi-Otu's *Fanon's Dialectic of Experience*, if many commentators actually read Fanon at all beyond a few excerpts in anthologies on politics, culture, and race. Should we not examine the possibility of thoughts peculiarly *Fanonian* today?

Fanon has been interpreted as a subordinate of nearly every European thinker whose ideas he engaged. Some commentators, such as Renate Zahar and Nigel Gibson, have deemed him a "left Hegelian"; some, such as D. A. Masolo, a "Sartrian Marxist"; and others, such as Homi Bhabha, a "Lacanian." In similar kind, Frederick Douglass was known as a "Garrisonian" and Du Bois has been known as every derivative from "Herderian" to "Hegelian" to "Marxian" (although he himself eventually adopted this last description). The situation with regard to black intellectuals seems hopeless. In my first book, *Bad Faith and Antiblack Racism*, I devoted ninety pages to the explanation of the concept of bad faith. Since

Jean-Paul Sartre presented the classic philosophical statement on the subject in *Being and Nothingness*, I provided copious references to his formulations so as to distinguish them from my own. Such efforts led to my being designated, in many book reviews, as "Sartrian," in spite of the text's many references to Fanon and Du Bois. Oddly, I have written more on Fanon's ideas than on Sartre's or any other thinker's, but have never been called "Fanonian."

There are many ways to read Fanon's thought. Consider this one: Fanon was an ironic writer who was struggling with the complex question of paradoxical reason and paradoxical historicity. The collapse of Reason and History into all things European represented a failure of Reason and History that required self-deception regarding Europe's scope. Put differently, Europe sought to become *ontological*—that is, *Being*. Such Being stood in the way of *human* being. It thus presented itself as a theodicy, as, that is, a system that was complete on all levels of existence; on levels of description and prescription; of being and value; of all there is, can, and ought to be. It presented itself this way while its incompleteness bled through its pores. The person of color, particularly the black, however, lived the contradictions of this self-deception continually through attempting to live this theodicy in good faith. This lived contradiction emerged for the black because a demand of this form of faith is that it be good without being *critical*. Critical consciousness challenges intrasystemic consistency by raising systemic critique. Take, for instance, rationality. Rationality emerges in many systems (especially those of the liberal kind) as being free of racist adulteration. What should we make, then, of racist rationality? A schism explodes in the soul of the black, a schism that leads to two souls, as Du Bois observed in *The Souls of Black Folk* and the earlier "Conservation of the Races," with a consciousness of pure exteriority in the face of the lived experience of interiority.

So, we find the following argument in *Black Skin, White Masks*: There is a white construction called "the black." This construction is told that if he or she really is human, then he or she can transcend the boundaries of racialized or colonial imposition—it is a consequence of constructivity. This construction is considered a leech on all manifestations of human identity-forming practices: language, sex, labor (material and aesthetic), socializing (reciprocal recognition), consciousness. In good faith, the black attempts to live each of these simply as a human being and discovers that to do so calls for living as a white. If blackness and whiteness are constructed, perhaps the black could then live the white construction, which would reinforce the theme of constructivity. Each portrait, however, is a tale of failure. And in fact, failure takes on a peculiar role in this text. Each failure is not necessarily Fanon's failure, for he is both a textual and a metatextual voice. Thus, although Fanon the black hero of the text constantly fails, Fanon the critic of Western discourses of Man, the revolutionary who demands systemic change, succeeds. Paradoxically, if the hero of the text wins, the theorist fails, and vice versa. So, after announcing in his introduction that ontogenic or highly individualized explanations and phylogenic or species-oriented explanations fail and instead need to be mediated by sociality/culture with a recognition of human agency, Fanon charts the course of the black with the theoretical idols of humanization. The black's effort at transgressive linguistic performance fails; instead of being a transformer of words, he discovers that he is considered an "eater" of words in a racist society and realizes himself as linguistically dangerous. He never speaks "white" as whites speak whiteness. Whites speak whiteness "bookishly," whereas people of color speak whiteness "whiteishly" or "whitelike." The significance of language is its inherent publicity. Failing a public retreat, the black may move inward, to the private sphere, perhaps to the sexual sphere for solitude from epidermalization or the alienation of complete exteriority. But there, on the level of the sexual, where the psychoanalytic reigns, the search for symmetry—to live equally, to live on a par with whites—fails; words of love, as a (white) woman or (white) man would offer a beloved, collapse into words of whiteness. The ontologizing of sexual difference meets its limitation—and, hence, its ontological failure—in the racial schema: masculine is structurally white, and feminine is structurally black. Jean Veneuse, the protagonist in René Maran's autobiographical Un homme pareil aux autres, should not be like Mayotte

Capécia in a patriarchal society. But he is: he seeks his words of being, love, and difference from the (since ultimately anonymous but paradoxically superstructural and suprastructural) White Man.

Fanon then explores the constitutionality of psychic life among colonial subjects and finds that the Symbolic is not psychoanalytical but colonial, that exploitation is not simply class structured but racial. Schemes of rational explanation are here finding their limits. In each instance, the black attempts to address a problem and encounters himself as the problem. So Fanon goes to a deeper level of interiority: his own experience *as lived*. He finds, in this autobiographical moment, a set of theses converging. The chapter "The Lived Experience of the Black" begins with a little white boy's use of language—of publicity—to enmesh Fanon in the realm of pure exteriority, the realm of the epidermal schema. There, Fanon's existence is a two-dimensional objectification, as in Euclidean geometry: he is "out there" without an inside. The irony here is that the moment is *autobiographical*, so its report is paradoxical. He announces the absence of his interiority *from the point of view of his interiority*. The paradox of experience is also raised: he experiences his historicity as a false history and his struggle with Theory, with Reason, as a cat-and-mouse game. Between Reason and History, Theory and Practice, there is experience, which in this case is the existential struggle against sedimented, dehumanized constructions. Fanon at first observes that he wants to laugh but cannot. It is not until he risks public harm by insulting the boy's mother, a white woman, that he is able to laugh and then move on to an engagement with assessing his situation—with, that is, Reason. Yet as we've already observed, Reason proves limited. Against History and Reason, Fanon then attempts poetic resistance through the upsurge of négritude, but there he finds structural symbolic imposition of a Manichean order: the Reality Principle, so to speak, remains—through Sartre and the skewed iconography of Senghorian négritude—white. Why couldn't the symbolism articulate, at least, *black reason?* So, at the chapter's end, he weeps.

That Fanon concludes chapter 5 of *Black Skin, White Masks* with weeping has not been commented on in the literature. Recall our point on laughter: it enabled Fanon to cope with his situation, to move on. The role of humor in oppressed communities is well known; there is not only the form of humor in which the oppressor is ridiculed, but there is also self-deprecating humor, humor that creates a paradoxical distance and closeness with their situation. A friend related a joke from a Jewish World War II concentration camp survivor in which a German officer yells to a group of inmates, "Hey—all of you—get out from behind that broomstick!" In many black communities, this "snap" or example of the "dozens" (the clever form of insult also known as signifying and dissin') appears: "Your father's so black that when he falls down, people hop over him for fear of falling in." In similar fashion, an obese man once said to another obese man: "Man, you so fat, when I tried to walk around you I got lost!" Another obese man said: "I don't nap on the beach from fear of people trying to push me back to sea." There has been slave humor; Gypsy humor; Jewish humor—as we see, even in concentration camps; varieties of immigrant humor; and there continues to be self-deprecating black humor. Humor stands in these communities as complex competitors of proverbs, but instead of wisdom, they offer distance. Fanon's text is loaded with this form of humor; the black sarcastically mocks the black's tragicomic efforts in this theodicean struggle. But humor has its limitations. It takes much to be able to laugh at oneself, and excess could lead to pathology. The struggle for liberation, for humanization, is structurally similar to therapy. Patients may, for instance, laugh at their situation while telling their story, but this laughter is to make them go on, although often without genuine confrontation; it is a practice of seeming closeness that leads to distance; the grin and the laugh also mean "too close for comfort." A "breakthrough" in therapy often occurs with tears, with catharsis. Fanon wept because he realized that every effort to avoid the truth failed. It was through such catharsis that he was then able to face the implications of his situation, in whatever form that situation may take. That is why Fanon's succeeding chapter was titled, "The Negro/Nigger and Psychopathology." Fanon was now able to face the psychopathological implications of his situation.

The first thing Fanon observes is that black psychology is abnormal psychology. Whereas there is a conception of normality for whites—that is, their being human by virtue of white normativity—there is no such thing for blacks. An adult black who is well adjusted is an "abnormal black." An adult black who is not well adjusted is a "normal black," which ironically means an "abnormal person," or simply an "abnormality." To be abnormal for a black and abnormal for a human being is to be in a Catch-22. The argument is similar to the black use of language: it is, as Fanon observes in the same volume, like The Thinker with an erection. In this chapter, as in "The Lived-Experience of the Black," all of the motifs of chapters 1 through 4 of Black Skin, White Masks are repeated but with more insight. If the black is sex, but repressed sexuality, then psychoanalysis and other Western human sciences find their limitations, for the sex there is not only structurally deviant, but also not symbolic. It is phobogenic, material, existentially "serious," real.[11] The search for recognition that emerges in Fanon's penultimate chapter fails, then, because the necessary conditions for self–Other relations also fail: neither the Hegelian Master nor the structural White Man wants recognition from blacks; each wants work, and bodies without points of view.[12] Here we see why the demands of classical liberalism and Kantian humanism fail: they depend upon symmetry. White–black relations are such that blacks struggle to achieve Otherness; it is a struggle to be in a position for the ethical to emerge. Thus, the circumstance is peculiarly wrought with realization of the political. Fanon's book ends, then, politically and existentially. Politically, like the author's romanticized African American, the call is to fight, to struggle against the system of his oppression. But in that struggle, Fanon calls for a pedagogy to build (édifier, "to edify," "to build") a questioning humanity. This building takes the form of a prayer. From anger, to laughter, to tears, he concludes with prayers—prayers to, of all realities, his body. Fanon beseeches his body to make of him a man who questions, a being that is open and, consequently, a being who is a human being. By 1960, in The Wretched of the Earth, he concludes with the same thesis, that material and conceptual struggles that open possibilities are needed to set afoot a new humanity.

There are many more insights in Fanon's writings. For our purposes, what is important is that he has much to say beyond the biographical and autobiographical moment, and that what he has to say stretches the meaning (and perhaps coherence) of his historical moment. That the black was born out of specific circumstances reminds us that the black has not always been here and, like other human formations, may not always be among us. This observation does not mean that Fanon's critique of the black's encounter with Western civilization—especially *as a product of that civilization*—does not have lasting significance and lasting value. For the literary theorist, but without surprise for other theorists, the writings of black intellectuals demand, then, engagement that genuinely requires a challenge to the self-reflection of our species; it demands more than interpreting and criticizing stories told, but interpreting and criticizing *interpretations* of how they can be told. Such engagement requires genuine revision of the canon of valuable literature as well as a critique of the criteria through which canons have hitherto been formed.[13] Douglass, Du Bois, Cooper, Fanon, and James would transcend the curiosity of experience to the engagement of ideas.[14]

Ideas shift black writing from perception to apperception. The former acknowledges that blacks have experiences, while the latter requires blacks' ability to *interpret* that experience. Such interpretation makes sense if it can transcend its particularity. Put differently, the dualism of black experience and white theory has to be abandoned here for the recognition that black reflections also are theoretical and informative of the human condition. The anxiety is not, then, over whether black intellectuals should be read but over *how* they should be read and *what* we should seek in such readings. For my part, I expect no more nor less from texts written by black authors than I do when I read texts written by white authors or other authors of color; some texts will, in other words, be more informative than others. Yet the projects of reading and theorizing are such that in their course the ultimate arbiters should be pragmatic. In the end, it is the usefulness of and challenges raised by ideas that transcend the authors and textual moments of their appearance.

What would signal progress? That Immanuel Kant could engage David Hume's and Jean-Jacques Rousseau's ideas to create his
critical philosophy; that John Rawls and Jürgen Habermas could
engage Kant's ideas to develop their branch of liberal and com-
municative rationalities; that Edmund Husserl could engage
Descartes's and Kant's ideas to develop his transcendental phenomenology; that Martin Heidegger and Jean-Paul Sartre could
utilize Husserl's ideas, along with Hegel's, Nietzsche's, Søren
Kierkegaard's, and Henri Bergson's as a point of departure into
their philosophies of existence, and that there are many instances
of such engagements represents the development of a tradition
that continues, but a tradition that is not, by far, indicative of the
human condition. Too much is excluded for this to be so. A
broader picture requires traditions that, by their historical specificity, have had to engage other traditions. Is this not the case with
the Africana tradition, especially given its antipodal status in Western civilization?

David Walker's appeal offered a critique of white Christian practices and influenced Maria Stewart's religious formulations of
equality and freedom, formulations that are essential for our understanding of religious dimensions of Africana humanism. Martin
Delany's efforts to formulate theories of liberation through an affirmation of blackness and a Pan-African agenda influenced thinkers
and liberationists well into the twentieth century. Frederick Douglass
authored a wealth of literature on topics ranging from the distinction between de jure freedom and de facto freedom, as well as
contributions to feminist philosophy and political philosophy that
challenge American conceptions of representative democracy.
Alexander Crummell's search for linguistic dimensions of raciality
(Anglocentric though they may have been) and emancipation, and
Edward Blyden's effort to understand the symbolism of blackness
and his distinction between religion and theology set the ground-
work for matters that concern Africana peoples to this day. Anna
Julia Cooper's reflections on human value, "What Are We Worth?"
and her formulation of a black feminist position have stimulated
contemporary discussion in the work of Joy Ann James and other

contemporary feminist thinkers. W. E. B. Du Bois's integration of all his predecessors and the complexity of his ideas on methodology in the human sciences, his phenomenological concept of double consciousness, his struggle to articulate a critical race theory, and much more, influenced Alain Locke's aesthetics, his pluralistic axiology, and his explorations of philosophical problems raised by the concept "Negro." Marcus Garvey's early-twentieth-century articulations of nationhood, prophesying, and political organizing led to the development of Rastafari, a philosophy of life and the human being that challenges many of the semiotic features of Western hegemony. The importance of the Rastafarian contribution should not be underestimated. Strong structuralist accounts of colonization and racism have misrepresented black people as incapable of a positive identity even on the level of their imagination and spiritual life. Rastafari proves otherwise, as Paget Henry has shown in "Rastafarianism and the Reality of Dread," and Joseph Owens has shown in his highly existential and philosophical *Dread*. Of note, as well, is Rastafari's interpretation of the lived body, which ironically emerges in the thought of many Afro-Caribbean thinkers' writings, including my *Bad Faith and Antiblack Racism*.

The black existential tradition, which is the focus of this book, could be traced from Walker's and Douglass's reflections on freedom through to Du Bois's discussions of consciousness and his effort to develop a humanistic sociology; Richard Wright's articulations of dread and existential paradoxes in race contexts; Ralph Ellison's explorations of invisibility and the search for an open humanism, Léopold Senghor's reflections on freedom; and Frantz Fanon's effort to develop a humanistic approach to the human sciences and revolutionary praxis. James Baldwin's protest and prophetic humanism continue today through, for example, William Jones's call for theorizing historical agency among the oppressed, Cornel West's prophetic explorations of dread, despair, and nihilism; Paget Henry's constructivist project with traditional African humanism and conceptions of predestination and agency in Africana thought; and bell hooks's project of a pedagogy of liberation in postmodern times.

What is religious thought in the twentieth century without the pressing questions raised by Du Bois on suffering and the iconography of religious figures; Countee Cullen's poetic articulation of the black Christ; Marcus Garvey's prophetic call for black religious transfigurations; Howard Thurman's activist conception of embodied spirituality and political resistance; Martin Luther King Jr.'s conception of the beloved community and the transcendental yet worldly impact of Goodness, James Cone's articulation of black liberation theology rooted in the economic, moral, and aesthetic demands of oppressed communities; William R. Jones's theodicean challenge as a *methodological challenge* to all theologies and his advancement of a historically embodied humanism, Jacquelyn Grant's womanist theological appeal through the symbolic force of the Gospels, and Cornel West's prophetic pragmatism, in which the effort is made to conjoin pragmatism, Marxism, and Christianity into a revolutionary praxis? There are, as well, the black radical poststructural and phenomenological traditions, which, albeit originally rooted in engagement with négritude (especially Senghor's and Aimé Césaire's search for what Sylvia Wynter has called "a science of the word"), drew sustenance from Frantz Fanon's reflections on language, consciousness, and sociogeny and continues in the work of Wynter, Thomas Slaughter, V. Y. Mudimbe, and the group who Paget Henry, in *Caliban's Reason*, has said practices the "poeticist" tradition—especially, for instance, Wilson Harris and Eduoard Glissant. The tradition of radical black political economy and historicism, in which C. L. R. James is the towering figure, includes figures like George Padmore, Kwame Nkrumah, Almicar Cabral, Eric Williams, Walter Rodney, Cedric Robinson, and Angela Y. Davis. And there are, of course, clear convergences of the poeticist and historicist traditions, as we find, for instance, in Claude McKay's literary and political writings, James's poetic rendering of the anticolonial experience, and Fanon's powerful prose. Think, as well, of the impact made on twentieth-century aesthetics by Richard Wright's, Ralph Ellison's, Lorraine Hansberry's, Addison Gayle's, Amiri Baraka's, Wole Soyinka's, and Houston Baker Jr.'s reflections on literature and music. And then there is the growing field of Africana metaphilosophy, where the goal is to set criteria and methods through which to assess and organize black intellectual production with prescriptions and suggestions for future research. This development includes the philosophical history of African American thought, in which the leading figures are Harold Cruse, with his challenge of African American intellectual independence; Leonard Harris, whose *Philosophy Born of Struggle* set the framework for such research; Cornel West, with his cultural studies approach; and the Afrocentrists Maulana Karenga and Molefi Asante ("Afrocentrism," after all, being a predominantly *African American* development)—the philosophical history of contemporary African philosophy, with V. Y. Mudimbe's explorations of African gnosticism, or ways of knowing; Kwame Gyekye's distinction between "traditional" and critical philosophy, and his articulation of African theistic humanism; Odera Oruka's notion of sage philosophy; D. A. Masolo's genealogical exploration of rationality; and Tsenay Serequeberhan's project of existential hermeneutics in the African context.

This list is not exhaustive, and it is certain that many readers may find some of these names unfamiliar. In truth, many of the names in the European canon have also lost their familiarity. We are in times, for instance, in which philosophy undergraduate majors and doctoral students from many of our prestigious universities have no idea who most of the names in the European philosophical canon are beyond a very small set of usual suspects. Nevertheless, it is the work of experts to produce the work that will provide a body of work for those who may develop interest in the ideas of such figures, ideas that may offer much for our understanding of the human condition. It is clear that, without the contributions of the Africana thinkers, reflections on such concerns as existence, ethics, aesthetics, politics, and human studies exemplify, at best, a false universal. Such a consequence is, however, of little relevance where, as in the Africana tradition, these thinkers are engaged and honored by the practice of a critique. For people of African descent, we need, then, an emancipation of ideas in which we can engage, without subordination, thoughts that we can treasure far into subsequent generations. A task faced by our generation is the liberation of such ideas.

Frederick Douglass as an Existentialist

The first phase of liberation must thus involve a rejection of
the material conditions and ideological images contrived in
the interests of the slave-holder class. The slave must reject
his/her existence as a slave. In the words of Frederick Douglass, "Nature never intended that men and women should
be either slaves or slaveholders, and nothing but rigid training long persisted in, can perfect the character of the one or
the other."

—Angela Y. Davis,
"Unfinished Lecture on Liberation—II"

I mentioned earlier, in chapter 1, my experience of sifting through
responses to the call for papers for Existence in Black, my edited volume on black existential philosophy. In the end, when chapters
were evaluated and edited and the work was in its penultimate stage
of production, I stared at a text containing many surprises.

One surprise emerged from composing the index of proper names. There was a clear list of influential figures in black existential philosophy. I have already mentioned some of them in the previous discussion. Particularly surprising were the many references to Frederick Douglass and W. E. B. Du Bois. Upon reflection, however, the surprise wanes when we think of the obvious, at least in the case of Du Bois. For his contributing motif of double consciousness holds many fruits for inquiry not only on the identity dimension of existential thought but also on its focus on lived experience. Double consciousness raises interesting considerations, after all, for our understanding of consciousness. Being simultaneously one identity and its outsider raises problems of anguish that permeate the writings of New World blacks from Phillis Wheatley through to Richard Wright as well as to Ralph Ellison and Toni Morrison. In black writing is the question of black consciousness, the idea that black people have perspectives on the world. The familiar acknowledgment at the beginning of some slave narratives—"as written by himself"—is but an instance of this reminder. Black consciousness' manifesting itself in black writing is not sufficient, however, for the substantiation of black existential thought; if that were so, then all black writing would be black existential thought. To show that a text is a contribution to black existential thought one needs to show that the work raises theoretical questions of an existential variety on the situation of black people. That Douglass is a major contributor to African American (and thereby Africana) philosophy is indubitable.

Unlike Du Bois, however, whose analyses focus explicitly on consciousness as regionally situated (in the United States) and globally situated (in relation to Africa), Douglass requires different intratextual resources. To situate Douglass's contribution to existential thought requires an articulation that addresses both slavery and struggle. In Douglass's lifetime, a transition from the combination of de jure and de facto slavery (the former sanctioned by the U.S. Constitution, the latter wrought via racism and economic exploitation) to only de facto slavery (de jure slavery having been done away with by the Thirteenth Amendment) was the underlying contradiction. In Du Bois, there is the added transition from colonialism to neocolonialism except in the case of prisoners, and Jim Crow discrimination to the contradictions of bourgeois democracy. In Douglass, one is pushed to a concrete challenge to existential thought. Slavery and its legacy must be studied by Africana theorists because of the historical role it has played in the formation of modern black identity. Douglass's life and thought had to be among the historical exemplifications of those reply letters I had written to skeptics in black existential philosophy.

In her "Unfinished Lecture on Liberation—II," Angela Y. Davis focuses on the impact of slavery and the significance of struggle in Douglass's thought. Albeit critical of Sartrean existential philosophy, Davis's discussion of Douglass utilizes many existential motifs.[15] Observe her formulations of Douglass's situation: "One of the striking paradoxes of the bourgeois ideological tradition resides in an enduring philosophical emphasis on the idea of freedom alongside an equally pervasive failure to acknowledge the denial of freedom to entire categories of real, social human beings" (p. 55). Here, there is not only the centering of the question of freedom, but also a critique of the practice of using abstract humanity to conceal what existential phenomenologists call "human being in the flesh." Davis's reading of Douglass focuses on the existential problematizing of philosophical anthropology, where the human being's "essence" of freedom militates against essentialism—the doctrine of necessary preclusions of possibilities. Freedom, like existence, is not a property and, therefore, resists essentialism. As Jean-Paul Sartre argued in his introduction to Being and Nothingness, existence is transphenomenal; it exceeds predications we ascribe to it. For Davis, the concrete implication of freedom is that it must be achieved. Her words are instructive:

> The slave who grasps the real significance of freedom understands that it does not ultimately entail the ability to choose death over life as a slave, but rather the ability to strive toward the abolition of the master-slave relationship. . . . The slave is a human being whom

another has absolutely denied the right to express his or her freedom. But is not freedom a property that belongs to the very
essence of the human being? Either the slave is not a human being
or else the very existence of the slave is itself a contradiction. Of
course, the prevailing racist ideology, which defined people of
African descent as subhuman, was simply a distortion within the
realm of ideas based on real and systematic efforts to deny Black
people their rightful status as human beings. . . . The most extreme
form of human alienation is the reduction of a productive and
thinking human being to the status of property (pp. 54–55).

Broadus Butler, in his essay "Frederick Douglass: The Black
Philosopher in the United States: A Commentary," makes a similar
assessment, but he adds a thesis on humanism. African American
thought, he argues, is human-centric, as opposed to the system
centrism that marks much of the thought of Europe. Douglass, he
adds, focuses constantly on the relevance of ideas for human welfare. The onus of human existence is thus borne by the human
being. The "unfinished" dimensions of Davis's assessments carry a
similar appeal: no lecture on liberation is ever a finished lecture,
since the human struggle for humanity ends only when there are
no longer any human beings. Douglass as a liberation text, then,
emerges from his efforts to understand human possibilities in the
midst of dehumanizing realities. Here we find ourselves on familiar terrain.

"Man is born free," announces Jean-Jacques Rousseau in Du con-
trat social, his classic eighteenth-century work, "and everywhere he
is in chains. . . . How can this be made legitimate?" (my translation). Yet for African slaves in that century and Frederick Douglass
in the nineteenth, the man who is born free is one to whom they
are only abstractly related in Rousseau's formulation. They face a
different question, which might be formulated thus: The slave is
born in chains but she has freedom within her bosom—how is
this possible? The chains that Rousseau wanted to make legitimate
were different from those faced by Douglass. Douglass's chains can
never be legitimated except through false consciousness and the

most crass form of legal positivism wherein the laws simply are "right" by virtue of being laws of the state. As Greg Moses observed in "Frederick Douglass and the Republican Heritage on Affirmative Action," Douglass struggled with problems of legal positivism on the problem of obeying the U.S. Constitution. His position, argues Moses, is that laws can be changed and interpreted and, hence, made more just. The Constitution is, thus, an interpretable document; that is why the democratic process is a struggle. Competing interpretations vie for public authority.

In his three autobiographies, Frederick Douglass had occasion to recount the significance of his conflict with the slave breaker Edward Covey. They are, from the earliest (1845) to the latest (1893), *Narrative of the Life of Frederick Douglass, An American Slave, Written by Himself*; *My Bondage, My Freedom*; and *The Life and Times of Frederick Douglass: The Complete Autobiography*. In what follows, I am less interested in the historical matter of Douglass's shaking loose from the ideological grip of the Garrisonian abolitionists, wherein his role as interpreter of his experiences was first denied and subsequently asserted. What is important here is the portrait that emerges from the interpretations, how Douglass reads this important event in his life. Douglass could have chosen many interpretations (for example, that his "nature" "compelled" him to resist his condition or that his resistance constituted no more than an individual success). Yet we find what is in the annals of existential thought a portrait that foreshadows some of the best of Richard Wright's and Frantz Fanon's reflections on struggle and freedom.

The fight with Covey raises as many questions as it addresses. Although a moral tale, it challenges many of our assumptions, much of what we take for granted—which, in the end, is a lesson that a slave's condition challenges all of us who fail to treasure our freedom. In teaching us about ourselves, Douglass's discussion raises questions on what it means to be a human being, and in that regard it carries a philosophical as well as anthropological leitmotif.

The anthropological question is a normative one here, for although we are biologically identified as members of the human species, the normative, existential credo is that one *becomes* a human being. Alone, alienated, a thing amid nature, the individual, onto-genically understood, lacks the social resources through which and by which even individuality can be realized. Thus, "first steps" are moments of existential awakening. The Hebrew analogy is well known: consider the story of Adam and Eve that emerges in Genesis 2. There, Yahweh has created a species high on the chain of being, but a species whose realization of self is absent.[16] An injunction is added: Do not eat the fruit from the tree of knowledge. In philosophies of sin from St. Augustine's *Confessions* and City of God, to Frederick Douglass, to Jean-Paul Sartre's *Being and Nothingness* and William R. Jones's *Is God a White Racist?* injunctions serve a unique, identity-forming role. The world that existed for Adam and Eve before the injunction is a boundless world, a world without distinction of self from the rest of the universe, a world without reason to fold inward toward self-realization, a world without negativity. When Yahweh admonished Adam and Eve, however, a new consciousness emerged (at least in this Eden). There was now the question of disobeying Yahweh, a question through which the question of *obeying* Yahweh emerged. Both possibilities ironically constituted a consciousness *beyond* Yahweh, for it was not—could not be—Yahweh's place to make the decision for them here. The decision in such a case would be Yahweh's. Thus, the Fall, if we will, preceded the actual consumption of forbidden fruit.

But what *is* the Fall?

The problem faced by Adam and Eve is that what they *should* do is *their* responsibility. In Kierkegaardian language, they are in anguish. Anguish is a struggle against making decisions that are constitutive of responsibility for the self. In anguish, we fear decision; we attempt to decide *not* to decide. The performative contradictions of an undecided decision, or a decided indecision, are familiar in philosophies of existence. The catch is that in either case responsibility is borne, for the struggle itself makes the denied more apparent. I am a slave. I know my options are limited. I am told that my existence is deserved because I am by nature a slave; I am by nature someone whose existence is so lowly, so inferior that

I am supposedly without courage even to resist my identity as a slave. Yet I feel in my bones that I am without courage so long as I do not try to escape or engage in some act of resistance. There are those who have taken the risk. Some are caught by dogs, brought back, whipped, sodomized or raped, castrated, maimed, vivisected, lynched, or burned. Others never return. Then there are those who help. They return to help others escape, and they provide stories of those who made it. To take that risk would be an act of courage, and ironically so even when throughout I may be frightened to the bone. However afraid, I would not be by nature one who performatively accepts the existence of slavery. Even though failure to act against slavery does not *logically* entail acceptance of slavery, it is a feature of all oppressive credos that one's actions proverbially speak louder than one's words, and one's words speak louder than one's thoughts. The anguish folds in upon the self. It is a familiar scene in all cases of oppression and victimization: the rape victim who "wants it" if she does not resist sufficiently yet whose rape is intense, exemplified more and more, over and over, each time she constitutes dissent by resisting. It is progress when verbal resistance has standing in courts of law.

Returning to Genesis and to slavery, the power of the injunction is the absolute relation, sedimented in anguish, that it establishes between Adam's and Eve's selves. It is the negative instantiation of their freedom, which here is, ironically, their humanity. Their humanity is the moment of maturation in which they realize, out of their lived experience, the responsibility of constituting, at least morally, who they are. For the slave, this moment is manifested in the distinction between the institution of slavery and the lived reality of being a slave. The slave, from his *inside*, is a rupture of an overdetermined exteriority the moment the slave simultaneously imagines his experience from the outside as *having* an inside, of seeing an Other.

Slavery denies the slave any status as an Other or a self. The slave is property, which means that the (unjust) legal system of slavery regards him as no more than a system of relations: a "life estate"; a "fee simple absolute estate"; a "fee simple absolute subject to conditions subsequent." These are terms in Anglo property law. Respectively, they mean that nonslaves can have access to slaves in forms of use but without rights of sale as long as the nonslaves are alive; have access with rights of sale; or inherit slaves upon meeting certain conditions, after which rights of sale are also acquired. In none of these relations is there a slave's point of view. To state a slave's point of view is to initiate a rupture in such a system. A correlate, as we have seen, is Frantz Fanon's effort, in Black Skin, White Masks, to articulate "the Lived-Experience of the Black." Recall that Fanon explored this point of subjectivity in response to the overdetermined reality of "epidermal schematization." The black, he argued, lives in conscious realization of denied insides, a reductionism premised upon surfaces. The rub of racialized property reductionism is that at times even property has more standing than slaves. Frederick Douglass tried to assert his lived-experience, and consequently his humanity, through his early Narrative with the addendum "as written by himself." His written text made its way through the Library of Congress and was protected by the laws of the land, but he had no standing before those laws (to the point of having to earn a living lecturing in Europe to avoid being taken back to Maryland under the infamous fugitive slave laws of 1850). Legally inferior even to his text, Douglass was what Fanon accurately described in his introduction to Black Skin, White Masks as "a zone of nonbeing."

For African American slaves, there were obvious similarities between the biblical injunction against knowledge and U.S. slave owners' injunction against literacy among their lot. Ironically, in antiquated times, slaves were often teachers; in the Roman Empire, for instance, one learned from a teacher who was also a Greek slave, of whom Aesop was the most popular. The uniquely dehumanizing project of U.S. slavery was such that the significance of literacy marked a peculiarly humanizing possibility. To pose an analogy between Yahweh and slave owners would, however, be remiss. The historical reality was that slave owners imposed their relation to slaves with a hubristic analogy of being on a par with Yahweh made flesh in the form of a white Christ. The obvious difference, however, is the interpretation of Genesis 2 as a loving act of indirection on Yahweh's part by his pointing to knowledge in the negative in order to achieve the positive consequence of human consciousness and freedom. However loving U.S. slave owners claimed to have been, the bottom line was that the injunction against literacy was for another purpose. Yahweh loves humanity and poses an injunction that initiates the humanizing process.[17] Conversely, the slave owners' relation to the slaves is misanthropic: he attempts, at all cost, to deny their humanity. It is perhaps this realization that enabled slaves to develop a syncretic adoption of Christian faith with great emphasis on the Hebrew Bible. The "re-Semiticizing" and, thereby, recoloring ("Palestinizing") of Christianity was underscored by the poignant realization that the God of the Hebrew Bible, Yahweh, was not misanthropic, and the white slave owners' appeals to curses on children of Ham or Jesus' supposed white skin began to wear thin in the face of Noah's having been a *human being* and Jesus' having been Jewish, colonized, a man of color, and poor. The terrain is familiar, so I will not here rehearse the tenets of black theology, which could easily be found through consultation of such volumes as Gayraud Wilmore's *African American Religious Studies* or Timothy Fulop and Albert Raboteau's *African-American Religion*. Of importance is that literacy—knowledge—is an initial humanizing moment, and in each of Douglass's narratives, he speaks of his entry into the world of learning via Sophia Auld, whose realization of what that literacy represented later led to her dehumanization into a de facto—rather than merely de ure—slave mistress. Douglass's description of her "fall" in *My Bondage, My Freedom* is full of biblical existential motifs:

> I was *more* than that [chattel], and she felt me to be more than that. I could talk and sing; I could laugh and weep; I could reason and remember; I could love and hate. I was human, and she, dear lady, knew and felt me to be so. How could she, then, treat me as a brute, without a mighty struggle with all the noble powers of her own soul. That struggle came, and the will and power of the husband was victorious. Her noble soul was overthrown; but, he that overthrew it did

not, himself, escape the consequences. He, not less than the other parties, was injured in his domestic peace by the fall. . . . In ceasing to instruct me, she must begin to justify herself to herself; and, once consenting to take sides in such a debate, she was riveted to her position. One needs very little knowledge of moral philosophy, to see where my mistress now landed. She finally became even more violent in her opposition to my learning to read, than was her husband himself. She was not satisfied with simply doing as well as her husband had commanded her, but seemed resolved to better his instruction. Nothing appeared to make my poor mistress—after her turning toward the downward path—more angry, than seeing me, seated in some nook or corner, quietly reading a book or a newspaper (p. 97).

Radically understood, we can also argue that Douglass began his humanizing path at the moment he could imagine an act that exceeded his masters' will. Punishment, however ineluctable, only intensifies that realization: "being" a literate slave was an act of disobedience. This was surely the position of the master of the household, who "unfolded to [Sophia Auld] the true philosophy of slavery, and the peculiar rules necessary to be observed by masters and mistresses, in the management of their human chattels" (p. 97). He continues:

Mr. Auld promptly forbade the continuance of her instruction; telling her, in the first place, that the thing itself was unlawful; that it was also unsafe, and could only lead to mischief. To use his own words, further he said, "if you give a nigger an inch, he will take an ell"; "he should know nothing but the will of his master, and learn to obey it." "Learning would spoil the best nigger in the world"; "if you teach that nigger—speaking of myself—how to read the Bible, there will be no keeping him"; "it would forever unfit him for the duties of a slave"; and "as to himself, learning would do him no good, but probably, a great deal of harm—making him disconsolate and unhappy." "If you learn him now to read, he'll want to know how to write; and, this accomplished, he'll be running away with himself" (p. 97).

Reading exemplified a transgression; it exemplified being able to do what was both denied and forbidden. But the moment the *possibility* that it could be achieved was raised, Douglass was thrown into a process of imagining himself beyond his condition. He became aware that there was nothing *inside him* that precluded reaching beyond his circumstance. His self became, as Sartre would put it, a project. He faced himself in existential anguish. But this realization, that disobedience raised an anguish-riddled relation to the system of oppression, also raised the question of how far he *should* go. Being secretly disobedient draws the weight of existence onto the self. Public disobedience needs to be waged at some point as absolute disobedience. Later on, exemplification of this disobedience on a group level took the form of black Union soldiers. But for Douglass, this absolute disobedience took existential, situational form, which we shall discuss below.

We have here, then, the basis of all existential theses: The human being emerges but must paradoxically be presumed if but for the sake of that emergence. Kierkegaard urged modern humanity to break down systemic dehumanization so that authentic individuals could emerge. But he was aware that such emergence depended upon contexts of universal, and then absolute, preconditions. In the same century, Douglass explored these issues through the developmental reality of human life: from birth through childhood into adulthood. His biographies provide details of the struggle of slave children and their grandmothers (since their fathers, mothers, older sisters, and brothers were put to toil as soon as they were able), struggles in which there was effort to nurture the human spirit in an inhumane world.

At this point, we find Douglass's thought bearing many similarities to one of his successors, Fanon, who, as I've argued, has perhaps written the most influential body of black existential texts. In an illuminating passage of *Black Skin, White Masks*, Fanon observes that "a black who quotes Montesquieu had better be watched. Please understand me: watched in the sense that he is starting something" (p. 35). "Starting something" is, of course, here an assertion of his humanity. The similarities between Douglass and Fanon lead to a question on the liberating project itself in both's work, for both start with autobiographical reflections that lead to reflections on violence. For Fanon, the latter is addressed in the discussion of violence in The Wretched of the Earth; for Douglass, it is the fight with Covey. Fanon's discussion of violence has its early formulation, however, in Black Skin, White Masks. There, Fanon brings to the surface the limitations of the sparks of freedom as struggle for humanity that Douglass experienced in his initial encounters with written literacy. The clue is in chapter 1 of Black Skin, White Masks, where Fanon discusses language. His argument is, as we have seen in our preceding chapter, a provocative performance of indirection. He explores what appear to be solutions only to point out their folly: that if they succeed, they have failed.

Let us look at Fanon's argument again, but this time with some additional considerations. He points out that the location of the human being in a colonial, racist world has been displaced: human being has distortedly collapsed into white. Thus, most of the structural resources by which the term human is designated have been infected by whiteness. The black then faces the problem of trying to overcome negative blackness when the linguistic and semiotic resources available for positive identity are white. Semiotically, to resignify oneself out of blackness leads to signifying oneself in terms of whiteness. "Nothing is more astonishing," observes Fanon in Black Skin, White Masks, "than to hear a black express himself properly, for then in truth he is putting on the white world" (p. 36). The semiotic project must be waged. Something is achieved through achieving what is deemed an impossibility, a feat against nature. All liberation struggles are to an extent that: a defiance of "nature" as ontological closure. Something ontological is achieved when black people read and write, when they do that which supposedly cannot be done. Yet the underlying limitation of this view is that it lacks a creative moment. It carries the sense of taking from instead of contributing and being entitled to. In Euro-mythological terms, the black's immediate satisfaction is Promethean. Prometheus has stolen fire. (His other transgression, in Hesiod's Works and Days, is an attempt to trick the gods into eating fat and bone.) He is punished, forever chained to a mountain where an eagle flies down and plucks out his liver, which grows back each day in order that the eagle may repeat the assault. Nature as repetition emerges here. Fanon's claim, however, is that the contradiction of a black speaking the language *as a contradiction* plays against the hopes of semiotic reconfiguring of racial reality. Famed *Morning Show* host Bryant Gumbel's speaking *simply as a news anchorman* has been the brunt of criticism—"Is he white?"— precisely because his blackness brings out the contradictions of semiotic assimilation. However much he tries to suppress black embodiment through white linguistic signification, he becomes just that: *a black who speaks like a white.* Fanon argues that the frustration of this realization first pushes the black inward to personal life, where he may try to escape racism through romantic, interracial liaisons. But even when it is the white beloved who produces value, it leads to an internal collapse. (Fanon does not, by the way, claim that interracial liaisons that are not premised upon white legitimation are impossible. He claims only that those initiated for the sake of escaping blackness lead to such self-defeating conclusions.) Turn, then, to the lived experience of the black where there is a struggle to instantiate a self as mundane self, as ordinary self concerned with everyday things in the face of constant impositions of semiotic, gestural, politico-economic, incarcerating limitations. The black attempts to live as a "yes," but emerges, almost always, as a "don't!" I say *almost always* since Fanon points out in *A Dying Colonialism* that it is the black, after all, who creates négritude, a conception of blackness that, in spite of its limitations, which Fanon uncovers in *Black Skin, White Masks,* and *The Wretched of the Earth,* is nevertheless a creative assertion of positive blackness. The semiotic limitations recur with a vengeance here, since even the négritude writers' conception of black positivity found its substantive elements from overdetermined, white interpretations of blackness. As Tsenay Serequeberhan later affirms, in his *Hermeneutics of African Philosophy* (pp. 42–53), Léopold Senghor's critique of Western civilization, for instance, turned out to be more Eurocentric than African in its Manichaean system of values. A dialectical resolve takes over here, a resolve that Fanon reluctantly conceded through Sartre, that the semiotic upsurge prepares one for struggle; it is a humanizing moment, but not achieved humanization.

The Sartrean model, in "Black Orpheus," appeals to a nonracial working class, which cannot work for Fanon since the semiotic reality in the historic antiblack world is that a "nonracial working class" remains white. The struggle must be waged, Fanon concludes, on two levels: the ontogenic level of individual struggle and the phylogenic level of structural and biological imposition. The mediating factor here bridges the gap between the two as sociogeny. Without the addition of sociohistorical considerations, the black does not appear and cannot consequently be understood through theoretical appeals to value/racial neutrality. At the end of *The Wretched of the Earth*, the restructuring of this conclusion is an appeal to new concepts and a new humanity. This is because Fanon recognized that purely physical levels of struggle, although necessary, require what Sylvia Wynter has identified in her essay, "Is 'Development' a Purely Empirical Concept or Also Teleological?" as the "liminal" struggle to restructure epistemic categories into new, *semioticbiogenesis*, into new forms of life. Freedom, that is, always calls for a new humanity to emerge out of unfreedom, a new humanity that is paradoxically the guiding *telos* underneath a humanity denied. Returning to Douglass's world of the slave, all this comes as the underlying realization that, when all is said and done, slaves are human beings.

My Bondage, My Freedom signals an early, biographical portrait of a similar existential journey. Douglass tells a tale, from bondage to a qualified freedom. The irony of "my freedom" is that Douglass was in the end free in the sense of self-recognition of the important humanizing activity of his life's mission. Two wars needed to be waged: one of moral persuasion and the other for resistance, survival, and liberation. The effort to persuade slave owners of the moral turpitude of slavery focused too much on their moral welfare instead of the ongoing misery of the slaves. Liberation of slaves had to be waged through force, and similarly the *text* of postslavery (Douglass's "freedom") laid foundations for future texts of postslavery, autobiographical texts that led to a conflict in African American and Africana thought to the present, including those of Booker T. Washington, Anna Julia Cooper, W. E. B. Du Bois, Richard Wright, Malcolm X, Lorraine Hansberry, Angela Y. Davis, and many others. Identity, in other words, emerges from struggle, but a subsequent struggle emerges over identity itself. This is the hallmark of existential struggles: existence preceding essence; praxis preceding concepts. The limitations of the early initiating of a freedom struggle through discourse, reading, and writing, are that they do not by themselves translate into freedom. They create an epistemic upsurge, but without a material/historical one, there is a gap that must be closed.

Having identified a certain level of consciousness of his situation through his learning to read and write, Douglass then moved on to the crucial moment of fighting for his self-respect through his encounter with the slave breaker Edward Covey.

The circumstances are classic. Douglass, deemed unruly by his owner, Thomas Auld (Hugh Auld's brother), was sent to Edward Covey, a former overseer turned tenant farmer, who had often been "lent" unruly slaves for the purpose of breaking their spirit, as one would in taming wild horses. Covey's methods were simple: he would subject the slave to prolonged misery in an environment of seeming order and regularity. Unreasonably arduous tasks would be assigned, the purpose of which was to lead to failure on the slave's part. Failure would then be addressed by severe corporal punishment. Moreover, Covey used techniques of manipulation and camouflage to create a sense of his omnipresence. As Douglass relates in My Bondage, My Freedom,

> He had the faculty of making us feel that he was always present. By a series of adroitly managed surprises, which he practiced, I was prepared to expect him at any moment. His plan was, never to approach the spot where his hands were at work, in an open, manly and direct manner. No thief was ever more artful in his devices than this man Covey. He would creep and crawl, in ditches and gullies; hide behind stumps and bushes, and practice so much of the

cunning of the serpent, that Bill Smith and I—between our-selves—never called him by any other name than "*the snake.*" We fancied that in his eyes and his gait we could see a snakish resem-blance. One half of his proficiency to the art of negro breaking, consisted, I should think, in this species of cunning. We were never secure. He could see or hear us nearly all the time. He was, to us, behind every stump, tree, bush and fence on the plantation. He car-ried this kind of trickery so far, that he would some times mount his horse, and make believe he was going to St. Michael's, and, in thirty minutes afterward, you might find his horse tied in the woods, and the snakelike Covey lying flat in the ditch, with his head lifted above its edge, or in a fence corner, watching every movement of the slaves! (pp. 133–4).

We see here Fanon's and Douglass's credo of liberation turned on its head. Covey starts with a brutal, material introduction to re-ality, but a reality designed to push the slave one step short of de-spair. Despair would mean giving up to the point of indifference to life itself, which would then mean that the slave would cease to be productive. Despair is one of the pressing concerns of existen-tial thought, from Kierkegaard's concerns in *The Sickness unto Death* to Richard Wright's book 4 of his misunderstood *The Outsider*. Covey's strategy is to break the slave's spirit, but break it only enough for the slave to remain "productive." Douglass makes a classic existen-tial distinction between remaining and living in *My Bondage, My Free-dom*—"I remained with Mr. Covey one year (I cannot say I *lived* with him) . . ." (p. 133)—the former analogous to *being-in-itself*, a form of being suited for "things," and the latter to *being-for-itself*, a form of being with open possibilities, with self-reflection—in other words, *human* being. Covey's goal is to convince the slaves of their inferiority, to convince them that they *are* equivalent to ani-mals on the farm, to make them identify with that existence. "Find your equality," he seems to urge, "below humanity."

Perhaps most telling are the events that led to the moments of anguish that the four-chapter account on Covey is meant to signify. Covey orders Douglass to gather wood in the forest and transport it back by wagon with some supposedly tamed oxen. The perversity of the command: Douglass is expected both to identify with the oxen and see Covey's position of having to tame him! The oxen took flight and Douglass found himself in the situation of having to retrieve them and negotiate his way back home with untamed oxen. He declares, "I now saw, in my situation, several points of similarity with that of the oxen. They were property, so was I; they were to be broken, so was I. Covey was to break me, I was to break them; break and be broken—such is life" (p. 132). Douglass managed to retrieve the oxen and make his way back to Covey's farm, but upon arriving, the oxen broke loose again and damaged the entrance way. The result was Douglass's receiving a severe flogging.

As time went on, and many floggings later, Douglass took ill one day and attempted to rest, despite Covey's kicking him and ordering him to continue laboring. Douglass resolved to appeal to Thomas Auld, his legal owner, issuing a complaint against Covey's cruelty. That Douglass did this at all is a sign of his unusual naïveté with regard to matters of justice, morality, and pity in his youth (he was approximately sixteen at the time). His appeal indicates a guiding motif of pacifist reasoning: always give the oppressor, violator, or colonizer the opportunity of doing the right thing; give him, that is, the benefit of the doubt. Auld's response, however, was to accuse Douglass of trickery and laziness and to order him to return to Covey.

Returning to Covey's farm, Douglass made some important resolutions. I won't here relate them all since they have been amply discussed in such places as Bernard Boxill's highly subtle reading of the tale in "The Fight with Covey" and Cynthia Willett's "Frederick Douglass." Instead, I shall focus on his decision to defend himself if Covey were to attack him again. We should note that this "defense" at first took symbolic form. He speaks of a charm handed to him by Smith, a fellow slave, to protect him from flogging. In addition, there was the expectation of Christian prayer—although Douglass mentions, throughout, the limitations of Christianity as a means of moral suasion: Covey was, after all, a devout Christian. In both the charm and Christianity, we see a restatement of the theme of semiotic limitations. They represent moments of resolve, but the concrete reality of contention is Covey in the flesh.

After a period's calm, typical of Covey's penchant for surprise, Covey charged Douglass from behind and attempted to tie him up. Douglass's account in *My Bondage, My Freedom* warrants a lengthy quotation:

> Whence came the daring spirit necessary to grapple with a man who, eight-and-forty hours before, could, with his slightest word have made me tremble like a leaf in a storm, I do not know; at any rate, *I was resolved to fight*, and, what was better still, I was actually hard at it. The fighting madness had come upon me, and I found my strong fingers firmly attached to the throat of my cowardly tormentor; as heedless of consequences, at the moment, as though we stood as equals before the law. The very color of the man was forgotten. I felt as supple as a cat, and was ready for the snakish creature at every turn. Every blow of his was parried, though I dealt no blows in turn. I was strictly on the *defensive*, preventing him from injuring me, rather than trying to injure him. I flung him on the ground several times, when he meant to have hurled me there. I held him so firmly by the throat, that his blood followed my nails. He held me, and I held him (p. 149).

Notice Douglass's observation that "*The very color of the man was forgotten.*" The existential dimension of the situation was such that it collapsed reflective, conceptual reality. It broke through the saturated composition of skewed, racist reality. Covey called for help; first from his cousin Hughes; then from his hired hand Bill. Douglass fought each off, leaving only Covey to contend with him. "Covey at length (two hours had elapsed) gave up the contest. Letting me go, he said—puffing and blowing at a great rate—'now, you scoundrel, go to your work; I would not have whipped you half so much as I have had you not resisted.' The fact was, *he had not whipped me at all*"(p. 151). For the remaining six months, Covey never struck Douglass again, and Douglass even gained a reputation as a slave who would have to be killed if anyone attempted to strike him. For philosophers of existence, Douglass's reflections on the incident are of great value:

> Well, my dear reader, this battle with Mr. Covey . . . was the turning point in my "*life as a slave.*" It rekindled in my breast the smouldering embers of liberty; it brought up my Baltimore dreams, and revived a sense of my own manhood. I was a changed being after that fight. I was *nothing* before; I WAS A MAN NOW. It recalled to life my crushed self-respect and my self-confidence, and inspired me with a renewed determination to be A FREEMAN. A man, without force, is without the essential dignity of humanity. Human nature is so constituted, that it cannot *honor* a helpless man, although it can *pity* him; and even this it cannot do long, if the signs of power do not arise. . . . After resisting [Covey], I felt as I had never felt before. It was a resurrection from the dark and pestiferous tomb of slavery, to the heaven of comparative freedom. I was no longer a servile coward trembling under the frown of a brother worm of the dust, but, my long-cowed spirit was roused to an attitude of manly independence. I had reached the point, at which I was *not afraid to die.* This spirit made me a freeman in *fact*, while I remained a slave in *form*. When a slave cannot be flogged he is more than half free. He has a domain as broad as his own manly heart to defend, and he is really "*a power on earth*" (pp. 151–2).

It should be borne in mind that Douglass does not take the position that a slave who does not defend himself deserves to be a slave, as Boxill reminds us in his "The Fight with Covey." For Douglass, slavery is a categorical evil. What Douglass focuses on here is the normative dimension of freedom, of its coextensive manifestation in the human spirit of responsibility and self-respect. His conclusions are not naïve. He speaks of "comparative freedom." This is because he is aware, always, like Rousseau, Marx, Cabral, Fanon, and C. L. R. James, of the need for structural change. He speaks of force, but force here is ambiguous since he also contrasts it with helplessness. Force here refers to will, to agency, to the human being as active. At the heart of the tale, then, is a statement on agency, and what is the point of any liberation project, as Sartre observed in his *Critique of Dialectical Reason* and as Fanon observed throughout his corpus, without oppressed people's agency?

There is much in this tale, which warrants perhaps a full-scale study in the form of a treatise. Douglass speaks of his experience as a rite of passage, and he speaks of two traditions—African (the charm) and Christian (the prayers). Extraneous to the context of oppression and violence is a leitmotif of West African and Christian rituals of spiritual maturation through physical trial. The possibilities may well be endless. For our purposes, the importance of the existential reading is that it accommodates all of these readings since they follow the actual act. In his discussion of Douglass's accounts of the battle, Bernard Boxill articulates this dimension through pointing out that none of the consequences of the act could have been foreseen in the act itself. Boxill is correct. I should like to add, however, that an added dimension of the accounts is precisely the explorations that Boxill and many others have pondered. Douglass's testimonies and reflections draw us not simply into a contemplation of the moral wrongness of slavery, but also into the metaethical level of morality's *relevance* in exigent situations. It is the hallmark of all philosophies of existence that the metaethical level is their terrain. The source of anguish here is the human capacity not only to judge morality, but also to go beyond it.

The battle concerned Douglass throughout his life. It returns in his final biography, *The Life and Times of Frederick Douglass* (1893), in pretty much the same form as *My Bondage, My Freedom*. In both accounts, he stands firm with regard to its liberating significance, but he is unsure about its significance for Covey. Douglass was here thinking in classical Christian terms about the moral welfare of his tormentor. To close, however, I would like to offer another consideration. Throughout our discussion, we have seen analogies between Douglass's expected existence and that of farm animals. U.S. slavery was a concerted dehumanizing project. It is this dimension that garnered its peculiarly *antiblack, racist* characteristic. The tale itself reveals much about racism. Racism, properly understood, is a denial of the humanity of a group of human beings either on the basis of race or color. This denial, properly executed, requires denying the presence of other human beings in such relations. It makes such beings a form of presence that is an absence, paradoxically, an absence of human presence. That being so, such beings fall below the category of Otherness, for an *Other* is *another* human being. With a being erased to a realm of property, even linguistic appeals—cries for recognition—are muffled, unheard; waving hands, gestures for acknowledgment, are invisible. It is not that they do not trigger impulses between the eye and the brain; it is that there has been a carefully crafted discipline of unseeing. The black slave is, thus, a paradoxically seen invisibility in this regard; seeing him *as a black slave* triggers not seeing him as a human being.

The fight with Covey, then, is a moment of scratching through this veil of nonseeing and raising the question of pushing the stakes up to Otherness. Whatever Covey may have said, he *knew* that Douglass was a human being, and Douglass *knew* that Covey knew it. The *physical* struggle dragged Covey into a moment of equilibrium; it was a point at which the only way for any of them to survive was by moving *upward*. For Covey, whether through fear, rational self-interest of preserving his reputation, or limited respect, it meant leaving Douglass alone. For Douglass, however, it meant, as he suggested, reaching for the heavens. His autobiographies are important ethical documents in this regard. They signify a testament that the voice from below is also an SOS from an Other.

The twentieth century has been marked by the continued struggle of that Other against projects of demotion. At this century's end, a message we can learn from the existential Douglass is perhaps best exemplified by a Haitian proverb, a proverb from a place fitting for closing this discussion, since Douglass later became a U.S. ambassador to that country: "Beyond the mountains, there are more mountains." So the struggle has been, and so it continues to be.

What Does It Mean to Be a Problem?

W. E. B. Du Bois on the Study of Black Folk

> I concluded that I did not know so much as I might about my
> own people.
>
> —W. E. B. Du Bois, *The Autobiography of W. E. B. Du Bois*

In his 1903 classic *The Souls of Black Folk*, W. E. B. Du Bois made a prognosis that has haunted the twentieth century. "Herein lie buried many things which if read in patience may show the strange meaning of being black here at the dawning of the twentieth century. This meaning is not without interest to you, Gentle Reader; for the problem of the twentieth century is the problem of the color line" (p. 41). When Du Bois wrote "Gentle Reader," he was being more than rhetorical, for this Reader, for whom there was once presumed a lack of interest and therefore (falsely) a lack of relevance, is here alerted that his condition, being other than black, was inscribed in the core of the problems in question. The black, whose "strange meaning" and "being" were also called into question, represented also a tension in the presumed order. Du Bois did not here write about *being* black but about its *meaning*. He announced a hermeneutical turn that would delight even his most zealous philosophical successors. This hermeneutical turn signals a moment in a complex struggle, a moment marked by its admission of incompleteness and probably impossible closure. The black, subject to interpretation, becomes a designation that could be held by different groups at different times and as such is both concrete and metaphorical. If the color line is at the mercy of interpretive blackness, then its boundaries carry risks, always, of bleeding into each other. The "Gentle Reader's" possibilities are announced, then, as paradoxically less fixed in their fixedness than he may be willing to admit. Such a reader may intensify, then, his effort to take "precautions."

Du Bois's announcement has played itself out, prophetically, in this regard. Race and color have marked a course through the twentieth century like a rift through the planet in whose wake and quakes corpses and heaps of ideological rubbish have piled themselves, like casualties on the Western front. Deny it as we may, as a consequence or cause of a multitude of evils the problem of the color line is a persisting problem — a problem that, in the eyes of a thinker such as Derrick Bell, in his *Faces from the Bottom of the Well*, is here to stay. Born from the divide of black and white, it serves as a blueprint of the ongoing division of humankind. The color line is also a metaphor that exceeds its own concrete formulation. It is the race line as well as the gender line, the class line, the sexual orientation line, the religious line — in short, the line between "normal" and "abnormal" identities.

The twentieth century was also marked by another pronouncement of grave import: the struggle for liberation and, hence, revolution. There were revolutionary struggles in Asia, decolonization struggles in Africa and the Caribbean, civil rights struggles in the United States, and indigenous struggles worldwide. Like the fate of Du Bois's announcement on color, many of the revolutionary efforts wrought at the century's morn have fallen into ill repute at its twilight. Yet the forces that gave them validity haunt our present. Global economic inequality intensifies in the face of First World dismissal of the *relevance* of revolution and, hence, revolutionary consciousness. We are in a sorry moment as the question of an active consciousness, of taking a stand, of resistance, has shifted its focus from systems to intrasystemic "critique." There is no longer the Leninist call of what is to be done. Instead, there is the pathetic retreat: What *can* one do?

Two announcements came at the twentieth century's dawn, announcements that have been serving as themes of our explorations thus far: identity and liberation. In spite of talking about "color lines," Du Bois's explorations have charted a genealogical thematic of fundamental thoughts on the twentieth-century subject of the twentieth-century self: His anguished voice was, after all, addressing problems of identity, the resolution of which later culminated in a voice of revolution. *The Autobiography of W. E. B. Du Bois* charts a course from New England liberalism in Great Barrington and Cambridge, Massachusetts, to communist internationalism in New York City's Harlem, and Accra, Ghana, though the closing remarks reveal a beautiful fusion of Marxism with African American existentialism:

> I just live. I plan my work, but plan less for shorter periods. I live from year to year and day to day. I expect snatches of pain and discomfort to come and go. And then reaching back to my archives, I whisper to the great majority: To the Almighty dead, into whose pale approaching faces, I stand and stare. . . . Teach living man to jeer at this last civilization which seeks to build heaven on Want and Ill of most men and vainly builds on color and hair rather than on decency of hand and heart. Let your memories teach those wilful fools all which you have forgotten and ruined and done to death. . . . Our dreams seek Heaven, our deeds plumb Hell. Hell lies about us in our Age: blithely we push into its stench and flame. Suffer us not, Eternal Dead to stew in this Evil—the Evil of South Africa, the Evil of Mississippi; the Evil of Evils which is what we hope to hold in Asia and Africa, in the southern Americas and is-

lands of the Seven Seas. Reveal, Ancient of Days, the Present in the Past and prophesy the End in the Beginning. . . . Let then the Dreams of the dead rebuke the Blind who think that what is will be forever and teach them that what was worth living for must live again and that which merited death must stay dead. Teach us, Forever Dead, there is no Dream but Deed, there is no Deed but Memory (pp. 422–3).

Identity and liberation are two themes that lay beneath the waves that announce seemingly other themes. Identity calls for the question of a being's relation to itself. Thus, as I've been arguing, we find identity questions in ontological questions, questions of being, essence, and meaning—in short, of the existential force of the question, in the end, "What am I?"

In the liberatory question, we head, too, through a series of philosophical turns. Although the two meet on the question of who is to be liberated, the liberating animus charts a course of value that at times transcends being although not always essence. Liberation is a concern about purpose, a concern about ought and why: Whatever we may be, the point is to focus energy on what we ought to become.

A powerful dimension of Du Bois's work is the extent to which he straddled both the identity and liberatory divides, divides of research and divides of policy. In his writings, the search reveals the normative and the normative reveals the search. His classic essay "The Study of the Negro Problem" offers several challenges on how researchers in the human sciences should go about studying racialized people. These challenges present a unique feature of African American thought; such thought raises the metatheoretical level of investigation even at the level of methodological involvement.

I have mentioned Du Bois's question of what it means to be a problem and I have reiterated it through discussions of specialized terms like "epistemic closure" and "anonymity" and "double consciousness" here and there. The following is a development of these terms through an exploration of the richness of Du Bois's argument for a humanistic social science.

The Young Du Bois's Situation

In 1896, the year in which the Supreme Court of the United States affirmed segregation of the races in the landmark case of *Plessy v. Ferguson*, W. E. B. Du Bois, then twenty-eight years of age, was called upon by the University of Pennsylvania to conduct a study of the black populations of the Seventh Ward, a ghetto, in the city of Philadelphia. Nearly seven decades later, he recounts in *The Autobiography of W. E. B. Du Bois* the invitation and the situation with the sensibility of an elder attuned to both the wisdom and naïveté of his youth, saying:

> It all happened this way: Philadelphia, then and still one of the worst governed cities, was having one of its periodic spasms of reform. A thorough study of causes was called for. Not but what the underlying cause was evident to most white Philadelphians: the corrupt, semicriminal vote of the Negro Seventh Ward. Everyone agreed that here lay the cancer; but would it not be well to give scientific sanction to the known causes by an investigation, with imprimatur of the University? It certainly would, answered Samuel McCune Lindsay of the Department of Sociology. And he put his finger on me for the task. . . . If Lindsay had been a smaller man and had been induced to follow the usual American pattern of treating Negroes, he would have asked me to assist him as his clerk in this study. Probably I would have accepted having nothing better in sight for work in sociology. But Lindsay regarded me as a scholar in my own right and probably proposed to make me an instructor. Evidently the faculty demurred at having a colored instructor. But since I had a Harvard Ph.D., and had published [*Suppression of the African Slave-Trade to the United States of America* a recognized work in history], the University could hardly offer me a fellowship. A compromise was hit on and I was nominated to the unusual status of "assistant" instructor. Even at that there must have been some opposition, for the invitation was not particularly cordial. I was offered a salary of $900 for a period limited to one year. I was given no real academic stand-

ing, no official recognition of any kind; my name was eventually omitted from the catalogue; I had no contact with students, and very little with members of the faculty, even in my own department. . . . I did not hesitate an instant but reported for duty with a complete plan of work and outline of methods and aims and even proposed schedules to be filled out. My general plan was promptly accepted and I started to work, consulting Lindsay regularly but never meeting the faculty. With my bride of three months, I settled in one room in the city over a cafeteria run by a College Settlement, in the worst part of the Seventh Ward. We lived there a year, in the midst of an atmosphere of dirt, drunkenness, poverty, and crime. Murder sat on our doorsteps, police were our government, and philanthropy dropped in with periodic advice (pp. 194–5).

Years later, Du Bois gave mature reflection on how he understood the so-called Negro Problem in his youth, saying, "The Negro problem was in my mind a matter of systematic investigation and intelligent understanding. The world was thinking wrong about race, because it did not know. The ultimate evil was stupidity. The cure for it was knowledge based on scientific investigation. At the University of Pennsylvania I ignored the pitiful stipend. It made no difference to me that I was put down as an assistant instructor, and even at that, that my name never actually got into the catalogue; it goes without saying that I did no instructing save once to pilot a pack of idiots through the Negro slums" (p. 197).

Du Bois faced a formidable task. That he was given only a year, without assistance, to present a systematic study of the black population in the Seventh Ward of Philadelphia betrayed the bad faith of the institutions that commissioned that study. In effect, Du Bois was set up to fail, but with the provision that his failure count as affirmation of the pathologies of the community under study. In other words, Du Bois's study was to serve as a theodicean legitimation of Philadelphian society (and by implication, U.S. society). Theodicy is the effort to reconcile the goodness of an all-powerful deity with the existence of evil. In modern times, theodicy has been secularized through making political systems or systems of rationalization stand for the fallen god, and by making social evils or contradictions stand for the annoying evils or imperfections of the system. Du Bois's labors were expected to demonstrate that Philadelphia's evils were extrasystemic, were features of the black populations, rather than intrasystemic, things endemic to the system and, hence, things done to the black populations. We see here an ironic relation to research, for if Du Bois were successful at what he was commissioned to do, he would have been a failure at what he himself had set out to do, which was to find out the "truth," as it were, of the Philadelphia black population's situation. The glitch in the institution's expectations was Du Bois himself; he was, after all, W. E. B. Du Bois, the future "dean" of African American scholarship. That title eventually came to him from the pioneering work he produced from The Philadelphia Negro (1899) through to Black Reconstruction in America (1935), and subsequent work in history, sociology, political economy, and philosophy. The twenty-eight-year-old Du Bois knew that he was hired as a lackey to legitimize policies premised upon black pathology, but, being a "race man," he knew, as well, that opportunities for black folk to succeed rather than fail were few and far between. He knew that any effort on his part to study and demonstrate the ordinary required extraordinary efforts, efforts that were no less than Promethean. Reflecting on the opposition he faced, he later wrote, in his Autobiography: "Of the theory back of the plan of this study of Negroes I neither knew nor cared. I saw only here a chance to study an historical group of black folks and to show exactly what their place was in the community. . . . Whites said: Why study the obvious? Blacks said: Are we animals to be dissected and by an unknown Negro at that? Yet, I made a study of the Philadelphia Negro so thorough that it has withstood the criticism of 60 years" (p. 197). Indeed, he had. Du Bois's work withstood sixty years of criticism because he not only studied the black populations in Philadelphia, but also questioned the study of black folk in the United States and, by implication, other antiblack societies.

"The Study of the Negro Problem" inaugurated a profound turn in the study of human beings in the modern era. The title brought the turn into focus succinctly by its focus on *study*. Du Bois, in effect, announced the metatheoretical question of how theory is formulated. There is something peculiar, he suggests at the outset, about how blacks are studied—key to consider is whether they are studied at all—which requires reflection on one's method more so than one would with normative populations. Practices of systematic inquiry and critical self-assessment are often put to the wayside by commentators in favor of opinionated statements of what supposedly must be so with regard to blacks. In effect, the Negro problems were thrown out of the sphere of human problems into the sphere of necessity premised upon pathologies. Consequently, Negro problems often collapsed into *the* Negro Problem—the problem, in other words, of having Negroes around. In this regard, it was, as commentators such as Fanon subsequently noted, a predominantly white problem.

Problematic People, or People with Problems?

The issues of problematic people are well known among existential and phenomenological theorists. It can be understood in terms of the spirit of seriousness. The spirit of seriousness emerges when there is a collapse in the divide between values and the material world. In such instances, the material world becomes a cause of values and their absolute limitations. In other words, there is such an isomorphic relation between values and objects of value that they become one. Thus, the object fails any longer to signify or suggest a particular value or meaning; instead, it *becomes* that value or meaning. In cases of a problematic people, the result is straightforward: They cease to be people who might face, signify, or be associated with a set of problems: they *become* those problems. Thus, a problematic people do not signify crime, licentiousness, and other social pathologies; they, under such a view, *are* crime, licentiousness, and other social pathologies.

How does one study problems faced by a people without collapsing them into the problems themselves? Du Bois begins "The Study of the Negro Problems" by offering a definition of social problems:

"A social problem is the failure of an organized social group to realize its group ideals, through the inability to adapt a certain de-
sired line of action to given conditions of life" (p. 2). That Du Bois
focuses on the social is already a theoretical advance. For in his time,
the tendency was to approach the study of a people in terms of either phylogenic or ontogenic considerations. The phylogenic focuses on species differences where, especially with regard to the
"racial" status of blacks, debate took the form of whether they
were members of the human species. The ontogenic consideration
had limitations in its focus on the individual organism. With such
a focus, one would address simply an individual organism that
works and another that fails—as can be easily found in any study
of a set of human subjects—but the meaning of "working" and
"failing" transcends the organism itself. The problems, matters re-
lating to success or failure, require a third mediating consideration: the social world. The social world mediates the phylogenic
and the ontogenic and presents, through the complexity of social
life—life premised upon intentions, actions, and the ongoing
achievement of intersubjective relations—a world of agency, deliberation, and contingency. It is a world without accident but
without, as well, necessity. It is a world that brings things into
being that need not have been brought forth. By focusing on the
social, then, Du Bois has, in one sweep, taken the U.S. discourse on
blackness onto unfamiliar ground.

This previously uncharted ground of social analysis required a
different method of reading problems; as Du Bois explains,

[A] social problem is ever a relation between conditions and action,
and as conditions and actions vary and change from group to group
from time to time and from place to place, so social problems
change, develop and grow. Consequently, though we ordinarily
speak of the Negro problem as though it were one unchanged question, students must recognize the obvious fact that this problem, like
others, has had a long historical development, has changed with the
growth and evolution of the nation; moreover, that it is not one
problem, but rather a plexus of social problems, some new, some

old, some simple, some complex; and these problems have their one bond of unity in the act that they group themselves about those Africans whom two centuries of slave-trading brought into the land ("Negro Problems," p. 3).

That social problems are not static raises the question whether it is possible to conduct systematic study of a constantly changing or metastable subject. The metastability of the subject here is a function of human reality. The human being is a subject that constantly challenges the permanent relevance of data. In effect, the tendency to stratify the Negro problem betrays a tendency to address black populations as though they were not human populations. As human populations, they are metastable. Such a reminder brings into focus important dimensions of the problem of studying black folk. If an error in studying black folk emerges from a failure to recognize their humanity, one might think that such an error could easily be alleviated by merely studying them as human beings. The question brings into focus the problem of racial formations. Can a racial formation be rigorously studied as a *human* formation?

Du Bois addresses this problem by raising another dimension of the human being that is not addressed simply by recognizing its capacity for change. After raising the social dimension he explores the historical specificity of blacks in the U.S. The historical reality of blacks in America is one of struggling against conquest, kidnapping, enslavement, and a constant reconstruction of racial hierarchies at each moment of seeming triumph over racial oppression. The Civil War, he points out, eradicated legalized chattel slavery without eliminating the conditions that racialized slavery in the first place. The result was, then, a reassertion of forces against the freedom of black folk. This dialectic between freedom and unfreedom is such that it raises, as well, the question of a dialectic between the past and the future. In taking heed of historical impositions and the possibilities sought in present inquiry, Du Bois brings another problem into focus—the problem of the political. "They do not share the full national life," he posits, "because there has always existed in America a conviction . . . that people of Negro blood should not be admitted into the group life of the nation no matter what their conditions might be" (p. 7).

The political problem, although not explicitly stated as such, has the consequence of political nihilism. Political nihilism is the view that one's political institutions are incapable of positively addressing one's social needs. Such nihilism is an understandable consequence of the nation's anxieties over black inclusion. Such anxieties rest, as Du Bois sees it, "on the widespread conviction among Americans that no persons of Negro descent should become constituent members of the social body. This feeling gives rise to economic problems, to educational problems, and nice questions of social morality; it makes it more difficult for black men to earn a living or spend their earnings as they will; it gives them poorer school facilities and restricted contact with cultured classes; and it becomes, throughout the land, a cause and excuse for discontent, lawlessness, laziness and injustice" (p. 8). A consequence of this social problem is the widespread credo, "Why bother?"

The equating of blacks with failure has played itself out over the course of the twentieth century. It is what troubled Fanon in the 1950s, when he reflected on the sociogenic conditions of failure in antiblack societies, and it has been a recurring theme in the 1980s and 1990s. Cornel West, in *Race Matters*, has, for instance, rearticulated this problem as one of nihilism in the black community, and I have examined this problem as a larger problem of political nihilism in a postmodern world in my *Her Majesty's Other Children*. Du Bois, however, links the problem of nihilism to a peculiar dimension of social reality that goes unnamed in his seminal article but which nonetheless serves as its subtext—namely, oppression.

A Phenomenological Detour

Before I state the theory of oppression that will underlie the rest of this discussion, some preliminary remarks are called for, because although my focus is existential, the way I go about conducting my analysis is phenomenological. For some readers, such an approach may require explanation, especially since by raising the phenomenological in my discussion of the existential, I bring forth also that which is existentially phenomenological and phenomenologically existential, two combinations that may make some specialists cringe.

By *phenomenology*, I mean reflective thought upon what can be called objects of thought. An object of thought emerges as such through suspension of certain kinds of interests in the world. In the everyday world, I walk to the store with an interest in the thing I would like to purchase. I drive to work in order to complete the tasks I have for that day. The reason I work at all is that I either like my job or, given my class status, must do so in order to survive. In this world, I meet people with expectations of conversation, to learn from them, to know what's going on, to strike a deal, to be, perhaps, a little less lonely. This world of interests and purpose is familiar among phenomenologists as the "natural attitude." The phenomenological moment begins when we suspend these sorts of interests; through suspension, we put aside these types of questions. It is not that we eliminate them; we simply do not make them our focus. Thus, through such suspension, we may wonder what it means to walk to the store, or instead of focusing on my interest in the thing to be purchased, I focus on the thing itself. I may think about what it means to drive to work. I may wonder *what it means to work*. I may ponder what it means to meet people, to strike deals, or to be lonely. As I suspend—or "bracket"—certain interests, I find myself approaching these objects of thought as phenomena. Phenomena, as most phenomenologists define them, are objects of thought or, better yet, objects of consciousness. I am conscious of these phenomena, and the form of this consciousness—indeed, consciousness itself—is "directed" or "intentional": consciousness is, always, consciousness of something. Without something of which we are conscious, we are left with, in a word, *nothing*.

Nothing. In *Being and Nothingness*, Jean-Paul Sartre explored this consequence of the intentionality of consciousness. He presented, first, as is well known, an ontological argument. If consciousness must be consciousness of something, and if consciousness by itself constitutes nothing, then the form of intentionality already points beyond itself. Indeed, even *beyond* connotes the limitations of idealism, where the world is reduced to an idea, for without transcendence, *beyond* makes no sense. An ironic consequence of this observation is that it raises an argument that undergirded the brand of phenomenology against which Sartre had rallied his brand of phenomenology—namely, Husserlian transcendental phenomenology. The argument that even the beyond makes no sense without the possibility of transcendence is one that goes back to Immanuel Kant's transcendental reflections on experience in his *Critique of Pure Reason*, and at its core is an insight that affected Edmund Husserl's *Ideas* and *Cartesian Meditations*—namely, that at the core of such argument is the idea that sense must make, in a word, *sense*. The appeal to making sense or having meaning is more than the *validity* of such appeals but their *viability* in projects of achieving, say, "rigorous" intellectual work. The transcendental argument is premised upon the necessary and universal conditions for an idea, conditions that make the idea objective, so to speak. But doesn't such a notion of objectivity presuppose a rationality to reality that fails to account for the negative moment that stimulates such reflection?

Sartre, it is well known, proposed a radical *existential* phenomenology. The existential turn goes to the heart of intentionality as a *pointing toward* that simultaneously embodies a *standing apart*. *Ex sistere*—the Latin etymology of *existence*—means to stand apart, and *existence*, the French cognate, is to exist and to live. To stand apart, the existential moment, challenges any preceding necessity, any preceding meaning. Thus, how could a transcendental presupposition be at the heart of such reflections? Sartre's way out was simply not to address it; he performed transcendental phenomenological work without reflecting upon it as transcendental. The *existence* of which he speaks is presented, for instance, as an *object* of phenomenological investigation— even though as such it is understood by readers who may lack the mediation offered by analysis. Since these readers also exist, they see the point as they stand apart from it in the paradoxical epistemological act of being drawn to a concept by differentiating themselves from it—the act, that is, of what Sartre calls "nihilation."

Case in point: If consciousness by itself is nothing, what, then, emerges when consciousness reflects upon consciousness? The formal move Sartre made was to point out the embodied prereflective moment that is objectified by the reflective moment. Thus, reflective consciousness reflects upon prereflective consciousness as its object. In effect, we have a negation reflecting upon a negation, which raises serious questions of whether it can deny itself as a negation or reduce itself to a negation. The denial and the reduction carry dangers, Sartre argues, of "bad faith."

Bad faith is a lie to the self, one that involves an effort to hide from one's freedom. One's freedom is at the heart of the absence of substance or a sedimented thing that we expect to conjoin us to the things of which we are conscious. We seek two things—the object of consciousness and consciousness itself. Yet consciousness, Sartre argues, is not a thing, so in such instances, there is simply one thing that remains—the object of consciousness. Freed from "thingness," we find ourselves facing a slippage of the self; our selves are not fully contained but, instead, always ecstatic—always, that is, facing their possibilities and past. Motivations abound on why such distancing might be unbearable, and many of us seek retreat in various directions. One retreat is into a pit of "thinghood," where we convince ourselves that we are, literally, full of ourselves. Or, we may deny all, convincing ourselves that we are so free from "thingness" that we can transcend everything. Such paths, as is well known among Sartre scholars, are respectively called a retreat to facticity ("thingness") and a retreat to transcendence (absolute freedom).

Sartre complicates matters by adding a requirement to consciousness, a notion that should already render Sartre's antitranscendental appeals suspect. Nevertheless, his requirement is straightforward: consciousness, he argues, must be embodied. The logic of embodied consciousness makes sense simply because without being embodied, consciousness cannot be somewhere; and without being somewhere, consciousness cannot be a point of view; and without being a point of view, there could be no position from which to be conscious of anything. Every there requires a here.

Here is where I am located. That place, if we will, is an embodied one: it is consciousness in the flesh. In the flesh, I am not only a point of view, but I am also a point that is viewed: I see, hear, and smell; and I am seen, heard, and (let us say without embarrassment) smelled. The one who witnesses me—through sight, sound, and smell—is the Other. And I do the same to him. Both of us, however, can be aware of another phenomenon, that of being seen, heard, and smelled. Implicit in that experience is the Other as a subjective point of view to whom I am presented as a self-aware object. Sartre identifies several forms of bad faith or self-lie connected to these relations. The first of these is sadism.

Sadism by itself is not a form of bad faith. One can engage in sadistic sexual play, for example, which means that one has, in principle, taken the position that one's role isn't absolute, isn't, in existential parlance, "serious." Recall that the spirit of seriousness is a bad-faith attitude that involves a collapse of values into material conditions of the world. With such an attitude, values are "caused" by the physical world and are "in" the world in forms similar to the release of energy from a split atom. Put differently, the serious spirit treats values as ontological features of the world. Values lose their force as judgments and become ossified reality; they *are* the way the world is. The bad-faith sadist is, therefore, serious. Sadistic sexual play is not bad faith, because in such an instance the erotic charge emerges for the sake of *playing*, which requires recognizing that one *chooses* the rules of the game.

Choice is an activity whose importance is so central to our subsequent discussion that I should take a moment to discuss its meaning here. A condition of one's freedom is that one is able to choose. Yet, choosing and having options are not identical: choices may work in accordance with options, but one may choose what is not a live option. The choice, then, turns back on the chooser and lives in the world of negation. There the choice at best determines something about the chooser, though it fails to transform the material conditions imposed upon the chooser. Theories that fail to make the distinction between choice and option carry the danger of using gods as the model for human choice. For gods or for that matter, God, there is no schism between choice and option, so whatever such a being chooses *is*, absolutely, what *will be*.

The sadist can, at best, *play* God, but the sadist cannot *be* God. The sadist who is not playing, however, situates himself on the level of God; such an obvious lie to the self affirms such sadism as a form of bad faith. The sadist of whom Sartre speaks is one who isn't playing; a sadist such as this desires to be the only eyes that function as eyes, the only standpoint of sight. Such a being "becomes" the point of view from which others are seen and thus manifests a desire to see without being seen, since a consequence of being the *only* point of view is the absence of others. To do that, the sadist must control the sight of others, force them never to function as a point of view. His credo? "I am the only point of view." Solipsism is, thus, another feature of serious sadism.

Then there is the serious masochist. Such a figure seeks to *be* through being seen. The nothingness of consciousness carries no "reality" sufficient to found being. Thus it is better to be the object of consciousness. The masochist throws him or herself beneath the eyes of the sadist, and where there are no willing sadists, the masochist attempts to create one. The irony here is that his desire to be pure object, to be a saturated existent, to be at the mercy of the sadist and thus give up agency, the masochist ends up manifesting agency; he ends up attempting to fix the sadist's vision and, hence, the sadist's freedom. We could think of the serious sado-masochistic paradox: "Beat me! Beat me!" pleads the serious masochist, to which the serious sadist replies, with narrowed eyes and a wry grin, "No."

The serious sadist wants to deny others' points of view, a task that would render others patently not-others. The world that he desires is a world without what phenomenologists in the Schutzean tradition call *sociality*. Sociality is the intersubjective world, the world of others, a world which requires the self *and* others, and the self as other to those other selves. The serious sadist cannot act out his sadism, cannot even emerge, without others. Similarly, serious masochism is a point of view with the interest of not being a point of view. Only the masochist could pull off this lie to himself, which renders the masochist's efforts performative contradictions.[18]

What Sartre leaves out of his argument, but we shall here consider, is this: if the precondition of sadism is another subjectivity and the precondition of masochism is a subjectivity that seeks to fix other subjectivities, then intersubjectivity is the precondition of these forms of bad faith. The argument is, in other words, transcendental. Seen in this way, the orthodox interpretation of sociality as a psychological phenomenon fails to appreciate the importance of nonpsychological foundations of the psychological appeal; in other words, it could only be purely psychological in *bad faith*. In Husserlian phenomenology, the point is put differently: psychological explanations are relative to the "factual" appeals of the natural sciences, appeals that are not absolute by virtue of their failure to raise radical questions of their own assessment. A psychologistic explanation of social reality is, in other words, blatantly not phenomenological, and by bringing in the natural sciences as modes of legitimation, they commit another phenomenological sin: they reintroduce the causal nexus of the natural attitude, a nexus that should have been suspended at the moment of initial reflection.

That sociality could not be denied without contradiction is the message we gain from the analysis of bad faith. Sociality is so much at the heart of human relations—indeed, their relationality, through which emerges their historicity—that we might as well add another definition of bad faith. Bad faith is the denial of sociality. Since bad faith is also a lie to the self, then to lie about sociality is also a self-lie. What type of self could be such that it is at one with social reality? It is at last what we know as human reality. In denying our sociality we deny our humanity.

At this point, all would seem fine and good but for a problem raised by the phenomenological approach. If sociality is linked to our humanity, does this mean that we must always be among others in order to be human? I recall a student informing me that he preferred "cooperative" housing during his years of study. I responded that such a way of living would have driven me crazy. In order to appreciate people, I need to be away from them now and then. For my fellow human beings to be staring me in the face without a reprieve, with no exit, as Sartre would say, would truly be hell.

Yet, it would be remiss for my student to have concluded that I was antisocial or a misanthrope. Paradoxically, an antisocial human being or a misanthrope could ironically manifest his ire through intense association with others. The intensity could be such that the sui generis dimensions of each human being would be lost. With such a loss, one need not pay the sort of attention to others as one would when each emerges as an individual human being. Karl Jaspers, in his *Philosophy* and in his *Philosophy of Existence*, has pointed to this saturation as simply *Dasein*, simply being there. His preferred existence, *Existenz*, calls upon us to look at each other as irreplaceable. Although not premised upon Husserlian and Sartrean phenomenology, Jaspers's observation affirms its insight: The irony of sociality is that although it is the world of others, it is also a world of irreplaceable others. It is the world that is the condition through which there are socially created phenomena to which I could refer in thought, memory, or imagination. The irreplaceable dimension suggests, however, a remarkable aspect of sociality and socially created phenomena. They are not simply here or there; they are *achieved*.

That sociality is an achievement raises a problem that is peculiarly phenomenological. Recall the phenomenological approach. We suspend certain interests in order to examine their phenomenal features. Let's give this approach another name. Let us call it *ontological suspension*. Ontological suspension means that we are less concerned with what something is and more concerned with its thematization, its meaning. With a rock, a chair, or a tree one could suspend ontological commitments and simply study its meaning. If one is uncertain, one could consult others for information regarding such an object. Could one do so with a person? Another human being? If one does so, doesn't that leave one simply with a flat surface? Could one intend a person without, say, moral commitments? How do moral commitments differ from ontological commitments when we focus on personhood? And finally, how can the Other appear as *other* without *being* another? In the course of our investigations, a curious possibility emerges for us that is absent from our investigations of rocks, chairs, and trees. Interrogation shifts from third-person resources—those of a set of explanations, of knowledge, of ways of the world offered in support of certain judgments—to the second person. Such another is no longer *such an other* but, instead, You.

And a Detour by Way of Race

The *You* with which I have concluded the last section is peculiarly absent in many discussions of race and racism. Although the racist's basis for such a violation is obvious—he does not want to recognize some people as *You*—a difficulty emerges in cases where there are antiracists who make a similar violation: the same people continue to be ignored in the discourse of antiracist reasonability. When many race theorists write about race, it seems as though they are not writing to racialized people. Race talk has that flavor of "Hey, take a look at this!" The problem is that "this" tends to be "them."

There is much that many of us, including those who theorize about race, claim to want to know but in fact do not really want to know about racial reality. The trajectories are familiar: the concept of race, for instance, is without natural scientific foundation and should therefore be abandoned. Race is divisive, so for the sake of unity, it should be abandoned. Race is a social construction, so it shouldn't be granted the same credence as things that are supposedly not social constructions. This last claim tends to ally itself with the first, since things that have natural scientific foundations tend to be treated as things that are not social constructions. And then there are the blatant racist versions of each of these: race is scientifically redeemable through measurements of normal versus abnormal groups of people, with, of course, the abnormal being those designated inferior races. Race is divisive, so blacks and other colored people should abandon their identities in favor of abstract, supposedly neutral identities. Race is a social construction, so colored races should abandon their race attachments. Why do I call these racist positions? It could easily be seen here that the latter set presents "neutrality" and "normal" as terms devoid of racial significance when in fact they are highly charged racial terms. Because, say, whites are normative in an antiblack society, it becomes superfluous to identify them when other groups are not mentioned. Put bluntly: The appeal of many so-called racially neutral terms— *man, woman, person, child*—is that they often signify whites, except where stated otherwise. They have a prereflective parenthetical adjective: (*white*)*man*, (*white*)*woman*, (*white*)*person*, (*white*)*child*. It is not the case that these terms *must* signify these subtextual markers; if that were so, then our position would exemplify the spirit of seriousness. It is that our life world, so to speak, is such that these are their significations. To advance the claim, then, that we should abandon the other designations in favor of the so-called racially neutral ones in no way threatens the unholy alliance between the racially favored group and normativity.

But what about the first set? How do they fare, given our criticism of their reactionary offshoots? From a phenomenological standpoint, the obvious flaw is that to reject race on scientific grounds is not a phenomenological critique, and, further, it achieves at best a claim to scientific modes of assessment. It tells us that something is wrong with race and with racism, but it does not transcend mere factual conceptions of error. The other objections, about divisiveness and social constructivity, fail phenomenologically because they simply scratch the surface. After all, divisiveness by itself is not an evil. One could easily think of some alliances that should be divided. And social constructivity itself is not necessarily fictitious. One could easily think of things that rely on social reality for their existence without being fictions. Is language, for instance, fictitious? How about community? Friendship?

What's more, there are instances of appeals to scientific validity that are hypocritical. For example, commentators who reject race because of its scientific invalidity have not scrutinized the type of race questions that many scientists ask. In a paper entitled "Anthropological Measurement," geneticist and anthropologist Fatima Jackson presents a reading of scientific treatments of race that chal-

lenge much that is presumed by both conservative and liberal proponents of a scientific resolution of race rationalizations. The standard liberal criticism, found in writers like Anthony Appiah and
Naomi Zack, rejects race on the basis of its failure to achieve an isomorphic relation between morphological differences and genetic
difference. People who look different may share genes, and people
who look alike may be genetically different. The conservative position uses the old racial morphological categories of Caucasoid,
Mongoloid, and Negroid, and then struggles through mixtures of
these three. And "origins" range from monogenesis in Africa and
then spontaneous differences of genes and appearance, or polygeni-
cally with different genes and appearances on each continent. Thus,
there would be Asian races, European races, African races, Australian
races, North American races, and South American races.

An implication of these ways of thinking is that one takes positions on race *because* of the scientific information available. We
already see, however, a divide in understanding the relationship
between race and racism here. For it should be clear that one
could take the position that there are distinct sets of races *and* that
we should respect them equally. One could then, as many of our
more progressive predecessors did in the nineteenth century,
fight against racism while believing in the existence of races. And
one's belief in the origins of races could be either monogenic or
polygenic.

Jackson's work argues, however, that the types of questions we
have been asking about genetics are dead wrong, and their wrongness is unfolding in one of the largest natural scientific efforts to
chart the course of the human species: the Human Genome Project. What the Human Genome Project reveals is that *all* human
genes originated from the same region: Southeast Africa. During
the period of our evolution, when human beings were in a single
region, conditions were ripe for the maximum diversity of our
gene pool. Subsequent patterns of movement and mating selections led to the focus on certain combinations of those genes in
certain regions over others until the gene variations spread across
the planet. What this means is that, from a genetic point of view,

there is indeed one human species that originated from a single region. But here is the rub: race critics have read this conclusion to mean that races do not exist. In one sense it is true; races do not exist. *One* race exists, and that race is "Negro."

Yep, *Negro*. How could this be? The standard pitch is to say that there is one race, the human race. But "human," from a genetic standpoint, is determined by the genetic diversity of *Homo sapien sapien*. Genetic diversity emerges at the point of origin, which here means evolution. After evolving, environmental conditions and mating selections affect formations. Thus, in the Negro or so-called "black Africans" is the genetic diversity that was subsequently reworked through such processes to create lighter Negroes—Negroes whom we have come to know as Caucasoid and Mongoloid. Or put differently, if Negroes were to disappear, we would not be able to reproduce the genetic diversity of the human species. If, on the other hand, all groups but Negroes disappear, it would still be possible to reproduce the genetic diversity of the human species.

Now although this may strike some of us as odd, it is something that many people who have been designated Negroes have long been able to "see." The social constructivists may point out that one could pick a socially mediating document like a birth certificate of a member of any group known today as "white" or "Northeast Asian" and notice the following consequence, should that birth certificate reveal two biological parents designated "Negro." Many of us would begin to "see" Negro features in that person. The hair, the lips, the buttocks, the feet; the way the person walks, talks—and, yes, dances and makes love—would take on new meaning in our race-inflected social reality. The families of many people who have been designated Negroes, especially in North and South America, tend to be morphologically diverse, but regarded (for the obvious reasons of being biologically related) as genetically one. In effect, such families are microcosmic versions of the human species.

The question emerges, What do geneticists now "see" when they look at their fellow human beings? And correlatively, what would race theorists who have supported scientism now advocate, given the growing body of evidence of our most ambitious natural scientific mapping out of the human species? Will many of them now realize that Abraham wasn't simply going to Canaan and Egypt, but that he and his company were also returning, that they were genes coming home? And more, would they now abandon, once and for all, stories of Egyptians' "Asiatic" and "Semitic" ancestry and face up to the fact that Semites and Asians could be looked at as Southeast Africans moving northward? But more to the point, would such theorists who have not been designated black now begin to look in the mirror and accept themselves as simply lighter-skinned Negroes? Could they now begin to think of "human" as "maximum diversity" and, hence, Negro?

Tough medicine, no?

It is with questions like these that the uniqueness of racial reality comes to the fore. As we have already seen, Frantz Fanon presented one of the best existential phenomenological treatments of this subject with the departing observation that between phylogenic explanations (the sort exemplified by natural scientific mapping out of the species) and ontogenic explanations (the sort exemplified by natural scientific portraits of an individual organism or theoretical study of an individual), there is sociogeny—that which emerges from the social world.[19] The social world is here understood as a dynamic medium of historical, economic, semiotic, and intersubjective forces. From the standpoint of the social world, the natural scientific support for humanity's diverse gene pool being synonymous with what we call "Negro" will be of little consequence if it does not affect the lived reality of how people negotiate their way through the social world. If, that is, the social world is premised upon there being people of different races and there being a major difference between Negroes and all other races, a difference of kinds, a difference that treats that group as subhuman, then the world would continue to be racially divided as such. An impact of social reality, then, is ontological; it transforms concepts—knowledge claims—into lived concepts, forms of being, forms of life. The geneticist might demonstrate the existence of one race, but the social reality is multitudinous: races and their mixtures abound.

The usefulness of a phenomenological analysis becomes obvious: It explores the intersubjective framework of meanings, the
impact of multiple intentions and sociality, to present interpretations that, at the same time, do not fall into the trap of bad faith.
This is so because phenomenology distinguishes between interpreting ontological judgments and making them. By suspending
the natural attitude, the phenomenologist is able to explore the
contours of the social world while keeping their contingency in
mind. It is with these considerations that we can now move further into the complex world of race and racial oppression.

Our first observation is that racism is a form of dehumanization, and that dehumanization is a form of bad faith—for to deny
the humanity of a human being requires lying to ourselves about
something of which we are aware. This observation debunks a
misconception in many presentations of racism. Racism, it is said,
emerges through an anxiety over the Other. The Other is supposedly a mark of inferior difference. The problem with this view is
that it fails to deal with the meaning of *Other*. Implicit in *Other* is a
shared category. If one is a human being, then the Other is also a
human being: here I am and there is *another human being*. Dehumanization takes a different form: here one finds the self, another self,
and those who are not-self and not-Other. In effect, as Fanon
points out in the seventh chapter of *Black Skin, White Masks*, there is a
schema in which self-Other relations might exist between whites
and between blacks, but white-black interaction does not signify a
self-Other relation. Rather, it is self-below-Other relation. A black-
white interaction, on the other hand, signifies a self-Other relation.
For the black, in other words, the white *is* another human being,
but the structure of antiblack racism is such that for the antiblack
racist, the black is not another human being. The struggle against
antiblack racism is such, then, that it involves an effort to achieve
Otherness. It is a struggle to enter the realm, in other words, in
which ethical relations are forged.

So racism is a context marked by a paradox of being a human relation of inhumanity. It is a human act of denying the humanity of
other groups of human beings. This human act can be structural

(institutional) and situational (between individuals). Although the addendum "on the basis of race" is usually advanced, it is important to note that most racists advance the superiority or inferiority of a racial group without advancing a concept of race. They may, in other words, not know what races are—only that they do not like black people or indigenous people, and so on. But more, that racism involves dehumanization situates it as a form of oppression.

Alas: Oppression

Oppression, often understood in terms of impositions of power, is a function of the number of options a society offers its members. I here speak of options because of the vagueness of appeals to power. Although many of us know power when we experience it, defining power is another matter. Michel Foucault, for instance, has spoken about power and knowledge as fused realities— "power/knowledge." But indeed, that does not tell us what power is, only that knowledge is one of its manifestations, or that one of the forms of knowledge is power. Worse, many discussions of power often speak more about *effects* of power, the result of which is our gaining little understanding of what power may be. It is my view that power in itself is an empty notion, and that words like *force, power, motion, gravity,* and *sunsum* (the Akan word for *spirit* or *force*) are simply ways of talking about things that are able to put other things into being. For some commentators, it is institutions that have this power, and for others, individuals do as well. From the standpoint of an oppressed individual, however, power makes no sense if it is of no consequence. Recall our discussion of the relation between choices and options. Where there are many options, choices can be made without imploding upon those who make them. If a set of options is considered necessary for social well-being in a society, then trouble begins when and where such options are not available to all members of the society. In effect, such options have an impact on membership itself. In a world where I only have two options, but everyone else has three, it is highly likely that my choices will exceed my options more quickly than would others'. Where there are only two options, I may use up two choices before I begin to make inward, abstract choices, such as "neither," or "I will choose X or Y *affirmatively* or *reluctantly*." Eventually, it becomes clear that to make more than two choices without collapsing onto myself and the *way* I make choices, I will need to expand my options. But to do so would put me in conflict with a world that has only given me two options. In effect, then, to live like everyone else places me in a situation of conflict. Here, we see the problem brought into philosophical focus. For, to live like everyone else, to live as "ordinary," as "normal," would require of me an "extraordinary" commitment.

Think of Jim Crow racism or U.S. apartheid. Jim Crow, in limiting the options available for blacks in the everyday negotiation of social life, increased the probability of black social life being in conflict with American social life; it increased the probability of blacks breaking the law on an everyday basis. Such limited options forced every black to face choices about the self that placed selfhood in conflict with humanhood. We could think, as well, of the debate on abortion: when abortion was illegal in the United States, many women facing the choice of whether or not to have an abortion had no option but an illegal one. The consequence was that the meaning of being a woman in the society was also marked by a high probability of an encounter with the legal system or having one's reproductive activities carrying high associations with being "in trouble."

In the post–Jim Crow era, problems continue as the collapse of blacks into pathologies is such that it limits the options available for blacks in civil society. Many blacks, for instance, in going about their everyday life, incur a constant risk of incarceration. The expression "DWB" ("driving while black") has become so much a feature of American society that it made its way to a March 9, 1999, broadcast on National Public Radio. Blacks here suffer the phobogenic reality posed by the spirit of racial seriousness. In effect, they more than symbolize or signify various social pathologies—they become them. In our antiblack world, blacks *are* pathology. The consequence is obviously claustrophobic. Under such circumstances, blacks are forced to take extraordinary measures to live ordinary lives; an ordinary life, after all, should not involve routine encounters with the criminal justice system.

It is at this point that we encounter dynamics of black invisibility. Black invisibility involves a form of hypervisibility. The black is, in other words, invisible by virtue of being much too visible, is not seen by virtue of being seen. Being seen is, however, ambiguous here. It means an act of reducing a feature of reality to absolute reality—of ontologizing that which is not ontological. In effect, it means to render something present through making something absent. Let us call this phenomenon *epistemic* closure. In an act of epistemic closure, one ends a process of inquiry. In effect, it is the judgment "say no more."

In contrast, epistemological openness is the judgment "there is always more to be known." Placed in the context of making judgments about groups, epistemic openness pertains to the anonymity that undergirds the social dimension of each social group. A social group is such that each member can occupy the role that exemplifies it. When the one encounters a member of that group and identifies, usually by virtue of the role the member performs, the social group to which he or she belongs, it is good practice to restrict judgments to the context and to the social role but not to extend them to the full biography of the individual who plays that role. Such aspects remain anonymous, nameless. Thus, to pass by a student and to recognize him as a student need not entail the role of student to cover the entire scope of that student's life and being. Such is the case with many other social roles and groups: there is always more that one could learn about the individual who occupies that social role. In the case of epistemic closure, however, the identification of the social role is all one needs for a plethora of other judgments. In effect, to know that role is to know all there is to know about the individual. In effect, there is no distinction between him and his social role, which makes the individual an essential representative of the entire group. The group, then, becomes pure exterior being. Its members are literally without insides or hidden spaces for interrogation. One thus counts for all. The guiding principle of avoiding the fallacy of hasty generalizations is violated here as a matter of course. Blacks become both effect and cause, cause and effect, an identity without dynamism, without possibility.[20]

The study of the "Negro problem" calls for a provocative form of human study—the study of a human population whose humanity is a structurally denied feature of the society in which they are studied. Implicit in Du Bois's call for such a study, then, is an indictment of the society itself; as he declares in "The Study of the Negro Problem," "The sole aim of any society is to settle its problems in accordance with its highest ideals, and the only rational method of accomplishing this is to study those problems in the light of the best scientific research" (p. 10). And what is the best scientific research? The best scientific research has criteria that will, at best, put into relief some (if not all) of the prejudices of the researchers. Du Bois adds to his appeal the claim that "the American Negro deserves study for the great end of advancing the cause of science in general. . . . [And those who fail to do so] hurt the cause of scientific truth the world over, they voluntarily decrease human knowledge of a universe of which we are ignorant enough" (pp. 10–11). The best research is guided by a search for the universal with a sensitive eye for the unique. Data that purport to cover the human species without inclusion of blacks and other peoples of color are at best true over a subset of the human species. The humanity of black folks, then, is a necessary addition for the rigorous practice of the human sciences.

Du Bois's insight has been repeated by many scholars and writers throughout the twentieth century. Each of them, from Alain Locke to Ralph Ellison through to the genealogical poststructural work of V. Y. Mudimbe and the black feminist arguments of bell hooks and Joy Ann James echo this point—that the structural collapse of universality into whiteness (and masculinity) has exemplified a false universal. One may find a full picture of a society in those places that its members often seek to avoid. In African American philosophy, for instance, one will find studies of both what (white) American philosophy is willing to face and what it is unwilling to face.

In effect, it requires a reenvisioning of both what America is and what it means to study philosophy in America; the same applies to social science and the human sciences in general.

Du Bois then returns to the question of study with an addendum of humanistic study. Humanistic study calls for recognizing the limitations of essentialistic claims across a social group. "[W]hat is true of the Negro in Massachusetts," he explains, "is not necessarily true of the Negro in Louisiana; . . . what is true of the Negro in 1850 was not necessarily true in 1750" (p. 17). He then advances two categories of study—the social group and the social environment. The four suggestions for the study of the social group—historical, statistical, anthropological measurement, and sociological interpretation—have been hinted at in our discussion thus far. Given the impact of G. W. F. Hegel's introduction to his *Philosophy of History*, it was a longstanding view that blacks were not historical. Du Bois's advancement of the historical here was, in this area of thought, Copernican. The quantitative suggestions were less problematic because of the dominant ideology that placed blacks in close proximity to nature. It seems odd, then, that Du Bois had to reiterate their importance. His advancement of quantitative analysis makes sense, however, if we consider another feature of the dehumanization of blacks, a feature that hits the heart of inquiry itself—namely, the impact racism has on epistemological openness and closure.

Epistemological openness, we have seen, pertains to the anonymity that undergirds the social dimension of each social group. Du Bois's counsel, then, is toward opening this space of inquiry. Our turn to anonymity brings us to sociological interpretation. To break out of epistemic closure, one needs to recognize that blacks have points of view on the world. Such an approach, explains Du Bois, "should aim to study those finer manifestations of social life which history can but mention and which statistics can not count, such as the expression of Negro life as found in their hundred newspapers, their considerable literature, their music and folklore and their germ of esthetic life—in fine, in all the movements and customs among them that manifest the existence of a distinct social mind" (p. 20).

The second category, the peculiar social environment, addresses the problem of options raised before. Du Bois ends the essay by issuing a call that has lost its power today in light of recent efforts to discard the study of races: "[T]rue lovers of humanity can only hold higher the pure ideals of science, and continue to insist that if we would solve a problem we must study it" (p. 23). The transition from Negro to Black to Afro-American to African American has been marked, as well, by the transition from races to contemporary claims of its scientific invalidity (e.g., Appiah's In My Father's House) and its so-called social and political irrelevance. In response, critics have issued the same objection Du Bois did a century ago: deny as we might the continued relevance of race and racism in the lives of large segments of the American population, how will those who continue to bear the brunt of discrimination present their case without data that identify such patterns against them?

Epistemic Limitations

The problem with data is that they must be rigorously gathered. "Rigorously," here, means that the process of gathering and interpreting data must be guided by an understanding of the challenges raised by human studies and an understanding of the logic of social action and claims of universality. Moreover, the challenge addresses the integrity of the theorist as well, especially the theorist who might be a member of the community under discussion. As Du Bois observed later in his Autobiography: "I became painfully aware that merely being born in a group, does not necessarily make one possessed of complete knowledge concerning it. I had learned far more from Philadelphia Negroes than I had taught them concerning the Negro Problem" (p. 198). A member of a group does not live his everyday experience in a way that constitutes the reflection of study. To study one's lived reality requires a displacement and a new set of questions about that reality that render one's experiences at best as data to be added to the stream of data being interpreted. But more, the theoretical questions raised may be such that there is no precedent for them, which means that by raising them, one has placed oneself outside of a privileged sphere of knowledge. How one lives in a community is not identical to the sort of knowledge involved in how one *studies* a community. A striking feature of Du Bois's recommendations for rigorous study, however, is that in the midst of all his almost positivistic conceptions of objectivity in the study of black folk, there are also the hermeneutical considerations and the experiential considerations of looking at blacks from the *inside*. These are concerns that Du Bois himself deploys in another essay from the period, "The Conservation of the Races," which he presented to the Negro Academy the same year as "The Study of the Negro Problems" which was presented to the American Academy of Social and Political Science. The two academies represented a historical reality that took existential and phenomenological forms in Du Bois's two essays. For it is "inside," so to speak, to a community of black intellectuals, that Du Bois brought forth the existential phenomenological reading of the nihilistic threat of denied membership as a struggle of twoness, of two souls, of double consciousness. Double consciousness raises not only the experience of seeing the world from an American point of view and a black point of view (from the point of view of the black diaspora), but also from the tensions encumbered by such experience. Must *black* be anathema to *American?* What black folks *experience* are the contradictions of American society; it is an experience of what is denied, an experience of the contradictions between the claims of equality and the lived reality of inequality, between the claims of justice and the lived reality of systematic and systemic injustice, between the claims of a universal normativity and the lived reality of *white* normativity, between the claims of blacks not having any genuine points of view and the lived reality of blacks' points of view on such claims.

By raising the question of black problems from blacks' points of view, Du Bois raises the question of an *inside* that required an approach to social phenomena that puts the theorist in a position to break down the gap between himself and the subjects of study. For in principle, if the theorist can imagine the black point of view as one that can be communicated, then already a gap between the theorist and the black subject of study has been bridged. The theorist, whether white or of color, must work with the view of communicability and, simultaneously, a process of interrogation that will bring forth what black subjects are willing to divulge. In short, the method presupposes agency, freedom, and responsibility, which transforms the epistemological expectations of inquiry. From the outside, one could receive limited data; from the inside, one could also receive limited data. Combined, one receives "good" data, "solid" data, "rigorously acquired" data, but never *complete* data. It is by staying attuned to the incompleteness of all data with regard to human beings that one makes the approach humanistic. It is a method that reveals that when it comes to the human being there will always be more to learn and, hence, more to research.

By Way of Some Conclusions

Our times are marked by a profound divide in approaches to human study. The sentiments, as we have seen, gear toward total abandonment of liberatory questions in favor of identity questions. Without the liberatory calling, identity questions become struggles over definition or the rejection of definitions, ironically, on supposedly purely theoretical grounds. The result has been, on the one hand, the continued, often reactionary influence of neopositivistic approaches, where the effort is to imitate the natural sciences through quantitative conceptions of objectivity. At the other extreme is the postmodern rejection of all totalizations and concepts like *progress* and *rigor*, and even the adjective *human* in *human study*. There, hermeneutics or interpretation has taken a path to the seemingly trivial.[21] For African Americans, the situation is particularly moribund, for how could a denial of humanity benefit a people who have spent more than three hundred years struggling for it? How can African Americans take seriously the constructivity of their situation when social reality continues to smack them in the face as a reality that is hardly fictitious? And as for neopositivism, with its demand of value neutrality, a similar criticism applies: It is only the powerful that can *afford* a world devoid of value since they are already situated in a position to be its beneficiary.

Neopositivism and postmodernism are not, however, the only alternatives. Interpretations can be socially situated by the complex network of questions that pertain to the study of the human being as a metastable subject that is coextensive with a set of values, including the values of freedom and expectations for the sort of life appropriate to mature members of a society. I say *mature* because without a coherent conception of maturity, all members of a social group, regardless of age, would be infantilized, which would require surrogacy, and, hence, be problematic. Such an approach requires both taking seriously the conditions of objectivity raised by the intersubjective dynamics of the social world and the existential problematic of how human beings live. I have argued in *Her Majesty's Other Children* that such a call is for an existential sociology.[22]

Now, a century after Du Bois's encomia, we face a population called "African Americans." This population has been studied to the point of serving, throughout the twentieth century, as the bedrock of much sociological and anthropological work. That African Americans have been reinscribed into the grammar of race signification is such that the forces that precipitated the "Negro Problems" are clearly problems that have made their way to the dawn of another century.

In his later years, Du Bois came to the conclusion that the study of a problem was a necessary but insufficient means of eliminating it. He did, as is well known, defy the adage of radicalism in youth and conservatism in old age by reversing its order. Du Bois became a revolutionary because, in the end, he saw that knowledge by itself does not compel action. For knowledge to become effective, it needs to achieve a degree of historical force. Part of the Du Boisian legacy is the rich body of texts on which to build our contemporary understanding of people of African descent. In effect, he contributed to the epistemic project of transforming a population of people through transforming the conditions of historic recognition. While the struggle for new social relations continues, the project of humanistic study is such that the possibilities offered by a richer understanding of human diversity may help set afoot, as well, the world for which Du Bois so faithfully struggled. It is with such thoughts in mind that I bring this chapter to a close with a repetition of his words:

> Let then the Dreams of the dead rebuke the Blind who think that what is will be forever and teach them that what was worth living for must live again and that which merited death must stay dead. Teach us, Forever Dead, there is no Dream but Deed, there is no Deed but Memory.

five

Mixed Race in Light of Whiteness and Shadows of Blackness

Naomi Zack on Mixed Race

Out in the world later on, in Boston and New York, I was among the millions of Negroes who were insane enough to feel that it was some kind of status symbol to be light-complexioned—that one was actually fortunate to be born thus. But, still later, I learned to hate every drop of that white rapist's blood that is in me.

—Malcolm X,
The Autobiography of Malcolm X

And Mayotte Capécia is right: It is an honor to be the daughter of a white woman. That shows that she was not "made in the bushes." (This expression is reserved for all the illegitimate children of the upper class in Martinique; they are known to be extremely numerous: Aubery, for example, is reputed to have fathered fifty.)

—Frantz Fanon,
Black Skin, White Masks

Victoria Holloway, a woman who in today's terminology would be identified as being of "mixed race," explained her misgivings with being called "African American" in a presidential address to the Yale chapter of a minority medical students association. "While some have recently overthrown this term [black American] in favor of African-American, I have not. I find it too simplistic. I am not an African with American citizenship. Please do not misunderstand. I embrace my African roots. However, the term African-American excludes the Native American, White Protestant, and Jewish components of my distant ancestry. And, I identify most strongly with a culture rooted in the American South. Since I have not yet thought up a term that like better, I still call myself Black."

This woman makes no denial of her being "mixed." Underlying her claim, however, is a prevailing view among American people of African descent, and that is this: most of us are mixed. This awareness of being mixed has taken many forms of expression that have become banal in black communities. But their banality signals language games that are rich with political significance. Black people often speak of being mixed, for instance, without specific reference to the term "mixed." But a specific hierarchy emerges in these descriptions, where the European and Asian and Native American genealogical connection will nearly always be placed in a privileged position over the dreaded African dimension. In the American context, that dreaded dimension translates into a specific point of socially constituted inferiority. Although the geographical parameters may shift, since black, in the Western context, save finance, means sin, malevolence, inferiority, low, or bottom, the African element signals the road to such a marker of hell.

There is a nasty scenario that emerges time and again inside black communities in all of the diaspora (in spite of Central and South American denial of racism in those regions). Racist aesthetics are conditioned from the moral matrices of fairness and injustice to the correlative color schema of white and black. In between is not gray, as some may think, but light and dark brown. Since white fundamentally signifies superior, to affirm one's connection to one's whiteness generally signals the articulation of one's superiority. Such superiority is linked, however, to one's inferiority, since one is more white in relation to the degree to which one is less black. In affirming one's link to one's blackness is, however, a complex affirmation by virtue of the dual significance of blackness as both sin and suffering. To choose blackness when one could choose whiteness seems to take the form of a sacrifice that carries complex ethical questions of its own. Mixed-race people who reject blackness are despised in black communities; that is true. But mixed-race people who affirm blackness have often gained something that they will never gain from affirming their whiteness in white communities. Claiming their whiteness would be like middle-class people's affirming an allegiance with the rich by virtue of their appearing rich in comparison to the wretchedly poor. It is no accident that the recent assault on the poor in American politics amid the moral rhetoric of protecting the middle class converges with an intensified assault on people of color, with the black welfare queen and the black convict at a polar opposite to the good, middle-class, white married couple.

Complexities emerge in many variations on these problems of both identity and identification. What is often missed, however, is the question of how racial concepts actually play themselves out in mundane life. Most theorizing on these concepts is already situated in the reflective, theoretical mode, and in that regard, it often fails to see the extent to which, even in the most hostile racial environment, the bulk of racial thinking is so unreflective that it operates, quite often, without the concept of race at all. For instance, I have always been aware of my genetic origins outside of my black ancestry. But at the moment of my first daughter's birth, where discussions with parents and grandparents emerged as everyone tried to see how much she resembled whom, special narratives also emerged that may seem very alien to many whites. For depending on whose eyes, whose hair, whose tone my daughter had, a complex political discourse prevailed. The only comparison I can think of is one in which a white family may recount the rape of an ancestor who decided not to abort the pregnancy, or a romantic union of an ancestor with an offspring of a most ruthless enemy.

"Your daughter has blue-rimmed eyes," announced a nurse, puzzled.

"That's because I have blue-rimmed eyes," I answered.

Two weeks later, I sat with my maternal grandmother as I recounted the conversation with the nurse.

"So," I said, "it looks like your eyes have gone through you to Ma and me and Jenny."

My grandmother went into a discussion of the complexion and hair and eyes of all of her children and also my paternal grandmother's children. Then she spoke of her mother, who had brown hair, blue-rimmed eyes, and very "fair" skin, and of how her mother got these features from her mother, who was a Jamaican slave of a plantation owner from Scotland. That slave master was my great-great-grandmother's father. My great-great-grandmother's mother was an African slave. We can think toward the future as much as we would like. But there was a part of me that was revolted by the reality that some of that slave-owner's genes are being carried on in so many people I love. And I thought more about the injustice of how those very features are often described—"fair skin," "good hair," "pretty eyes," as they are called in black communities—as marks of biological "refinement," as if our African side were some crude muck in need of a good genetic cleansing. My response was not connected to "mixture" per se, no more than Victoria Holloway saw her mixture—for my paternal grandmother, a Chinese woman, never occasioned such a response. I've never looked at my father nor his brothers as indicative of something negative because of their being a mixture of African and Asian ancestry. The context, that is the story to be told, connected to questions of stories that are being told.

In her influential book *Race and Mixed-Race*, Naomi Zack takes on the philosophical question of exploring the conditions of telling such a story. The book is of historical importance in that it is the first systematic philosophical study of this social formation. In that regard, it will serve as a suitable context for our philosophical explorations of this phenomenon.

Race and Mixed-Race is separated into three parts, "The Existential Analysis," "The History of Mixed Race," and "The Philosophy of Anti-Race." The structure of the book reveals some dimensions of its theoretical stand, for the distinction of the existential situation from that of history locates the work in a particular conception of existential thought. Existential philosophers like Jean-Paul Sartre and Frantz Fanon, for instance, regard the existential analysis as fundamentally linked to the historical situation, and in Zack's actual discussion, we find a great deal of historical analysis. In either case, since the existential dimension of Zack's text comes to the fore, we find already another historically significant dimension of the text. It stands as the first explicitly existential book-length work by a professional American woman philosopher of African descent, and perhaps one of the major texts of a new wave of American existential thought. There are ironies here, for Zack adamantly rejects identification beyond the scope of chosen identities, but as we all know so well: neither Martin Heidegger nor Martin Buber ever referred to himself as an existentialist.

Following Kwame Anthony Appiah's rejection of racialism, Zack summarizes her book's thesis as being "that black and white racial designations are themselves racist because the concept of race does not have an adequate scientific foundation. If racial designations are racist, then people ought not to be identified in the third person as members of races, then individuals in the first person ought not to have racial identities" (pp. 3–4).

Given that racial designations are awful afflictions upon humanity, Zack asserts that: "the question arises of why rational and otherwise well meaning Americans still make the racial designations that they do" (p. 5).

This question of rationality is buttressed by an appeal to "science" in terms of "empirical facts"; as Zack notes that "the oppressiveness of some racial designations and the immanence of all of them, combined with the lack of an empirical foundation for the concept of race, entail that no racial words are appropriate designations for human beings" (p. 8).

And this dialectic works its way through to the existential conclusion that "[i]f the existence of certain human beings causes problems for certain concepts or systems of categorization, then it is the concepts or systems of categorization and not the human existants [sic] which need to be criticized and changed" (p. 17). This conclusion, existential though it may be, raises some problems early on in relation to the first claim of rejecting race because of its *scientific* invalidity. In effect, the existential argument suggests that "existents" should have precedence over concepts. But the scientific appeal suggests that scientific validity should have precedence over existential reality. If most people live their racialization well, why should race be debunked for those who do not, especially since the conceptual-existential tension is such that there will always be people who do not stand comfortably within conceptual schemes?

So we face the raison d'être for the existential turn, which is to explore the forces behind the choice of such designations of identity and identity formation in the face of their supposedly debunked scientific validity. I say *supposedly* primarily because *scientific* society has not proven to be any less racist historically than *lay* society. For instance, when Zack says, "What scientists now view as the mythology of race is closely intertwined with the historical conditions under which the now-disproved scientific theories of race were formulated" (p. 12), I find myself asking the question, Which scientists? We would be begging the question if we were to respond, "The enlightened ones." Unlike Zack (and Appiah), I do not have confidence in the general scientific community when it comes to speaking out on race matters. That same community is dominated in spirit by a form of physicalist naturalism and biological determinism that underlay various forms of racist intellectualism from the advancement of quantitative intelligence testing to insidious racist Darwinism. One wonders how far and wide are the distances between phrenologists of the nineteenth century and recent gene detectives who seek "artistic" and "rational" genes.[23] Even if such genes were generally distributed among the entire species, the eugenics claim is that one can genetically construct a

combination that will constitute at least, for that specific set of individuals, a "superior" combination of those very genes, and that
superior combination will be white. I don't see where there can be
a scientific objection to such a thesis, but I do see how, say, a fundamentally existential, ethical, and phenomenological response can
be made.

From the existential and ethical standpoints, one doesn't fight
against racism simply because race is a scientifically problematic
concept. Are we willing to say that if race were not a scientifically
problematic concept, we should then not fight against racism? Recall that one hundred years ago, both science and religion were
rock-hard appeals to racial realities, and that most human beings
believed in the reality of races as one would the reality of atomic
matter. Yet that didn't negate their fight against antiblack racism.[24]

From the phenomenological standpoint, the problem rests in
the very notion of a scientific instantiation of a concept as onto-
logically basic to begin with. We may call this "the problem of
constructivity." Like Appiah, Zack refers to races as "fictions," as
unscientific. The implication is that that which is not fictitious is
that which is scientifically determined. But what are the conditions
of these determinations? It would be an error, for instance, to
claim that social phenomena are invalid because of their "social"
status—which usually means that they have a dimension of subjectivity versus supposed "objectivity"—since implicit in that very
argument is the view that constructivity in itself lacks objectivity.
The world of the natural sciences would thus be advanced as, literally, preinterpreted worlds, as if scientific systems aren't systems
constructed with specific domains of meanings and (intrasystemic) reference. The constructivity of race does not in and of itself constitute the ontological conclusion of a fictitious reality.

What can be readily observed in race discourse, however, are the
clever ways in which value constructions are concealed and passed
off as "factual" or "value-free" constructions. The equivocations are
obvious when we reflect upon the terms that flow out of discussions on "purity," "superiority," "inferiority," "strength," "weakness," "rationality," or "affect." Zack explores some of these hidden

dimensions through an analytical treatment of race and a critique of origins. She points out that whites are defined as "pure," in terms of having no colored ancestry. "Coloreds," specifically blacks, are defined in terms of having at least one colored ancestor. She laments that "This schema unjustly excludes people with black forebears from white designation" (p. 9). One can ask, however, why this is a case of injustice. Given the earlier claims that racial designations are inherently unjust, why would it be just to achieve white designation? We can go even further and point out that there is clearly something unsettling about the treatment of whiteness in terms of purity. Other races function as pollution in relation to whites. Given the array of associations of blackness with dirt, the consideration of pollution is essential for the existential—that is, situational and intentional—features of racist designating.

The theme of pollution also carries, by the way, a thesis of "blood mixing," which Zack discusses throughout the text. On the level of myth and literature, Zack's investigations led me to wonder whether the paradigm Western sentiment toward miscegenation is embodied in vampire mythology. In most versions, to become a vampire one must first be bitten by a vampire (that is, suffer through a cannibalistic ritual) and then one must drink the blood of a vampire (that is, perform the cannibalistic ritual). Through the process, one is transformed into a vampire, a creature of desire who is also able to elicit desire from others. What happens, however, if one is bitten but does not die and one does not drink the blood of a vampire? Is one left partially standing in both worlds? Who stands as the mythical correlate of mixed-race here? It is possible that there are two levels of mixture here, since even the vampire was once a human being. But the verdict against being mixed is the same in both cases, for, in the final analysis, aren't both vampire and almost-vampire *unnatural* forms of existents?

It is not entirely the case, however, that white is determined by the provision that there is no black ancestry. True, there are whites who claim that their race evolved from entirely different ancestors than blacks, but for the most part, many whites, and especially those who are Darwinian white supremacists, take the position that all people evolved from Africa. They simply add that whites (and sometimes Asians) are the ancestors of those who progressed better on the evolutionary scale than the rest. In Zack's book, for instance, there are numerous allusions to white racist associations of blacks with apes, and, as Jan Nederveen Pieterse has shown in White on Black, the literature on blacks as the primary subhumanoid group is immense. The individual who is a mixture of white and black finds himself, then, in more than a construction of mixture by itself. He finds himself facing a mixture of clearly unequal terms. He is thus simultaneously less and more of an animal, in the American (and global) racial hierarchy of evolutionary humanoids. His choice of identity, then, functions in relation to blackness in dual forms of denial: affirmation of whiteness is a rejection of base blackness, but so too is affirmation of being mixed, since in either formulation the black stands as a point at which both white and mixed-race designations will stand, like a renaissance humanity that reaches at the gods in a flight from the animal kingdom, in a world "above." It is not that one is less of an animal in the extent to which one is a human being, but that one is less of an animal in the extent to which one is white.

Problems of contamination and biological preservation lead to a particularly powerful political construction in the United States: the family. Zack issues a powerful critique of the American presentation of family as fundamentally the white family: "The official American white family, which is a publicly sanctioned private institution for breeding white people, enjoys a preeminent position in American culture" (p. 34). Such a family is treated as the locus of values, security, and, above all, purity. In addition, the white American family structures patriarchy as a normative ideal, an ideal which some designated black social theorists, like E. Franklin Frazier in his The Negro Family in the United States and Orlando Patterson in his Rituals of Blood, accepted as axiomatic. The culmination of this standpoint of normativity that is well chronicled in the literature on American racism is the infamous 1965 Moynihan Report, The Negro Family in America: A Case for National Action.

Zack's response to the centering of the white patriarchal family is twofold. First, she attacks the socioscientific enterprise of demographic assessments of forms of family organizations: "The problem with demography as a tool for studying families is not that it fails to document feelings of alienation but that it fails to document forms of family organization that are not the dominant form in a given culture" (p. 45). On this matter, a text that would have been an interesting addition is Herbert G. Gutman's *The Black Family in Slavery and Freedom 1750–1925*. In that work, written as a response to the failures of the Daniel Patrick Moynihan Report and the limitations of E. Franklin Frazier's normative assumptions on which Moynihan's work was based, Gutman researched the written correspondences, by their own hand and through amanuenses, of thousands of slaves and freedmen, as well as the official documents on their filial relationships. A credit to that work is its taking to heart the Du Boisian admonition against treating the people one studies as the problems instead of identifying the problems they face. In the course of following that counsel, Gutman addressed the variety of conceptions of family that prevailed among slaves. He observed, for instance, that slaves developed different sets of mores for sexual behavior versus child-rearing behavior. For American slaves— who, being designated as property lacked legal protection over their sexual availability—marriage was primarily an institution for raising children.[25] This conception of marriage wasn't entirely far afield from the Anglo conception of marriage that evolved in the industrial revolution—that a man was able to procure a wife after he had procured land or some other means of livelihood. In contemporary terms, one should get married if one can support the children who will emerge from that union. This conception continues in terms of the dream of owning a home, which situates marriage and family in an economy that indigent populations, with up to five times the unemployment rate of the dominant group, cannot maintain. For the slaves, then, the question of "mixing" was not a major area of concern, since they didn't have the power to dictate the terms of such mixing; instead, the question of the offspring's survival was paramount. As a consequence, the discourse on race mixing was a fundamentally white and freedmen's discourse. We can think of a correlate in the contemporary discourse on racial mixing that emerges around affirmative action. Affirmative action is fundamentally a white discourse since the resources with which to implement affirmative action programs are, for the most part, in the hands of whites. Its structure then, with terms like "qualification," "disadvantaged," "best candidate," often dictates the inferiority of the colored element whose inclusion constitutes social "mixing." From the point of view of color, their inclusion or diversity actually *raises* the standards of institutions.

The second response comes out of the near positivist conception of science that underlay the claim that the concept of race is fictitious. "What is needed," writes Zack, "is a neutral definition of the family" (p. 46). The problem with this appeal is that family by itself is not a neutral concept. The very notion of neutrality signals conceptions of family that on its face calls for the rejection of certain inquirers on the question of family. For instance, here are some questions that Zack claims a neutral definition of family can be expected to settle:

> Are kinship, coresidence, and legal marriage necessary for a group to be a family? Are deceased family members and divorced family members part of an individual's family? Are sexual relations necessary between individuals who are not related biologically for those individuals to be family members? If sexual relations are necessary, must they be heterosexual? Do family members have to be of the same race or culture? Must they have a common language? Can animals be family members of the families of human beings? Who has the authority to say, "No, there is no family here," or, "Yes, this is a family"? Can new forms of the family come into existence or even be deliberately invented? Must the family be defined as an objective, observable unit, i.e., *positivistically*, or can the family be defined in terms of individuals' concepts of their own families? (p. 47).

The appeal to neutrality signals the direction in which the argument is headed, and it is where the text itself later concludes: liberalism in the philosophical sense, as an appeal to value neutrality in the assessment or adjudication of political or cultural phenomena. The problem is that liberalism is far from a value-neutral standpoint on the construction of families. It's like asking the conservative capitalist and the communist to put aside their differences and engage in nonjudgmental discourse. For the conservative or the communist to do so would constitute both's being liberal, as though they were both not in a quarrel with liberalism in the first place. Can the Muslim, the Jew, the Catholic, or the Mormon, for example, treat family as neutral choices without embracing a form of secularism? How about the Akan, the Hindu, the Hopi, and the Zoroastrian? Or how about our nineteenth-century families on slave plantations; what would constitute a neutral conception of the family for them? To claim that family is, as Zack defines it, "those sentient beings the individual feels most close to, thinks about most, and would suffer the loss of or separation from most grievously" (p. 47) betrays the far-from-neutral values of individuality and subject-centered social (or antisocial) formation. One can ask, for instance, whether this definition holds up in cases where the sentient beings offer no recognition of such a relation. Are we filially related, for example, to people who are obsessed with us or who have a crush on us or who may have affection for us in spite of our not even knowing that they exist?

Moreover, Zack's reference to the limitations of positivistic approaches to family while defending the individual's intentional constitution of filial relationships raises the question of constructivism that we advanced earlier. If we accept her arguments against race, even where individuals construct racial realities, why should we not also accept them against the construction—whether socially constituted or individually constituted—of family?

On these matters of choosing our constructions, Zack refers to the work of Martin Heidegger and the work of Jean-Paul Sartre. Zack appeals to Heidegger's distinction between science and technology, wherein our age is identified as an age of technology functioning as "the tail that wags the dog of modern science" (p. 152).[26] This appeal suggests that Zack simultaneously has two conceptions of science at work here; one narrow, one broad. In the narrow sense, races are designated to be realities that are without referents. I've already advanced my view that this conclusion fails to account for the other dimension of scientific language, where we can point out that the constructivity of race alludes to assessments of the multiple meanings of referents. I do not, however, wish here to criticize Zack's appeal to Heidegger, nor the philosophy of language that undergirds her position.[27] Instead, I would like to raise the question of some considerations that emerge as we examine the existential situation of mixed-race people's relation to technological domination.

The technological dimension has been lurking in the undercurrents throughout our discussion, but most especially so in our earlier references to eugenics. On the standpoint of the people to whom Zack refers as "designated black" people, the following observation by Fanon is informative: "For several years certain laboratories have been trying to produce a serum for 'denegrification'; with all the earnestness in the world, laboratories have sterilized their test tubes, checked their scales, and embarked on researches that might make it possible for the miserable Negro to whiten himself and thus to throw off the burden of that corporeal malediction" (Black Skin, White Masks, p. 111).

The technological vibrations echo "denegrification" in ways that make our remarks on the aesthetic significance of mixed-race designation return to the fore. There are skin creams for lighter skin, hair tools and chemicals for straighter hair, blue- and hazel-colored contact lenses, and surgical techniques for the transformation of lips, hips, or any feature of the body that is interpreted as an indicator of blackness. Although these technological innovations allude to whiteness, since they are worn, or in phenomenological terms lived, by people of color as colored presentations—their social meaning, as Alfred Schutz would say, is that of literally passing for mixed. And in fact, most people of color aim less to pass for whites as much as to pass for mixed, which is ironic since many multiple-generation people of color in the United States are, in fact, already mixed. That being mixed needs to be made phenomenologically apparent signals a living technology of mixed-race construction within the designated black social sphere. Within the white social sphere, the technological innovation is ironically similar: the objective, whether in the form of the white actress Bo Derek's wearing cornrows or the current wave of hairstyle and tanning techniques to don the look of mixed-race, is not to be taken for actually *being* mixed but instead to be taken for *looking* mixed. Although in both cases black and white function penumbrally, as it were, being mixed is nevertheless extended as an *attractive mode of being* (for whites, sexual; for blacks, both sexual and of higher social status). A dichotomy of sex–power relations emerges in which the mixed-race individual is structured technologically as a symbol of successful possession (think of the status symbol of the black cliché of the light-skinned wife, or perhaps even the mulatto concubine of the nineteenth century) and power (the status symbol of the light-skinned husband, who, in black communities has been the historical recipient of educational, spiritual, economic, and political resources), which, in stream with Zack's provocative discussion of the white patriarchal family, promises a future of less and less blackness—in a word, *denegrification*.

The Sartrean considerations emerge when we consider the implications of such choices. Zack focuses on Sartre's *Anti-Semite and Jew* for some insight into the question of an authentic existence for a mixed-race person. In considering Sartre's positions on freedom, Zack argues, "If freedom is a higher value than racial identity and the two are not compatible, surely the person of mixed race will continue to choose freedom. This means that anyone in the position of having to deliberately construct a racial identity must remain *race-less*" (p. 159). On this basis, Zack concludes, "An American who identifies herself as mixed black and white race is a new person racially, because old racial categories do not allow her to identify herself this way. It is such a person's very newness racially that gives her the option of racelessness. To be raceless in contemporary racial and racist society is, in effect, to be *anti-race*. If 'authenticity' is a definition of the self in the face of oppression, then the authenticity of a person of mixed race may rest on her resistance to biracial racial categories—the racial authenticity of mixed race could therefore be the racial position of anti-race" (p. 164).

If the individualist references strike the reader as liberal, perhaps even libertarian, it is not without foundation. Zack makes it explicit that she regards liberalism as the antirace philosophy, and she is absolutely correct. For liberalism demands a conception of the moral and the political person that renders nearly every determination of his particularity irrelevant. The rejection of race as fictitious is, in part, the quest for the value-neutral, tolerance-spirited individual.[28] It is easy to see why it is the case, then, that a certain group of race theorists—namely, theorists like Appiah, Henry Louis Gates Jr., and to some extent, Cornel West—embrace liberalism. Yet Zack also interprets a rather unusual crew of European philosophers of freedom as standing among liberalism's allies: "Sartre, de Beauvoir, Leiris, and Picasso were all champions of human freedom—they were all liberals" (p. 167).

It is a feature of Sartre's philosophy that he did not interpret freedom in the narrow, Anglo sense of liberty. Sartre in fact theorized in a framework that distinguished liberty from freedom. One is sometimes responsible for one's lack of liberty, but one cannot lose responsibility for one's freedom. Given Sartre's antibourgeois stand, which he maintained from *Nausea* straight through to his *Family Idiot*, as well as his relentless, albeit critical defense of socialism, the situating of at least Sartre (and Pablo Picasso) in liberalism is a very problematic taxonomy. Freedom means liberalism provided, in advance, that one is a liberal. For a Marxist, or even an existial Marxist, freedom fundamentally means the breakdown of the alienation of human beings from each other. Although it is clear to me that such positions entail antiracism, it isn't clear to me why they would be, whether liberal or Marxist, antiracial. And in fact, in practice, liberalism in itself hasn't demonstrated its antiracist calling, if the murderous history of the founding fathers of the United States and their expansion westward continue to stand as historical authority. Moreover, Sartre himself provides an array of arguments that would call for the construction of such a turn on the part of a mixed-race person to be a classic form of bad faith, a consequence that the conclusion was meant to reject. Not only does Sartre speak in *Anti-Semite and Jew* of the insidious self-concealment of the democrat (who, by the way, is the liberal who rejects race, ethnic, and class identities while espousing a liberal ethic of tolerance that preserves the status quo), but he also advances, in *Being and Nothingness*, a devastating critique of individuals who stand in positions to regard their sense of being unbounded as a clear indicator of being unbound. He calls such a turn the "anarchic consciousness," and says about it that "[t]he 'bourgeois' is not only defined as a certain *homo oeconomicus* disposing of a precise power and privilege in the heart of a society of a certain type; he is described inwardly as a consciousness which does not recognize its belonging to a class. . . . It is only when the oppressed class by revolution or by a sudden increase of its power posits itself as 'they-who-look-at' in the face of members of the oppressing class, it is only then that the oppressors experience themselves as 'Us.' But this will be in fear and shame and as an Us-object" (pp. 554–5).

Bad faith is not only the evasion of one's transcendence. It is also the evasion of one's facticity. Some commentators on Sartre's work, perhaps because of the popularity of his awful lecture *Existentialism Is a Humanism*, have unduly interpreted Sartre as a defender of radical freedom. Radical freedom is an evasion of situational reality. It is a form of bad faith.

There is a political dynamic in mixed-race contexts that unfortunately parallels Sartre's description of the bourgeoisie. Although there are no designated black people who are properly members of the bourgeoisie, there have been and continue to be designated black people who are part of what E. Franklin Frazier, in *The Black Bourgeoisie*, ironically called the "lumpen bourgeoisie." These were and continue to be individuals whose power is indexed asymmetrically among blacks. The term designates a pseudoclass that has wealth and a degree of social prestige without power. This class has been, as Zack chronicles well in her book, historically dominated by people of mixed black, and other, races. The historical "place" for these individuals has been black communities for the same reason that, on the plantations, their place was among the slaves: white communities disowned them. That experience of rejection was the constituting experience of "us" (as opposed to "we") blacks. But it is at the moment that these individuals reject the call of black membership (that is, "we," the reciprocally recognized community of blackness) that the anarchic dimensions emerge. This dimension is conditioned primarily by the rejection of blackness. Mixed-race anarchical consciousness is therefore conditioned by rejection of their designated inferiors. In short, their relation to blackness. Although in this age of what I call "equal opportunity racism," it has become good etiquette always to present blacks as equal sources of racism as whites, it is hardly the case that white people are suspicious of mixed-race people because of a sense of the latter's "superiority."

I have had many a discussion on the suspicions that many black folk have of mixed-race people, particularly those who are purportedly physiologically capable of passing at least for a "dark" white person. On one occasion, I asked a colleague who was defending the view that such behavior is a source of mixed-race alienation, Why should people who are treated like dirt because of their dark complexions trust a person who seeks also to identify with people who function every day as institutional symbols of their oppression? If the working class should be careful of people who function as their bosses, why should dark-skinned people be any different in virtue of the historical, supervisory role of light-skinned people? It is not that black people are morally right in having such a suspicion; it's simply that they may be no more unusual than any other group who is constituted as society's bottom. To make matters worse, however, it is this dimension of the argument that makes Sartre an especially problematic appeal in the effort to defend a mixed-race antiracial platform. For in the scenarios I've spelled out, Sartre's position may prove more offensive to the mixed-race person who espouses it, for the term Sartre uses is slime. It is not that mixed-race people are "slimy." It is that the conditions that Zack has spelled out for their authenticity are the very conditions for sliminess, sliminess that I would say is at the heart of the kind of distrustful figure that, say, Toni Morrison articulates in The Bluest Eye in the person of Reverend Whitcomb, a descendant of light-skinned colonial civil servant privilege in the

Caribbean. Here are two instances of the description of slime in *Being and Nothingness*:

> Slime is the agony of water. It presents itself as a phenomenon in process of becoming; it does not have the permanence within change that water has but on the contrary represents an accomplished break in a change of state. This fixed instability in the slimy discourages possession. . . . The slimy flees with a heavy flight which has the same relation to water as the unwieldy earthbound flight of the chicken has to that of the hawk. Even this flight can not be possessed because it denies itself as flight. It is already almost a solid permanence. Nothing testifies more clearly to its ambiguous character as a "substance in between two states" than the slowness with which the slimy melts into itself (p. 774).

> What comes back to us then as an objective quality is a new *nature* which is neither material (and physical) nor psychic, but which transcends the opposition of the psychic and the physical, by revealing itself to us as the ontological expression of the entire world; that is, which offers itself as a rubric for classifying all the "thises" in the world, so that we have to deal with the material organizations or transcended transcendence (p. 773).

These passages ironically undergird the existential force of Naomi Zack's argument against U.S. racism in an interesting way: American antiblack racism constructs people of mixed-race as slimy. And that is because, in such a world, racelessness *is* slimy. For people of color know what to expect when we hear conservatives and liberals declare that they are going to be "color-blind" and disregard racial designations in their response to the current condition of racial injustice. It means for sure that they will use racelessness to *preserve* racism, and that is exactly the force behind the 1995 California (Anti) Civil Rights Initiative and its successors in Oregon and Illinois. It is also why racism has been exacerbated at the end of the twentieth century.

How can that be?

In a provocative essay, "White Normativity and the Racial Rhetoric of Equal Protection," Robert Westley makes a claim that may unmask this insidious dimension of racelessness in the present age.[29] He first points out the familiar observation that since whites function as the *normative* standpoint of humanity, they normally live as raceless. Like Sartre's bourgeoisie, who find it difficult to think of themselves as a class, whites "normally" find it difficult to think of themselves as a race. Yet when the legal remedy and the struggle for equal protection emerged in the public discourse of the 1950s through 1970s, a strange phenomenon emerged: whites became *racialized*. In the previous world, things were simple: there were whites, and then there were races; there were human beings, and then there were *blacks*, and then other coloreds. But to be treated equal to blacks could not mean, in the prevailing ideology, going "up" to their level, nor could it mean bringing blacks up as well, since an impossibility of such lurks in the undercurrents. The conclusion that became apparent was that whites were being asked to *come down* to the level of blacks. It is that "fall," if you will, a fall chronicled in Zack's and many other texts in race theory, that constitutes the experience of racialization. Needless to say, many whites can't take it, and the fallout since the Civil Rights Act of 1964 has continued straight through to the *Regents of the University of California v. Bakke* case (1978) and the slew of antirace and so-called reverse discrimination constructions that persist.

How does this dialectic play out in a mixed-race context?

Given the argument advanced thus far, to affirm being black is to affirm being a member of a race. To affirm being white, on the other hand, means to affirm the normative standpoint. One can see straight away why there is an incentive to deny blackness altogether. Thus, at this point there is no *mixed* assertion. But let us now say that a mixed-race person decides to affirm both, not as races, but as *equals*. The problem is that to equalize whiteness with blackness is to racialize whiteness, which thus loses its normativity. There is a Catch-22 here: whiteness can only be affirmed as normative through the rejection of blackness, for at the moment it is equalized—that is, racialized—blackness is affirmed. The solution cannot, therefore, be to reject racialization, since that would only affirm whiteness (which continues to be normative). Instead, perhaps a more direct liberatory scheme of overthrowing the normativity of whiteness is needed. What would better accomplish that than racializing whites?

Perhaps the politics of racialization comes to the fore most on questions of the national census. Much of the designated black population has some form of mixed-race background. Let us suppose that mixed-race people were designated a racial category that is separate from white and black. Although Zack has in various stages of her argument suggested the choice of mixed race as a category by itself, there is the simultaneous social benefit of being designated *not black*. It is a waste of time to discuss the social losses of being designated white, since the global distribution of resources continue to fall disproportionately in favor of whites. So, even if one won't be accepted as white, it is still of paramount importance *not* to be designated black. To quote the familiar adage, "Well, at least you're not black." Among blacks, there is some effort at flexibility, with the addendum, "At least you're not a nigger," but as we know, being black makes one a great deal closer to that designation than all the rest. For people of mixed race, then, such a category will constitute a legal move "upward" even though the argument in defense of the mixed-race category in the census may be in the form of appealing to a lateral move.

So, what is the consequence?

My suspicion is that one would find a great affirmation of racelessness in the midst of more intense racial discrimination against the designated bottom group. This is because the top continues to function as normative, while the perceived middle increases in numbers, and the bottom shrinks in determined numbers. This is what has happened in the Caribbean and South America, although one would be hard-pressed to find people from those regions who would admit this—except, conspicuously, the black ones. If it is important to have people fighting the conditions of racism instead of being its perpetrators, why not increase the probability not only of the racialization of each upper level of the racial hierarchy, but also the probability of their embodying the racialization they hate the most? Why not apply the one-drop rule with a vengeance by claiming *any* black ancestry? Why not simply "blacken" or "color" as much of the U.S. as possible? How about electronically affecting as many birth certificates as possible, making a black nation in which there will be more and more need to respond to racism in all of its anticolored forms? Why darken the world? Because lightening our racist world will be perceived as a positive thing, which will increase the probability of differentiating the lighter from the light—in short, a new set of black folks. Whereas, to do the negative thing, to do more than darken it, to *blacken* it, will surely be perceived as an act calling for decisive action. To adapt a prescient cliché, "Negativity is the mother of invention." I would say that the insight of some of the leaders in the previous generations of mixed-race people is that they knew that no justice was to be attained in any contemporary society through the affirmation of a white identity. They knew they were mixed, but they also knew that, when it comes to political action and the fight for social change, one has to work with those dimensions that will effect social change.

So we come to our final concern. Throughout the text, Zack treats the concept of race as the governing fiction to be abolished. Yet most racist behavior does not even raise the question of race as either a direct or indirect reference to racist behavior. Race tends to emerge when rationalization begins. When my son is harassed for being dark and therefore supposedly ugly, race in itself is hardly a consideration in his juvenile white harassers' minds, even though they are identifying my son as black. When Europeans plundered nearly nine-tenths of the globe and slaughtered, in some cases, nearly 90 percent of the indigenous colored populations, neither race nor racism was on their minds, but they were able to identify and kill Native Americans, Africans, Indians, and Southeast Asians with cruel accuracy and efficiency. The concepts were rationalizations of the deeds, but they were not the source of the deeds. I doubt very seriously that whites of the past, especially such liberal whites as George Washington and Thomas Jefferson—would have refrained—any more than many of their descendants would today—from enslaving or slaughtering me if they identified me as X instead of black. But if the response is that I should not have been nor continue to be identified at all, I don't see how such a turn wouldn't be a case of making me, instead of my oppressors, the problem. For them to refrain from harming me would rest upon their being drastically transformed. It is clear, then, in a wickedly ironic way, that perhaps the world would have been more just if their identity had not emerged since their identity is fundamentally conditioned by hating mine. And why should anyone continue to defend any identity that is premised upon being the primary agent of hate?

The irony in all this is that the natural sciences of which I was critical in the early sections of this chapter are in fact providing the foundations for a turn in these concluding directions, for, as we saw in our discussion of Du Bois and human sciences, genetics and physical anthropology are revealing that there is, indeed, a valid scientific notion of race. It is the notion that there are human races that is wrong. The human species is not only one race, but that race turns out to be the one most hated by most of the globe. In effect, that the human species is basically dark and light black people from Africa challenges much of what is written in the name of science on mixed race. From the point of view of genetics, there is no such thing—in the very way that Zack and Appiah refer to there being no such thing—as mixed-race people because there is only one human race. But more, genetics is also challenging how we look at mixture in a different way. If blackness means maximum heterogeneity of the species, then the move away from blackness is in effect an effort to construct the very purity that mixed-race policies are supposedly designed to avoid. Like whiteness, then, mixed race, too, stands as a version of the road to purity.

six

Can Men Worship?

An Existential Portrait in Black and White

A religion may teach the men of one tribe to torture and kill men of another tribe. But even such a religion would pretend to teach right conduct. Religion, however, gives us more than a moral code. A moral code alone, with its "Thou shalt," would be no more religious than is the civil code. And what it adds is, first, enthusiasm. Somehow it makes the faithful regard the moral law with devotion, reverence, love. By history, by parable, by myth, by ceremony, by song, by whatever means you will, the religion gives to the mere code life and warmth. A religion not only commands the faithful, but gives them something that they are glad to live for, and if need be to die for.

—Josiah Royce, *The Religious Aspects of Philosophy*

The Greek expression from which we have gained the term "enthusiasm" is *entheos*. *Theos* is the Greek word for a god or God, *entheos* literally means "to be filled or entered by a god or God." To be enthused is to be imbued with a god, to be open, to be entered by a spirit. If a man were to regard himself as a closed being while enthusiasm—a precondition of worship (which from the Old English *weorth* means also "*to value*")—and religiosity require an "open" body, a susceptible or vulnerable body, how would or could such a man stand before God?[30] If this man's posture is the posture of masculinity, we find ourselves abruptly facing a sticky problem: Can one worship God and remain masculine too? Can a male maintain his masculine identity and worship God in good faith?

These questions have thrown us already into a specific area of philosophical concern: existential phenomenology. This is because our questions call for a form of anguish on the part of men over their identity. Existential phenomenology, as I have been interpreting it throughout the preceding discussions, explores the implications and the possibility of studying the phenomenon of beings that are capable of questioning their ways of being. I have raised the question of the existential situation of a male figure who attempts to reach out to God, or perhaps more accurately, a male figure who faces the dilemma of losing himself insofar as the possibility of choosing to lose his identity as a closed identity, a closed being, is concerned. Is there something erotic, or perhaps homoerotic, about "letting God in"? The project of reaching God or letting God in may hold its own, frustrating existential features. The problem raises two existential concerns: the problem of bad faith and the problem of critical good faith.[31]

Jean-Paul Sartre has examined the concept of bad faith in contexts ranging from our attitudes toward our presented images (in his *Imagination*) and emotions (in *Outline of the Emotions*), to our attitudes toward our neighbors and different races and creed (in, for example, *Anti-Semite and Jew* and the appendix on American blacks in his *Notebooks for an Ethics*). As we have seen, bad faith is generally a lie to oneself that involves a flight from freedom and responsibility. The two forms of bad faith that will be of special interest to us are those that involve a flight from one's presence and the assumption of a thing-like existence or completeness in various situations. A "situation" is tentatively defined as a confrontation of freedoms, which for Sartre is a reality with human significance. Let us first look at a theory of the male body implicit in those two forms of bad faith; I will then offer an interpretation of the male body as a theological figure in bad faith.

The Body

Consciousness, phenomenologically understood, is always consciousness of something. Put differently, a world without objects is also a world without consciousness. A consequence of consciousness' requirement of an object is the reality of perspective. Consciousness always exists, that is, from somewhere; being other than consciousness, an object is always "there," whereas consciousness is always, simultaneously, "here." We shall call that somewhere in which consciousness seems to be located—or, perhaps better, situated—a *perspective*, and we shall call such a perspective *the body*. The body is one's perspective on the world.

The body can be understood in terms of three dimensions. The first we have already mentioned: the body as one's perspective on the world. The other two are the body as seen by others, and the body's (consciousness') realization of itself as seen by others.

A peculiar aspect of my perspective is that I cannot surpass it. It is, in effect, nonpositional *by me*. Take away the perspective of my eyes, for instance, and I see nothing; take away my nerves and I feel nothing. But these aspects of perspectivity can be extended. My ocular perspective can be extended by a telescope; my fingertips can be extended by a walking cane; my height, by platform boots. These extensions are not identical with me. They are artificial, but they enhance my perspective on the world. Without a perspective, I will be an anonymous consciousness without a point of reference. I will be a view, literally, from nowhere.

Since I cannot surpass my perspective, I, in effect, live my perspective; it is simultaneous with my choices. My movement and my perspective are one; my choices, my feelings are the same. I can live myself freely—as, metaphorically, fluid—or I can live myself unfreely—as, again metaphorically speaking, congealed, slimy.

Think, first, of fluid movement. We can live our body as freedom. We stride, with such an attitude, with grace and a simultaneous sense of responsibility. We move because we will ourselves to do so. But suppose our sense of movement takes the form of self-denial. We do not walk; we are "pushed" on by either circumstances or an imaginary presence as though we were effect to an external cause. The more causally affected we move, the more we live and regard ourselves as linked to a chain of events that we may claim is beyond our control. I don't raise my hand; my hand is raised. It is not I who hesitate to get out of bed on a cold morning; my body is either asleep or held hostage by the chill. Bad faith in this context is the assumption of our body's being a thing in the world, a thing no different from wood floating on water. This form of bad faith is the assumption of presence (facticity) with a denial of absence (transcendence). Sartre discusses transcendence, however, in ambiguous ways. Transcendence can pertain to that which is other than consciousness, in which case it could be an object or a fact, which suggests that a transcendent object can also be factical; but it can also pertain to that which transcends or is constituted beyond facts or the present moment, in which case it can be (for Sartre) "nothingness," the future, possibility, or freedom. Our use will be restricted to nothingness.

The body is a lived ambiguity. The body can be seen, heard, smelled, felt. In this regard, the body appears as a thing-in-itself. The body, living, breathing, acting, choosing, intending—that body, manifesting all those significations of the human being as a metastable, elusive intention—comes to the fore in the single advancement of the body as freedom. A corpse, for instance, is not a body in the sense in which we are considering body. Such a thing is unsituated, since a situation is ultimately an anguish-riddled confrontation with choice. Corpses, for rather obvious reasons, don't choose to do anything. Yet a consequence of assuming or choosing the existence of a corpse is the denial of the transcendent aspects of the body: the body appears, but it appears also as the locus of possibilities in the world.

The possibilities of a seen body are not physiologically holistic. In semantic terms, the body has a variety of interpretations, although its spatial-temporal coordinate is a single referent. The body signifies different meanings in different situations.

The final dimension is that of awareness of objectification: the body understood as an awareness of being seen by others. This last dimension has a rich history in philosophy and psychology—think, for instance, of Simone de Beauvoir's The Second Sex and The Ethics of Ambiguity, and Jacques Lacan's Écrits. The consequence of this dimension is a sense of the self as an Other; the face that we think of when we think of ourselves is an understanding of ourselves from the outside. It is an estranged intimacy.

The Spirit of Seriousness

The spirit of seriousness is a twofold attitude. In one form, it is the view that values are external, material features of the world. Values, from this point of view, exist independent of human beings. Another form of spirit of seriousness is the notion of self-importance beyond the scope of judgment. With this attitude, one's existence becomes "necessary," "justified." "It is not simply that I exist, but," such a serious man might say, "I must exist; I ought to exist." We regard the spirit of seriousness as a form of bad faith because it calls for the elimination of the anguish of responsibility over values: objectified values negate the anguish of being responsible for those values by living them. Do or die, we encounter good in the world, under the serious attitude, but we are not responsible for it.

The classic case of the serious spirit is the cosmogony and theodicy of the Persian Mani, "the Apostle of God," from whose name we have gained the term manichaeism. Mani's system was based on a dualism of material good and evil in the world. Under such a model, one can rid the world of evil as one can remove bacteria from water by heating it. In *The Respectful Prostitute*, Sartre's misogynist/racist character Fred declares the Manichaean credo; looking at the bed in which he has just spent the night with the prostitute Lizzy, he announces that "It smells of sin." Why? The odors of semen, discharge, and sweat permeate the room. Sin literally invades his nostrils and violates his lungs. On blacks, he advances his ontology: "A nigger has always done something." Why? *Because* he is a "nigger."

Serious values needn't be limited to attitudes toward people. We regard some material things as food and others as not-food, even though we can eat either. Instead of admitting that we make certain things food by desiring them, we treat their desirability as an intrinsic feature. "For the spirit of seriousness," writes Sartre in *Being and Nothingness*, "bread is desirable because it is *necessary* to live (a value written in an intelligible heaven) and because bread *is* nourishing" (p. 706). With such an attitude, we face "inedible" objects as though we don't play a role in their determination or, in phenomenological terms, "constitution" as food. We act as though the anguish of whether to eat or not to eat certain things were not in our hands. There are many nourishing substances that we don't desire or consider to be food.

The ultimate figure of seriousness is Absolute Consciousness—one that has achieved itself as its object of desire: God. God serves as an external, objective impetus of all value. But if God were to shout, "Do X!" the reason *why* cannot be God.

Recall our discussion of the story of Adam and Eve. Until Yahweh posed the problem of eating from the Tree of Knowledge of Good and Evil, there was no existential situation posed. We can go further: there were no human beings, in the sense of mature creatures of self-reflection. There was liberty without freedom. At the moment of Yahweh's command, they were placed in anguish and were thrust into freedom. For Yahweh could only serve as his own justification at this point: whether it was right or wrong to obey Yahweh was posed to Adam and Eve as a problem *for them* to decide. It is in obeying Yahweh that they would have substantiated the command, *Thou shalt obey*, but it is also in disobeying Yahweh that they instantiated their own responsibility. The very possibility of disobeying Yahweh thrust them beyond Yahweh. They were thrown into the negativity of their own freedom. Ironically, their freedom was established by the restriction of their liberty.

Yet our problem goes deeper. For now we see that the very possibility of Yahweh is insufficient for the elimination of anguish. Anguish is a confrontation with the self; it is a confrontation with one's responsibility for making choices in one's situations. Even if there were God, we face the question of how to act toward "Him." If we disobey, we reduce the value of God's command *to us*. If we obey, we make it valuable *for us*. Thus, if we claim that the commands were valuable by virtue of their source—God—we would be in bad faith. We would be lying to ourselves.

The Sartrean formulation is atheistic in a strangely religious way.

Manliness

We now consider a bad-faith situation of manhood. A human being, we say, defies identity. Sartre expresses man's existence as a defiance of identity rather awkwardly as man being what he is not and not being what he is. Only objects of consciousness—seemingly, things-in-themselves—are properly beings whose identity is one-with-themselves, beings that are "solid" in their being. Yet a man qua his masculinity appears unequivocal. He is solid. He fills things. Nothing enters him. He is closed.

Let us imagine a figure who accepts such an identity, such an interpretation of himself. His "closedness" makes his perspective that of an emanation from the center of reference. As a being whom he regards as invulnerable to entry, he thrusts himself into the world as pure, closed flesh—a protrusion of being—the modus operandi of the phallus. Such a man lives himself as sealed, as a being without holes. His very movement through space has the sense of a spear in flight, or light jabbing its way through vacuous darkness.

Woman, in this scheme, becomes an absence—in old Jungian and Adlerian jargon, holes. Yet the fleshiness of woman—her breasts, her inclined stomach's fat lining, her buttocks—defies such an ascription. So we may add that whereas the male flesh protrudes, the female flesh, seen under this schema, lives under the threat of implosion; it is regarded from the standpoint of a masculinity of seriousness and power as flesh caving in, flesh "succumbing" to invasion.

We should note that this analysis is of a particular form of interpretation of gender identity—one that is premised upon bad faith. Men and women are reduced to binary existents of power and weakness. It is a form of bad-faith reduction for the obvious reason that it fails to admit the viability of alternative, lived interpretations of human beings. Penises are, after all, not always "hard." It is odd, as well, that masculinity has been so focused on the penis when just below it hang testicles—organs of unparalleled vulnerability. One could imagine what would happen to male studies if theorists shifted from the penis to the scrotum. Similarly, a hole needn't, in our studies of women, be passive. It can also be inviting, swallowing, and the like. As Sigmund Freud remarked, in his *Civilization and Its Discontents*,

> We are accustomed to say that every human being displays both male and female instinctual impulses, needs and attributes; but though anatomy, it is true, can point out the characteristic of maleness and femaleness, psychology cannot. For psychology the contrast between the sexes fades away into one between activity and passivity, in which we far too readily identify activity with maleness and passivity with femaleness, a view which is by no means universally confirmed in the animal kingdom (p. 59).

The masculine-feminine dynamic lives on the level of the symbolic. This masculine-feminine dichotomy also has racial form. Whiteness is regarded as presence, as being. Blackness is regarded as absence of being. Frantz Fanon has observed in *Black Skin, White Masks* that there is a homoerotic dimension of antiblack racism. In the presence of a white man, a black man stands as a gaping black hole of being to be filled by white presence. Let us take this observation to another level, one on which the white man confronts the black man as a symbol of the feminine. The confrontation would not necessarily be homosexual; it could also be misogynist. This would mean that the black male or the male of color may be situated as woman or the symbol of the feminine in an antiblack world.

Consider an example. In the popular film The Crying Game (1992), a white Irish terrorist discovers that a black woman whom he has been seeing turns out to be a man. But is s/he? Throughout the film, dimensions of masculinity and femininity are preserved. The white protagonist's identity as a man isn't threatened; the leitmotif is that any man can understand why the protagonist would maintain a relationship with this transvestite. The film drew great attention from "mainstream" audiences. Would the film have been popular and would the significance of the characters maintain its integrity if the transvestite were white?

At the end of the film, a white female Irish terrorist confronts the black British transvestite. It is clear in the scene that she is a "man" and he is a "woman"—though in the scene the terrorist is dressed in black leather and the black transvestite is in a white cricket outfit. Both hold black guns. Where, in this scene, stands the phallus? The phallus cuts through the confusion of decoy phalluses. If both characters were stripped down to their ontological essentials—that is, their bodies—the matrix of power emerges in full bloom. The phallus appears to be white skin.

Gender identity is more complex, of course, than bodily presentations. It should be clear, for instance, that the hallmark of the phallus in The Crying Game example is power. But how could a white woman have power in such a way that makes her stand as a man before a black man?

Sartre is instructive here. In Being and Nothingness, he observes that it is the hallmark of power to be able to regard boundaries as fictions. From the standpoint of the bourgeoisie, for instance, the proletariat's assertion of a class struggle is misguided, since there are supposedly no classes. But for the proletariat the reality of classes is confronted, is lived, every day. Thus, when the bourgeoisie deny that they have more power than the proletariat and assert that there are no class distinctions, they *make* themselves bourgeois in their attitudes, for they can act upon their assertions, which reinforces their delusions. They don't have boundaries; they constitute them. *They* are who all must contend with, and eventually surpass, in order to live and to make a living in their society; this is what it means to have social and political power. Similarly, a white woman may have fewer boundaries than a black man in an antiblack world. She stands before him as a presence when it comes to matters of recognition before the law. She knows that in the eyes of her society her life is more valuable than his. A similar phenomenon occurs among blacks. Middle-class blacks have more options than working- or so-called underclass blacks. In relation to other blacks, then, a middle-class black may say that race doesn't matter, but that is because he has the luxury of dealing with a set of racial dynamics that differ from the link between race and poverty. Such a person knows that his economic status makes him appear more valuable than lower-class blacks. Yet he also knows that in an antiblack society, class status doesn't tear down all boundaries. Cornel West's reflections in his preface to *Race Matters* is instructive here:

> I waited and waited and waited. After the ninth taxi refused me, my blood began to boil. The tenth taxi refused me and stopped for a kind, well-dressed, smiling female fellow citizen of European descent. As she stepped in the cab, she said, "This is really ridiculous, is it not?" Ugly racial memories of the past flashed through my mind. Years ago, while driving from New York to teach at Williams College, I was stopped on fake charges of trafficking cocaine. When I told the police officer I was a professor of religion, he replied "Yeh, and I'm the Flying Nun. Let's go, nigger!" I was stopped three times in my first ten days in Princeton for driving too slowly on a residential street with a speed limit of twenty-five miles per hour (p. x).

In the context of race, gender significations betray their symbolic character. One is not simply a man or a woman.

A Serious Man's Worship

Imagine a man who regards his "manliness" to be a material feature of his being. He is the objective value—white, masculine. If he is objectively masculine—a white protrusion of flesh and power sticking itself out at the world—how does he stand in relation to God? If he permits God to enter, so to speak, his identity could be lost. But if he penetrates God, then either God is black or woman or homosexual, or he regards himself as God.[32]

At this point we need to take a pause and contract the parameters of our discussion. I should like to say that I suspect that the relativism implicit in cultural anthropological approaches to the question of religious variation is fallacious. There is the false dilemma of an exclusive disjunction between a single religious *Weltanschauung* and a multiplicity of cultural monads, each distinct and epistemologically problematic to the other; these are not necessarily our alternatives. There is also the possibility that religions have both shared and different features—if not in their intrinsic structure, certainly because of the historical fact of cultural cross-fertilization. Thus, to translate another religious worldview into one's own is not identical with either claiming it *as* one's own or claiming that it is a version of what is the *other's* in the first place. It could be the discovery that it is neither one's own nor the others' exclusively. Thus, my decision to restrict my discussion to the Judeo-Christian tradition is a function of the simple fact that I simply know more about it. My restriction doesn't entail its universality or particularity, only this author's particularity.

Let us consider Genesis 1:1–5 of the King James version, in which Yahweh is introduced as a *presenting* or *constituting* substance.

In the beginning God created the heaven and the earth.

And the earth was without form, and void; and darkness *was* upon the face of the deep. And the spirit of God moved upon the face of the waters.

And God said, Let there be light: and there was light.

And God saw the light, that it was good; and God divided the
light from the darkness.

And God called the light Day, and the darkness he called Night.

And the evening and the morning were the first day.

Whatever the author(s) may have meant in this passage, it is
clearly the case that a great deal of what has been discussed thus far
follows almost axiomatically from this cosmogony.

It is theologically problematic to claim that Yahweh "enters"
anything. Yet in the Genesis story something is added that was previously absent. Yahweh is clearly a positive force, a force that sticks
out (or in), protrudes, and enlightens. Yahweh is powerful. Yahweh is masculine. Yahweh is white.

There is obviously something problematic about engendering
and racializing God. Although God needs neither skin nor penis,
"He" certainly needs power. In fact, the orthodox interpretation is
that God is potency—a concern that led William R. Jones, as we
saw in our preface, to raise the provocative question, *Is God a White
Racist?* That the phallus is not necessarily a penis and that gender is
not necessarily a function of genitalia (despite the etymological relationship) enable us to deal with an obvious Catch-22; even if
Yahweh had female genitals, "She" would still be a "He." And if
God had black skin?

Yahweh is linked to the light. It doesn't help matters to retort
here that this linkage is only symbolic, for our point is that gender, race, and power are symbolic realities as well. That one symbol can take on an identity relation with another in bad faith is
conceded. That doesn't mean that the identity relation cannot be
critically interpreted.

We now face several problems. We cannot say in the abstract,
Can men worship with enthusiasm? This is because "men" has
been revealed to be a complex, ambiguous concept. We must now
ask, Can whites worship with enthusiasm? It is clear that white
women are already constructed with a dual problematic situation
in our analysis, for they are "men" into whom it is generally considered legitimate to enter. I say "generally" because there are com-

plex rituals around legitimate entry of white women. In Christianity, for instance, the association of cleanliness with God's relation to Christ's mother has left a symbolic heritage of a master's or power's accessibility to all women and the relegation of some women to the trap of becoming sacred artifacts. They are the epitome of the object of violation. But note that it is generally legitimate to enter white women when their symbolic whiteness has been eliminated. A white woman "womanized" is symbolically an emasculated male. She is, at that point, "colored."

So we are left with the white man as our focus. How can such a figure receive God? Perhaps we should discuss what is at stake if he is rendered incapable of receiving God. Let us consider the Christian notion of salvation.

Salvation is more than the situation of being brought back to life by God. It is also the realization of both *deserving* to be in the Kingdom of God and being there; one needs first to commit an act of repentance. From the Sartrean standpoint, repentance is loaded with futility in a world in which, at least morally, losers win. Only the oppressed, it seems, can have salvation. Each individual bourgeois cannot, for example, change the relationship between the bourgeoisie and the proletariat, yet he is nevertheless responsible for such a relationship. Should he choose to fight on behalf of social justice or working-class emancipation, his project appears bankrupt in the realization that revolution is not *for* him. The white faces a similar circumstance; in the end, there is the realization that racial justice is not *for whites*. And "men" and "women"? To be a black woman, it has been argued, is to be at the bottom of the racial/gender hierarchy. This, argue some black women theologians (for example, Jacquelyn Grant in her *White Man's Christ and Black Women's Jesus*, and Marcia Riggs in her *Arise, Awake, and Act*) means that they are the embodiment of Christ. To be a white man may ultimately mean, in this historical moment, to be theologically condemned.

The white man finds himself facing three possibilities, if he seeks salvation: (1) an identity relation with God, (2) recognition of an ambiguous human situation, or (3) rejection of the whole theological problematic. Sartre, as is well known, opts for the third, but he retains a great deal of religious baggage in his conception of what it means to be human: the desire to be God. Sartre is thus in support of the third possibility above, but his philosophical conception of man stands firmly in the first. Since our focus is on the theological problematic, the third will not concern us except insofar as it relates to the Sartrean interpretation of the first.

If the white man opts for the first possibility, he attempts not only to become God, but he also makes himself Man. The history of the white man as Man need not be spelled out here. Suffice it to say that it is, in the least, the history of antiblack racism. If the white man becomes God, then there is no need to let God "in." He, the white man interpreted as God, enters others. But the white man knows that he is not God. He knows this, from the Sartrean perspective, not only because he is in fact not God, but also because as a conscious being he is able to pose God as an object of his desire, one with which he is not identical. The argument is complex, but in brief form it is that in order to be conscious of an object, we must be able to nihilate the object. We must be able to put it at a distance from ourselves. Joseph Catalano summarizes Sartre's complex argument this way in his important article "Successfully Lying to Oneself: A Sartrean Perspective":

> One of the most striking things about Sartre's notion of being is that he maintains that the principle of identity is synthetic. A is A; a tree is a tree. True, Sartre claims, but this identity is constituted by its relation to consciousness. Consciousness is consciousness. False, Sartre claims, for who or what could constitute its identity over time. Who or what could hold it in existence? God? Perhaps. If he existed; but, I believe that a proper Sartrean answer is that not even God could create a knowing being that would be a knowing being; it would always have to be at a distance from itself to be aware of itself. Without this lack of identity, knowledge would collapse into an in-itself of a mechanical force (pp. 665–6).

To take the route of an identity relation to God is a form of self-deception. The white man may be white and hence powerful, and God may be powerful, but the white man is not God. Yet, if God is powerful, would not God then be white and therefore symbolically identical with the white man? If this is so, then how could a white man be deceiving himself if he declares himself God? Wouldn't he be recognizing the social reality behind the lived experience of whiteness, as Fanon urged everyone to admit the lived reality of the black? How can he be deceiving himself by recognizing the symbolic truth of himself?

We raise here an equivocation that pushes the white man into the second option above, to stand before God in a way that enables him to recognize his incompleteness—that he is existentially nothing but socially situated as something. He is existentially absence, but he is socially presence. The antiblack world throws blacks/women into the nonrealm of the existential. To bring God "in," therefore, requires a recognition of his existential situation. His existential situation is that he cannot be saved as a white man.

If he cannot be saved as a white man, can he be saved as a human being? Here the problem takes on a different dimension. For the human being is an embodiment of presence-absence. If we interpret the body as presence, then we face the same stock of problems. The human body has to be regarded in different terms; it has to be capable of being entered—not in the sense of having a hole or being possessed, but in the sense of being open in its embodiment. The human body has to be the embodiment of critical living, of critical practice.

We are now compelled to reconsider some of our previous observations. Recall that it is a form of bad faith to deny one's embodiment. It is also a form of bad faith to deny one's transcendence. Consider also that bad faith is a chosen attitude; otherwise, we would not be responsible for our bad faith. If it is bad faith to make oneself closed (because it is to live on the level of substantiation) and also to make oneself completely open (for the same reason), then the notion of the spirit of seriousness has to be revised, a point on which Sartre agrees in Notebooks for an Ethics.

The problem of bad-faith worship is raised—a problem that could not be raised if worship in itself were bad faith. But how could this be, since worship depends on the conception of the self as open—that is, as enthusiastic? We have already seen that, given the interpretations of masculinity and femininity, white and black, power and weakness, presence and absence, the white male figure is mired in a situation of bad-faith worship. We have added that for him to be responsible for his situation requires the possibility of bad-faith worship. What would this be?

Bad-faith worship is the reduction of human reality to any one aspect of its mode of living. Thus not only is the presentation of the self as pure presence a form of bad faith, it is also a form of bad faith to present the self as pure absence. The striking conclusion, then, is that worship is in bad faith. But we seem to have come upon a paradox. We have argued that pure openness is an inhuman mode of being. If we were open without choices that constitute being open, then to be open to God would be a mode of being that is no different from water's being open to our plunging ourselves into it. A human mode of existence emerges where there is choice. Authentic worship must therefore be a form of presentation of one's responsibility for one's relation to the object of one's (presumed good) faith. One lets the spirit in.

Conclusion

The possibilities of worship considered here are meant to raise some questions about religious practices that may have an impact on gender/race identity. They are not meant as any definitive statement on male religious ritual. What I hope the reader has begun to consider is the complexity of the problem of interpreting gender and racial roles in religious contexts. If the symbolic becomes ontological, then the array of rituals available may experience what Judith Butler describes in the preface to her influential Gender Trouble as "trouble." She uses the term in the Sartrean sense, where consciousness is "clogged" and lives itself as unfreedom. The body lives in many ways that betray such trouble. We see it in its posture, its motion, its intensity—flesh attempting to live on the level of an ideal that it is not. What the male subject, and particularly the white male subject, faces from this standpoint is the problematizing of his religious experience. For him, worship is—should he attempt to maintain his masculine identity in the process— a homoerotic ritual. He is a phallus who lets a phallus "in." The psychoanalytical significance of this observation is obvious, but it is my hope that examination may follow beyond the realms of homophobia, misogyny, and racism. If the symbolic functions on a level that seems almost ontological, it may be fruitful to consider the possibilities of a phenomenology of the worshiping body. I leave that for further study.

seven

Recent Africana Religious Thought

Existential Anxieties of Pan-Africanism and Postmodernism at the End of the Twentieth Century

. . . you may change the Theology of a people, but you cannot change their Religion.

—Edward Blyden, *African Life and Customs*

God is dead; but given the ways of men, there may still be caves for thousands of years in which his shadow will be shown—and we—we still have to vanquish his shadow too.

—Friedrich Nietzsche, *The Gay Science*

An area of Africana study that has followed a similar progression as Africana philosophy is Africana religious thought. Here questions of identity and teleology emerged at the turn of the century regarding the "meaning" and "purpose" of blackness, primarily in Christological terms. Most histories of Black Theology show a path from early formulations of a "colored" to a "black" Christ to questions of the *liberatory significance* of a black-centered hermeneutic of the Gospels and Christian eschatology. Although the identity question did not always take theological form—as we find in works that simply study black religions, whether as syncretic forms or as examples of retentions of African religions—anxieties over studying things African in the U.S. academy have been such that positivism has never been a feature of black religious thought. The historic reality of black folk is too serious to afford "value neutrality." The consequence is that such thought has always been in dialogue—whether critically or affirmatively—with black liberation thought. James Cones's black liberation theology, for instance, received much criticism from William R. Jones's critical humanism in the 1970s, and Cornel West's prophetic pragmatism and cultural studies approach has led to subsequent debates over the expectations of theology and religious thought. The rest of this chapter will examine two contemporary efforts to develop this legacy.

A Pan-African Theology

My aim here is to examine Josiah Young's *A Pan-African Theology: Providence and the Legacies of the Ancestors* as an example of one of the best efforts to forge a systematic example of African America's relation to Africa and the impact of such a relation on African American religious thought. An added feature of the work's importance is the unique way in which Young reads nineteenth-century African American thought's relation to contemporary Africana religious thought. Recall that Caliban studies require engaging not only Prospero's language but the language of Caliban's forebears. Young's work—his methodology and his suggestions—calls for a renewed understanding of the complexity of thought that preceded us and the social world in which we now theorize.

Young's argument comes to the fore early in his text. He urges his reader to consider a theology of liberation that is open to the diversity not only of people of African descent, but also of the diversity of humankind. This is because the theological project must come to grips with itself as not only a formulation of theoretical positions, but also an effort to persuade others to join its counsel. Young begins by affirming a distinction developed by the nineteenth-century black Pan-Africanist and scholar of religion Edward Blyden. Blyden argued that long-term emancipatory efforts at social transformation call for a transformation of consciousness in the people to be liberated. On the cultural level, this means addressing the binding force of religion in their lives. To present a theoretical case as to why a people should transform (if not abandon) their religion throws one into theological work that may be self-deluding, for although a people may find the theological position persuasive, they may nevertheless maintain the religions to which they have been culturally bound. One can, in other words, change a people's theology, but not necessarily their religion. This is an insight Blyden brought with him from the Caribbean, where avowed Christians (a changed theology) lived many Africanized versions of Christianity and where, when it came to day-to-day practices, African retentions reigned. In stream with Blyden's distinction between religion and theology, then, Young advances a distinction between "acculturation"(Africanization) and "inculturation" (Christianization):

> I understand acculturation as the *spontaneous* force of traditional values that naturalizes missionary Christianity within the substratum of national culture. This grassroots process is observed within the African independent churches. Among BaKongo influenced regions of Zaire, for instance, "Kimbanguism" has represented an African Christianity precisely because of the preponderance of things African in its expression. Inculturation signifies the Christianization of traditional BaKongo religion, without obscuring the acculturative force of ancestral values. Without inculturation, African *theology* is not Christian; without acculturation, Christian theology is not *African* (pp. 18–19).

The task of a good theology, Young argues, is acculturation—to draw upon, that is, the cultural formation that is already present. That acculturation tends to be the religion of the people and inculturation the reflective theological project means that the liberation theologian's task is already situated by socio-cultural reality. For liberation theologians and anyone who theorizes about liberating human communities, this sociocultural reality is the fact of human diversity. There are no longer (if there really ever were) such formations as homogeneous nations of people.

The challenge of recognizing human diversity becomes acute when one considers the proposals and failures of discussions on Africa's colonized indigenous and settlement communities and their relation to other such communities. This challenge pushes the liberation theorist to the metalevel; to considering problems of theory and method. To be rigorous, liberation theorizing must be consistent with its goals. In that regard, argues Young, a decisive shift emerges between what he considers the old guard and the new guard. Echoing Karl Marx's eleventh thesis on Ludwig Andreas Feuerbach, he advances, as an epistemological claim, that the old guard's methodological and teleological goals were simply to interpret the world, whereas the new guard's (from the late 1960s onward) have been to change the world through interpreting it. We could term this approach *liberatory epistemology*—a theory of knowledge that is liberating.

A goal of liberatory epistemology is to challenge reductionistic and absolutist conceptions of meaning, what are at times called, echoing the language of European existentialism and postmodern criticism, "essentializing" and "totalizing" meanings. Methodologically, this means resistance to totalizations that militate against cultural diversity or heterogeneity. This approach does not suggest that community consensus be discouraged or deemed impossible, for in either case the point is for it not to be treated as closure or the conclusion of Caliban's work. As Young points out, "Even if one assumes an ideological consensus among [for example] revolutionary Pan-Africanists, nuances of meaning are bound to emerge" (p. 14). The method must, therefore, accommodate nuances and diversities of meaning. Such accommodation is, of course, necessary in a project that attempts to work through complex cultural, and even metaphysical, conceptions of reality—conceptions that lead to the affirmation instead of the rejection or occlusion of human differences. Young's liberatory epistemological commitment necessitates, then, a principle of interpretation or hermeneutic instead of a dogmatic system of claims to a practice of "Absolute Truth." The hermeneutical method he offers is, in the tradition of Africana thought from Du Bois through to Fanon, James, and West, social analysis. Young writes, "Social analysis includes levels of examination of distinct contradictions of an unjust international matrix. Social analysis focuses on the contradictions of given contexts in order to demarcate theo-political options related to the liberation of the oppressed" (p. 17).

We may wonder why, given Young's position on the nuances and diversity of meaning, he would place privilege on the "oppressed." Young's response would be connected to his multicultural commitments: oppression is a relational designation, which means that oppressed communities are constantly shifting as social relations change. A stark example is provided by his discussion of the nineteenth-century North American black settlers in Liberia who were regarded by the African indigenous populations as "white." The hermeneutical method of social analysis requires constantly reminding oneself that meanings change, and that someone who may stand as oppressed today could stand as oppressor tomorrow.

Young then examines the nineteenth-century roots of the contemporary problems of semiotic and material liberation. From postcolonial and cultural studies we have learned that when we seek liberation of oppressed people, we face the task of doing so in nonoppressive language—language that affects how they are read and who they "are" in theoretical terms. For black liberation, this means articulating a black liberation project without collapsing into white supremacist (or antiblack) terms. To illustrate his point, Young provides a critique of the "tragic" figure of Alexander Crummell, whose "demonic" notion of Providence emerged within his Pan-Africanism. At its heart is the lure of symbolic transformation: to be human and to be saved is to be "washed," "cleansed," and "whitened," in the process of cultural transformation (see pp. 44–6).

The project of constructing a Pan-African liberation theology thus requires the positive articulation of the semiotic features of African identification. Africa must be transformed from the nega-

tive blackness signified by "Dark Continent" to a treasured blackness. This means advancing not only European Christian resources
in one's theology but also African cultural resources—for example, the rich array of proverbs and customs from Africa's many ethnic groups.[33] Without such transformation, Pan-Africanism would
be "demonic," a foreign force with colonizing aims over Africana
communities, a human manifestation of false salvation. Young situates this task in the Christian context through two biblical formulations. The first is from Romans 7:19:

> For I do not the good I want, but the evil I do not want I do.

The second is from Psalms 68:31:

> Princes shall come forth from Egypt;
> Ethiopia stretches forth her hand to God[34]

The first formulation points to what black religious thinkers
should avoid ("the evil I do not want") and the second signifies
what they should strive for—a connection with Africa. Crummell
exemplifies the first formulation. The second formulation requires
respect for Africa and serves as a biblical foundation for Pan-
Africanism. The impetus for a Pan-African identification is the material and spiritual misery of the dark wretched of the earth.
Young articulates this identification through the relational theory
of racism in classic liberation theological terms: the least advan-
taged in every social context is the manifestation of "the blacks."
The relational theory of race is a syntactical, semiotic theory; it
points to the contingency of those who occupy racial roles and appeal, instead, to the grammar that gives those roles meaning. As the
grammar requires that one avoids the lower and seek the higher,
one is high to the extent that one is not low and vice versa. By sub-
stituting black for low and white for high, the relations are exemplified by their contingent occupiers. Thus, in the U.S. it is the
"underclass" who signify blackness, and in Africa and the Afro-
Caribbean it is the peasantry. Young calls this the "transcontextual"

dimension of Pan-Africanism; it has a global message. The Christian credo of the meek inheriting the earth is clear here. In its liberation theological form it incorporates the humanistic dimensions of the classic Marxist theme of ushering in egalitarianism through the universalizing potential of a dominated group. It then re-Christianizes that theme through the existential and ethical category of oppression. The struggle here is for a recognition of the humanity and value of those whose humanity and value have been, and continue to be, denied.

At this point, a theodicean problem emerges. Young's project emerges out of the black Christian experience, but the history of the relation of Christianity to people of color—especially Africans and Native Americans—is hardly a glorious one.[35] It stands historically as Prospero's religion instead of Caliban's. Given that history, why should people of color (descendants of Caliban) become Christians? Young appeals again here to the distinction between acculturation and inculturation. Recall that he has argued that in Africa, Christianity must draw upon acculturated dimensions of African peoples in order to become an inculturated part of their reality. How would this inculturating consequence of acculturation play itself out in the context of the U.S.? Couldn't one argue that Africa is no more acculturated in the U.S. than is Europe, or perhaps that Europe is more normatively so? Cornel West, for instance, attempts to deal with the acculturated dimensions of U.S. society through pragmatism and Christianity, and when he speaks of "African American," the *African* dimension is peculiarly absent; for West, it is the syncretic prophetic traditions of the New World that serve as his basis for inculturative concerns. But more, since Christianity is a dominant feature of the Americas—especially since the Americas exist only as a consequence of the modern reality of global conquest—isn't the acculturation-inculturation gap for North and South Americans here bridged through simply an appeal to Christianity? Is not the *historic* cultural reality of many people of color in the Americas one of inculturating traditional colored identities, which makes inculturation here a distinct problem from inculturation in, say, Africa?

The concrete response would be to issue a critique of the Americas and other societies that are consequences of conquest and colonization. The Bible and the sword, as C. L. R. James has shown us, are together a familiar motif of demonic Christianity. Christianity has spread Europeanism more than it has Christian ethics. Whatever the norms of Christian doctrine may be, its historical manifestations have been by way of the sword and economies of exploited labor. The theodicean question thus returns: "How could a religion whose historical growth is wrought with such evil be good?" Young addresses these theodicean elements through a discussion of Alexander Crummell, who regarded the path of Christian hegemony as a quintessential good: "The opacity of the problem of theodicy endures, and I appreciate Crummell's eschatological effort to make the benevolence of God transparently clear: 'You meant it for evil but God meant it for good'" (pp. 34–5). Young argues that we need to come to grips with the failings of Alexander Crummell as characteristic of the man. After all, other African American theologians, philosophers, and revolutionaries shared his concern for black liberation without relying on his anti-African attitudes. Young's example is Martin Delany, the father of black nationalism, whose efforts to liberate Africa never capitulated from a love for and devotion to traditional Africans and other dark-skinned peoples.

According to Young, Crummell had several limitations. Although he did not condone slavery, Crummellian missiology called for the introduction of Christianity into Africa and, in doing so, supposedly justified Christian colonization of Africa. Second, Crummell believed that Anglo-Saxon culture offered a benevolent form of cultural imperialism to the colored world. Like Jean-Jacques Rousseau's view of political society forcing its citizens to be free, Crummell thought Anglo-Saxon society would make Africans free. Third, he argued that even in places where Christianity did not end slavery, the Christian God restrained the wrath of slave owners. Slavery could have been worse. (This makes one wonder at the very least about Crummell's actual knowledge of slavery.)[36] Fourth, he tried to mitigate Anglo-Christian antiblackness through arguing that the Canaanites rather than the descendants of Ham were the truly cursed people. The standard mythic explication of black inferiority in Crummell's day was traced back to Noah's curse on Ham. Crummell rationalized that curses fell upon the youngest sons (those who received very little of the family inheritance), which meant that the Canaanites had to be the most cursed.

We may wonder what Young hopes to achieve in his explication of Crummell's faults in the midst of his strengths. Perhaps Young's analysis falls within the sphere of the Hebrew prophetic tradition. Although flawed, the prophets were men and women through whom the message of redemption was carried. Many prophets never entered the proverbial promised land. This motif is embodied in the historical significance of Malcolm X, Martin Luther King Jr., and Ella Baker in the U.S. On the other hand, Young's position is connected to a commitment to truth and testimony. Testifying undergirds much of black religious thought and protest. In many black Christian churches, it is called "bearing witness." A third point, which Young presents, is that: "Pan-African theologians today must overcome the terrible twoness that blinded Crummell to the redemptive ways of the ancestors: a second sight achieved in the removal of the alienation responsible for the veiling of the integrity of the ancestors. Their integrity is the a priori of the pretext of enslavement and colonization, a pretext which dissimulates itself in equating oppression with Providence. . . . Today, Africans will teach African-Americans, so that the latter may divest themselves of the Prometheus syndrome and understand more of the precious ancestral spirituality edifying for a Pan-African Theology" (p. 47).

Young sees Crummell and Blyden as offering two distinct positions on Du Boisian twoness. Crummell shuns the idea and potential reality of an Africa rich with indigenous cultural resources, while Blyden engages the African dimension of Pan-Africanism. Like Crummell, Blyden has difficulty shaking off the shackles of Eurocentrism. But unlike Crummell, he sees the breaking of these shackles as essential to the liberation struggle. Blyden saw the "Westernized Negro" as the bearer of a new civilization that would take root in Africa, while still appreciating the significance of the

African past. Much of his thought on African history, particularly with regard to Egypt, served as a forerunner to more recent forms of black nationalism. Unfortunately, he supported the racist view that Africans should focus on agriculture and affect and leave industry and rationality to Europeans. The political and economic flaws of such a view are obvious (see pp. 58–9). Blyden's black nationalism also involved a hatred of mulattoes, which, aside from its obvious moral flaws, also resulted in flawed political decisions. Perhaps the most tragic example was Blyden's collaboration with European colonialists against the mulatto settlers in Liberia. Blyden's hatred of mulattoes was guided by resentment as well as a political realization that could be illuminated by the relational theory of racial oppression: in time, he thought, mulattoes would become a group of whites who would replace the current significations of whites. Indeed, as we have seen, the black American settlers were referred to as "whites" by the indigenous black population.

Young applauds Blyden, however, for his rejection of all missiologies that require the extinction of indigenous cultures. He also applauds Blyden's aim neither to reject nor valorize Europe. Writes Young, "When blacks are no longer ambivalent toward Europe and themselves, they will have greater incentive to work for black liberation" (p. 69). The goal is to develop an appreciation for and an understanding of the African ancestral heritage and to replace the model of the Europe of Blyden's day, which strove for a socialism with capitalist values, with a socialism with socialist values.

The conclusion drawn from Young's comparison of Crummell with Blyden and his advocacy of an acculturative approach toward inculturation is that liberation theorists should bear in mind that black religions are wrought with African retentions that have enabled African Americans to develop aesthetic and spiritual resources of resistance to their oppression. Important examples of these retentions are the sense of ancestral obligation (respecting the elders) in black communities, and the aesthetic exemplifications of worship in both the avowedly religious art form of Gospel music and the supposedly secular art form of jazz. Jazz, according to Young, is, counter to popular representation, an artistic expression of black spirituality that draws upon retentions from Africa. It provides a musical link between African Americans and Africans. Moreover, participation in jazz transcends cultural specificity and, in so doing, provides a model for positive black identification across the Atlantic. It is positive worship from the black experience. Since the core evil affecting black people is not only the exploitation they have suffered under white supremacy and European capitalism but also the self-hatred incurred by generations of their own, Young concludes that, in order to achieve liberation, African Americans and Africans must learn to "love themselves tenaciously because the swelling ranks of white supremacists and the cancer of self-hatred growing in black hearts impede human liberation. Love-for-self is not an idolatrous love, but a prerequisite for participation in a new humanity—the promise of the Beloved Community in which all humankind will celebrate the gift of Being in peaceful coexistence. Blacks' love of themselves concurs in the Spirit's providential work of regeneration" (p. 163). The modern world is marked by a hatred for black people. Black people, however historically constituted their identity may be, must be loved in order for antiblack racism to erode and eventually disappear.

Beyond Ontological Blackness

Whereas Josiah Young's project involves utilizing developments in Africana thought and European hermeneutics to articulate a viable liberation theology, Victor Anderson's work questions the compatibility of liberation and theology. Like Cornel West, Anderson believes that the danger faced by African American communities is not a failure to identify with the acculturative legacy of Africa, but is instead an absurd attachment to an episteme that has outlived its usefulness for any community but those who are antipathetic to black communities. That episteme is the notion of ontological blackness. By *ontological blackness*, Anderson means the collapse of black identity into an essentialized being whereby black existence is foreclosed by narratives of necessity, homogeneity, and totalization. Like Young, Anderson's argument offers methodological considerations for Africana religious thought. The notion of the episteme, for instance, announces a clear affinity to Foucauldian genealogical poststructuralism, where orders of knowledge manifest power relations in different ages. Ontological blackness is thus also a way of ordering blackness, a way that could be overcome by another way of ordering reality. Foucault, as it is well known, also refers to these ways of ordering reality as "power/knowledge" because of the control and discipline (power) that stand symbiotically with knowledge.

Anderson urges us to reject ontological blackness because it impedes the progress of African Americans. It locks African Americans into an essentialized narrative of suffering and analytically stratifies them in a constant, negative relation to whites. In effect, he is thus criticizing the relational theory of race, which sets blacks in opposition to whites. The problem with this view is that even African Americans' achievements are rendered negative, analytically, by virtue of African Americans having achieved them, which is in effect to render the achievements void. This totalized narrative of negative location has dominated African American theological reflection, Anderson argues, by constantly locating African Americans in the symbolic role of black suffering as Jesus on earth.[37]

In contrast to narratives of suffering and redemption, Anderson advocates a postmodern cultural studies approach to African American religious thought, which, he argues, challenges black essentialism. Echoing Cornel West, he further advocates a prophetic pragmatist consolidation with postmodern cultural studies to articulate challenges at the roots of African American social problems in the thickets of American society and culture. This route supposedly calls for a rejection of systematic and existential theologies because of the transcendental, metaphysical commitments of the former, and the asocial, anguish-riddled narratives of black suffering that emerges from the latter's role in African American religious thought. He argues that both systematic theology and existential theology lead to the elevation of false epistemic claims that gain the normative force of false gods. In short, they are prone to idolatry.

Those idols—racism, ontological blackness, exploitation—must be destroyed on the grounds that any god presented as a supreme iconography in the face of a heterogeneous population is bound to become idolatrous, which makes Anderson's theological project a form of antitheology, a project, that is, of political secularization. This destruction raises the possibility of African American citizenship by providing a properly secular category and a place for the practice of the good life for African Americans.

Such is the short version. The road taken by Anderson to his conclusion is, however, a complex one of skillful weaving in and out of the array of interdisciplinary resources needed to defend his postmodern cultural studies approach. The decision in favor of African American religious studies as the academic study of religion, where by *academic* is meant the most influential scholarly developments in human studies, is well set here. His avowed method draws upon genealogical poststructuralism (Nietzsche, Foucault, and, to some extent, Hans Blumenberg), critical theory (Jürgen Habermas), prophetic pragmatism (West), and African-American cultural studies (West, Henry Louis Gates Jr., and bell hooks). His actual arguments are, however, guided by a motif that he hurls at sites of ontological blackness as a classical reductio ad absurdum. In effect, the argument is that human beings are incomplete, open possibilities. A theory that appeals to completeness, closure, and necessity appeals to something that is not human. Since African Americans *are* human beings, such inhuman appeals must be false and should, therefore, be rejected.

Anderson pursues these sites through a critical genealogy of the ontologizing of humanity in Western intellectual history. One site that receives special attention is the notion of "genius." Genius, here, does not mean individual genius, as we find in Kant's discussion of the sublime in his Critique of Judgment, but group genius, whether ethnic or racial, as found in some of the proponents of Johann Herder (see pp. 123–4).[38] The danger of African American genius is that this genius, rehearsed through many portrayals of African Americans as the opposite of Euro-Americans (as found in the Senegalese correlate of the négritude narratives of Léopold

Senghor, where blacks are the opposites of whites) locked African Americans into a set of attributes that are persistently, predictably stereotypical. The relevance of the appeal to African-American genius in African-American theology emerges in the black theological notion of the redemptive qualities of symbolic blackness—that African Americans, as a black people, bring the genius of redemptive suffering to the world.

What should African American intellectuals do? They should aim their intellectual energies at facilitating African American cultural fulfilment. To that end, Anderson ironically advocates the cultivation of a "public theology," or reflective thought on African American religious experience in the service of the public good. What could "theology" mean here? The conception of theology is similar to what Blyden has in mind in the epigraph to this chapter. Anderson's epilogue is worth a lengthy quotation in that regard:

> The black theology project attempted a grand synthesis when it proposed the union of Marxism with the existential theology of Karl Barth and Paul Tillich in the interests of a theology of black self-consciousness. The synthesis has not been successful. . . . The identification of ontological blackness with *ultimate concern* leaves black theology without the hope of cultural transcendence from the blackness that whiteness created. . . . There is a need for an African American public theology that goes beyond black crisis and existential theology. *Beyond Ontological Blackness* is for me a platform from which to clear a critical path for a more constructive work on African American public theology. Such a theology will require resources from a wide variety of fields. It will seek to get beyond prior preoccupations with existential hermeneutics and its racial politics that have controlled the productions of African American theology until recently. Such a theology will seek to explicate the content of liberation not only in terms of positive self-consciousness at the various levels in which African American life is lived: class, ethnicity, gender, and sexual orientation. It will also place itself at the risk of public irrelevancy when its emancipatory aims are tested within the often compromising realm of public policy (pp. 160–61).

This message from Anderson raises several critical concerns. First, we see here a path from ontological blackness as ultimate concern to a rejection of existential hermeneutics, particularly of the Tillichean (and I presume Ricoeurian) variety. If by this rejection Anderson also means the trenchant advancement of a postmodern rejection of ultimate concern itself, the following consideration then emerges: with the elimination of ultimate concern from religious reflection and the centering of the agonal place of public policy, we here witness a return to the trope of liberal politics as "the religion" of the present age. A serious question is raised as to whether public policy is another form of idolatry. That the project is not a transformation of the American public sphere but an effort to be included into it reflects a robust optimism regarding the possibilities of justice in U.S. civil and political society. If the system stands for God, we will find ourselves facing a theodicy of the system; theodicy, after all, is the project of accounting for an omnipotent and omniscient God's goodness in the face of evil. Similarly, a theodicy of the system involves accounting for evil as that which is not structural but a function of the epistemic and misguided commitments of members of a system. Postmodernism means, then, a rejection of revolutionary projects (which always address systemic evil) and a warm embrace of neoliberal ethics of aesthetic political play. The critic of this position could immediately question the status of an individual who could *afford* this play in the contemporary U.S. political milieu. I suspect Anderson would say that he does not advise African American religious intellectuals to ignore the travails of the American poor. He would probably argue that part of the public debate should be the rallying of American institutional resources for the alleviation of poverty, which, for Anderson, militates against cultural fulfilment and should, therefore, be considered among items of cultural stultification and underclass stratification; it should be addressed through the political process. To Anderson's credit, then—whether one agrees with his politics or not—he appears immune to the political cynicism that often undergirds postmodernism.

Anderson's rejection of the synthesis of Marxism and black theology is, however, highly problematic. Black liberation theologians never laid claim to effecting emancipation by theological means alone, and Marxists never laid claim to effecting emancipation without crises in capital over a series of mediating points in history. In short, there is much that both Marxism and black liberation theology admit they do not know. The goal of synthesizing a black liberation theological project with Marxism is to foster a revolutionary consciousness in the black, and antiracist white, populations. This black population includes not only church congregants but also the development of intellectual capital in the service of the liberation struggle.[39] Black liberation theology has not, that is, presented itself as a form of practical reductionism. It is not the *only way*, but one among the many necessary for social change.

What has happened to the discourse on Marxism in the 1990s is hardly a failure of black theology. That postmodernism has been the dominating academic discourse of the most elite, empowered, cultural studies figures cited in *Beyond Ontological Blackness*—Houston Baker, Henry Louis Gates Jr., Cornel West, Alice Walker, bell hooks, Michael Eric Dyson, and others, all of whom ascended during an age of entrenched conservatism, heightened opulence, distraught public education, and nearly absolute antipathy to any project of social emancipation—should entail, by at least verificational historicism, a similar, resounding conclusion on the synthesis of postmodernism with African American thought; whereas the Marxist synthesis produced protest and grassroots movements, the postmodern movement produced textual critique and a politics of systemic adjustment.[40] Could the charge of conservatism and antirevolutionary (if not counterrevolutionary) practice ultimately be refuted by cultural critics when even the point of the charge is that even their avowed political diversity is epiphenomenal—indicative, perhaps, of a new episteme with its own will to power?[41] If African Americans abandon a protest discourse on fundamental social change, how could they be politically emancipatory? Again, haven't African Americans, as Bill Lawson has argued in "Disappointment in the Black Context," struggled through the political sphere from the eighteenth century and most of the nineteenth century to the present, where they continue to align themselves in critical good faith with liberal (and even conservative) politics?

The ability to continue the struggle against racism in the face of recurring disappointments raises an existential commitment, evinced as well by Anderson's and others' work against the antipolitics of despair. Anderson's attack on existential thought is, then, curious in this regard. Although his target is specifically Tillich's systematic religious existentialism, his position does not hold against other forms of existentialism. Recall that Anderson's problem with ontological blackness is, in the end, that it functions as a form of epistemic, social, and metaphysical closure. How can one progress on a human problem if one fails to address that problem in human terms? Ironically, at the heart of this rejection of ontological blackness is an *existential* appeal: The human being does not have an essence; therefore, any effort to instantiate an essential feature of existence that precedes the lived reality of how human beings forge meaning in their lives—in this case, the public sphere—is destined to encounter what Judith Butler has called "identity trouble." Jean-Paul Sartre's classic formulation, "existence precedes essence," is perfectly compatible with Anderson's antiontological blackness. Anderson thus makes a paradoxical appeal: he rejects existentialism through an existential argument.

Anderson's other existential appeal is by way of Friedrich Nietzsche.[42] The existential Nietzscheanism that undergirds his argument emerges through what he calls an "aesthetics of the grotesque," by which he means an aesthetics that "holds in tension the ambiguities between attraction and repulsion, and exposes both the light and dark sides of culture. It recognizes that things can be otherwise than how they appear. Ambiguity and difference constitute the normative gaze of the grotesque figure" (p. 17). The connection between an aesthetics of the grotesque and recognition of the complexity of human reality drawn by Anderson is, in a word, brilliant. "For Nietzsche," he writes, "the grotesque must open up creative possibilities for a Dionysian genius if critical philosophy is to fulfill its iconoclastic and creative intentions. The grotesque requires a transvaluation of values whereby the heroic qualities of the Apollonian cult of genius are preoccupied in the grotesque. Nietzsche asks, 'What makes a hero?' His answer is: 'Going out to meet at the same time one's highest suffering and one's highest hope'" (p. 131). Here, Anderson provides an argument for the importance of reading African American aesthetic productions, and perhaps all African American intellectual productions, in their complexity. Why, for instance, are the blues also happy, though they emerge from suffering? Why is "doing the dozens"—in which African Americans insult each other with wit—also an aesthetic form that can be appreciated, enjoyed, and passed on from generation to generation? We find here, then, Anderson's affinity with Young in an unexpected way: both of them call for a nuanced discussion of African-American cultures that is attuned to the complexity of human idiosyncracies.

Conclusion

Our portrait of these examples of recent African American religious thought reveals a complex struggle over its relation to theology and a heterogeneous social world. At the heart of this struggle are the problem of secularism and the metatheoretical problem of whether theory is facing its twilight. What is outstanding about Young's and Anderson's projects is that they have placed problems of method into focus. Each project is, however, legitimated by the transformative project of the authors, wherein God seems more like an afterthought. Young announced God as his ultimate concern, although his arguments have sent a theodicean message of theistic assessment.[43] There are religions without a formal deity, but there are no religions, to my knowledge, without ultimate concern (or an ultimate set of concerns). Perhaps this makes Anderson's apperceptively written work the most prescient representative of an age of grotesque religious secularism.

eight

Existential Borders of Anonymity and Superfluous Invisibility

Nationhood is the only means by which modern civilization can completely protect itself. Independence of nationality, independence of government, is the means of protecting not only the individual, but the group. Nationhood is the highest ideal of all peoples.

—Marcus Garvey, *Selected Utterances of Marcus Garvey*

*B*orders and nations have an intimate relationship premised upon the survival and meaning constitution of groups of people—at least with regard to the dictates of classical international law. Contemporary dissatisfactions with nation-state analyses often fail to appreciate that failures in nation-states elsewhere do not constitute eradication of the nation-state everywhere. A point of dissatisfaction is the oft-cited complexity of "indigenous" peoples and racialized peoples—especially with regard to so-called black–white dichotomies. Dissatisfaction usually identifies the failure to achieve "appearance," which, in effect, is premised upon invisibility as a paradoxical site of border presence and absence. For the indigenous person the matter is starkly presented in terms of land and conquest. For the racially formed, the sites are often the body and a metaphysics of group association. For both, there is an epistemology of closure and a dialectic of disappearance and extinction. Such will be the themes to follow.

A Reminder of Method

The subject at hand has been dominated, for obvious reasons, by the disciplinary resources of law, political science, and history. The political significance of nations and their borders, whether positivistically (i.e., legislatively or adjudicatively) or, as one would say today, "imaginatively" determined, are products of complex struggles of interests whose impact has forged the historical visibility— Hegelian style—of governments and the people they govern. As such, statecraft and its accompanying bands of legislative authorities and documenters and defenders (namely, the military) are familiar players in the game of theorizing nations and borders.

In our age, the hegemony of legal, political, and historical approaches to the study of nations and borders have fallen sway to a multitude of approaches, most noteworthy of which is the global dimensions of literary theory in the Anglophone academy. The nation-state and its borders have become "textual" and have, thus, been hoisted up from their cozy nests in realms of necessity to the realms of textual openness. The result has been that one can now study nations and borders without appeals to legally, politically, historically, or even humanistically drawn lines of distinction. (When I mentioned to some friends that I was writing something on borders, they quipped, "Yeah, those are really good bookstores.")

I am not interested in criticizing here the turn to textual nationhood and borders. It is clear that insight can be gained from suspending certain questions in favor of others, and the focus on textuality surely affords a way of "reading" borders without some of the baggage of defending or rejecting them. There is, however, an implication of this turn that is worth considering—that is, its hermeneutical significance. That one can offer interpretive resources for the study of nationhood and borders opens the door to methodological approaches beyond the textual as well. Contrary to approaches that solipsize texts in the name of textual rigor, "intra-textual reality" points beyond texts and is, therefore, intertextual, which suggests an "outside" beyond texts. One such approach is phenomenology.

A subtext, if we will, of all nation and border talk is the human significance of these phenomena. Even in its geographical manifes-tation, the field of inquiry here is a human one or, as the Germans prefer to say, a *Geist*, or spiritual one—a matter of *Geistwissenschaaften*, which is often translated as the "human sciences" but could also be translated as "the science of spirit or sociality," or, as I often pre-fer, "human studies." The word *science* is hopelessly narrow in the English language. Another lesson emerges here from the textualists: translation is a tricky affair. That we are engaged in a human study raises some questions about the vantage points of our analyses. Without the possibility of first-person assertions as genuinely first-person assertions, our phenomena lose the ontological upsurge that represents the limit known as the human being; they become that which is acted upon without emergence, without defiance, resis-tance, and agency. It's a familiar problem: some of our approaches to human studies are "inhuman." Phenomenological appeals have the distinct advantage of recognizing intentional dimensions to human phenomena. They entail an appeal to the intersubjective foundations of meaning, to their constitutive features manifested, biconditionally—as we saw in our discussion of Du Bois's search for a humanistic social science—in the realm of sociality.

Moreover, like the textual appeals, phenomenological ones afford a space for openness by suspending ontological commit-ments to the phenomena beyond their status as phenomena. In phenomenological language, that means stepping out of the "nat-ural attitude" of exigency into the realm of meaning and variation.

The important point here is that although the descriptions of phenomena that follow may carry appearances of "essence," they are not "essentialistic"—they do not, that is, make claims to "being" but instead point out the errors of collapsing beings into "substances" ("necessary beings").

An implication of these appeals to agency, description, and ontological suspension is that they culminate in the ever-present possibility of bad faith. Bad faith, as we have seen, is the effort to evade human reality through the denial of agency; in bad faith, we deny responsibility for that which depends upon our denial. The agency factor undergirds the web of social relations that constitute society itself. As Frantz Fanon reminded us in the introduction to his Black Skin, White Masks, "Society, unlike biochemical processes, cannot escape human influences. Man is what brings society into being."

Nation-States, Borders, Movement

We are a species puzzled by movement and hence puzzled by change. The dialectic of being and nonbeing has often taken the qualitative synthesis of nothingness, where we struggle at the precipice of nihilism and despair. The modern world, once wrought with optimism and vigor, finds itself at a Heraclitean theoretical impasse of constantly changing permanence. Long gone is the permanent divide, as in the biblical invocation of light constituting a first day and recurring days of division into neat divides of land and sky, earth and heaven, low and high. Lines drawn in the sand are, in the final analysis, lines that can be washed away—if not by water, by the force of laughter with regard to the folly of lines that are, in the end, well, lines. (I recall a comedian speaking of the dividing stick on a cashier's conveyor belt in the supermarket. One of those can stop anyone in his tracks. The comedian suggested using such dividing sticks at the nation's borders instead of guards and dogs.)

Enrique Dussel, as we have seen, has spoken of the modern moment of nationhood as a complex affair of technology and conquest. The New World's constitution as "new" began in 1492 by a civilization that had the technological wherewithal to enforce its conception of universality on communities elsewhere.

Conquest is an unusual project. Its aim is to seize nothing but the land. The problem with such seizure, however, is that people often occupy lands. Such occupation poses a moral problem. This problem is usually resolved through an act of bad faith. The conquering people simply choose not to see the people they are conquering on the land. Thus, there often was, and continues to be, talk of conquered *lands* instead of conquered *people*. The land is treated as "peopleless." It is this form of denial that enabled the persistence of the misrepresenting motif of Columbus's having "discovered" America. It's a similar denial behind such historical acts as the Louisiana Purchase, in which Thomas Jefferson, on behalf of the United States, simply "purchased" much of North America west of the Mississippi from Napoleon Bonaparte.

Today acts of displacement continue as borders are drawn and redrawn without recognition of the populations who live on the land. Although the concept of the nation-state emerged as a means of determining the scope of protectorates' jurisdictions, the complexity of protection has not always fared well in this regard. The scenario is classically Hobbesian: the sovereign, Thomas Hobbes argued in his *Leviathan*, can reign so long as it is able to protect those who live within its borders. In modern political philosophy, the classic challenge to this view emerged in Jean-Jacques Rousseau's observation in *The Social Contract* that sovereignty is also a matter of legitimacy, and protection alone is insufficient for legitimacy. A sovereign must be "right," which for Rousseau meant that it must work in the interest of human freedom (which he characterized as the "general will"), a notion that enables sovereignty to extend way beyond its borders. By the time we arrive at Antonio Gramsci's twentieth-century reflections on hegemony in his *Prison Notebooks*, the foundations have already been laid for transborder assertions of sovereignty.

Of course, *borders* in this context mean specifically those defined by international laws and quasi laws. Gramsci's insight is that borders are also normatively defined; they are spaces that function, as well, as epistemic limits. Some borders—if not all—are also cultural: they are points beyond which a society may not be willing to go, which, quite often, is where such a society is unable to go. A case in point is the global status of U.S. hegemony today. This nation's cultural and economic influence is seemingly without limit; its currency is the global currency, and in spite of the rumblings about multilinguality, in truth, English—*American* English—is, with all its imperfections, the earth's current lingua franca.

The results are inevitable. As culture and economy fuse to "culture as economy" and "economy as culture," U.S.-centrism requires a U.S. Mecca, which, in the end, isn't Mecca but the U.S.A. itself. Egypt, Rome, Madrid, Paris, and London have fallen sway to the triumvirate of New York, Washington, D.C., and Los Angeles. The mass immigrations and efforts at immigration that follow are obvious consequences of this cultural-economic fusion; economic capital can no longer be supported willy-nilly, if it ever has, by an economic system, which means that those efforts to bolster national consciousness, to call upon community fervor to save dying worlds like sandbag walls against a swelling river, find themselves swept under the weight of cultural capital whose source is always elsewhere. Ironically, immigration to the center isn't necessarily a flight to a foreign land but a sojourn, like moths to outdoor lights at night, to an uncomfortable home.

The search for home needn't be rehearsed here beyond the observation that in today's world it is a hopeless ideal. Most people "visit" home, and those who are "stuck" there often realize that that is their condition—a condition of being "stuck." We experience feelings of home, here and there, but our times are restless because we are always aware of our cultural connections elsewhere. To the insult of our neighbors, the underlying reality of globalism is clear: more and more people are becoming American even in lands whose legal borders declare them "un-American." And as Americans gain increased understanding of those elsewhere, they find themselves ironically attempting to escape America by seeking *Americas* elsewhere—and everywhere.

It is no wonder that critics of the nation-state are emerging in droves. Many nation-states have been rendered ineffective on Hobbesian and Rousseauian grounds: they cannot protect their people, and their legitimacy has been invalidated by U.S. cultural hegemony. How many times must we see the *simulacrum* of the U.S. Constitution abroad for this point to become evident?

What is often forgotten in the midst of this deterioration is that the U.S. continues to function according to Hobbesian and Rousseauian dictates, if only in an ideologically confused way. The U.S. nation-state is as strong as ever, to the point of being invasive, for without *interglobal* threats (except for those of you out there who have spotted extraterrestrial ones) the inevitable direction is implosive. We are witnessing a heightened intensity of state implosivity on a global level as information and other technologies have rendered the totalitarian personality of mass culturation the order of the day. (I am not particularly worried about protection from extraterrestrials right now since my efforts to encounter such visitors have been fruitless, although living in Indiana for two and a half years should have guaranteed me at least one sighting.)

Another Look at Anonymity, Race, and Superfluous Visibility

The transnational dimensions of Americanism are such that we will need to take seriously some of the unique shortcomings of Americana. Although conquest and racism are not unique to the U.S., they do function as the nation's founding moment in a way that challenges many classic interpretations of hegemony and exploitation. Take, for instance, the race-class debate. It is no accident that the terms of this debate encounter contradictions in "New World" environments. In Europe, class is so indigenous to its environment that it emerges even in European efforts at socialism. One can "feel" class in Europe as one can the air that one breathes. In the U.S., however, the effort to escape (yet retain) Europe took the form of homogenizing European identities into a whiteness framed on the premise of racially fallen beings. Race, then, became an endemic motif of New World consciousness, and that is why one can "feel" race here as one can the air that one breathes. Thus, class dynamics are conditioned more by mass categories of rich and poor, government and people. The agony experienced globally, then, is not simply one of intensified class division but also one of an asserted New World consciousness on those not indigenous to it. Think, for example, of how the discourse on race has worked its way through other communities in U.S. form.

Something new is being formed. Just as a new oppressive relation emerged when Europe expanded westward (and subsequently, eastward), so, too, are new oppressive relations emerging as the New West goes global. Is it racism? Classism? Sexism? In my view, it is none of these uniquely, but instead a pervasive ethos *against* humanistic solutions to any of them. In short, it is the ethos of counterrevolution and anti-Utopia.

We will do well to examine the U.S.'s guiding motifs, then, since they are no doubt playing a role in the development of new social formations worldwide. Two motifs I would like to explore here are occluded indigeneity and race.

First and foremost, North America and South America are founded on conquest. What this means is that legitimacy in the U.S. context requires an act of theodicy, an act of writing away the evils of the system for the sake of the system. In this case, a single exercise reveals a pathology of exorcism. That the North American indigenous population was reduced to 4 percent by 1900 makes the case for moral legitimacy difficult without challenging the indigenous population's right to exist. In effect, rendering the indigenous people "illegitimate presence" on the land problematizes indigenous people themselves; from the U.S. perspective, the implosive problem of indigenous people is their ever-present call for justice in the form of reacquisition of land. Indigenous Americans are so fused with land identity that their peoplehood is inseparable from it. The land isn't simply theirs; they are also the land—the land protesting, the land agonizing, the land hiding. Indigenous Americans find themselves in the position of a *necessary* invisibility.

This invisibility resides, always, in the realm of anonymity as a border of moral consciousness. The system depends upon the bad faith of most of us knowing and denying their history.

Let us reexamine anonymity. Anonymity literally means to be nameless. In this context, however, we will use anonymity to mean a point of epistemic limitation that affords certain levels of generalization. For instance, when one encounters a student in an ordinary context, one admits a certain level of epistemic limitation. The definite article *a* affords the student to be part of the type, "students." But the type "students" is insufficient for a complete judgment of the student beyond the reality of his social role as a student. To know more about the student, information that would transform the student from a type into a unique individual requires interrogation, which, again, concedes epistemic limitation. Indigenous people's invisibility emerges from the force of being a people whose borders are temporal; since the presumption is that indigenous peoples *should not have been here to begin with*, their emergence is one of questioned or problematic existence—in other words, "You should not still be here." Borders for indigenous peoples, then, are not simply geographical but temporal: they are people trying to cross the past into the present, in order to found a place for the future. It is no wonder that the iconography of Native Americans is nearly always spiritual: they are ghosts in their native land.

It is this dimension of temporal border-crossing that indigenous people share with black people. I am using the term *black people* because of the unique role they play in U.S. racial formation. As the indigenous American represents the reality of conquest and unjust acquisition of land, the black in the U.S. context represents the nadir world of racial dilution. One is white to the extent one is not black, which enables whiteness to reemerge from many other mixtures, but rarely ever with blackness. Blackness is the primary racial marker; it has categorical implications. Unlike Native Americans, blacks carry a threat of reproductive potency; quantity translates into prodigious presence, which enables a form of anonymity that is complete and thus leads, paradoxically, to blacks as a form of absence. The more present a black is qua a black, the more absent he is as a point of epistemic limitation and assertion of agency. One doesn't *ask* a black; one *concludes* about him. The consequence is that one black is always superfluous, is always one black too many. Because Native Americans' extinction is treated as a fate accompli by virtue of their hegemony being *pre-American* and the fact that there are now *Americans*, the presence of Native Americans isn't treated as superfluous at all; it is treated, simply, as nonexistent, which enables little risk for those who routinely play with Native American cultural formations as "relics." Blacks, however, are some potent possibilities wrought with sexual anxiety. The modern black is born at the birth of the Americas, and is indigenous to "America" and other New World formations. The irony is that the very institutions that created the black are also those that detest blacks; the black is, thus, always deemed on the prowl for reproduction. As a result, black reality crosses borders of quantity.

For example, when I was a professor at a university in the Midwestern United States, I noticed that most of the black faculty responded to the hostile environment there by parking their cars right beside the buildings in which they taught. They often raced right out of the building to their cars and disappeared. I took it upon myself to stroll across campus as often as possible. I recall a semester in which I taught two courses on opposite ends of the campus. I walked over to one in early afternoon and returned after class. As I walked back and forth, editorials began to appear in the school newspaper voicing anxieties over affirmative action and the "deluge" of black faculty (there were seventeen black faculty out of two thousand faculty members). After a while, I began to realize that each time I crossed the campus, I became *another* black faculty member; my number went from one to many. I was that deluge of black faculty at the university since I was "seen" exponentially by students and faculty as I crossed their paths each day. The school newspaper was, by the way, called *The Exponent*.

Exponential blackness is one of the perverse forms of quantitative borders. It signifies achieving goals for black communities through a single black body. In a world whose objective is to distance itself from blackness, *any* blackness is too much blackness for comfort. This blackness is a stain whose shadow appears in places where it may not even seem apparent. Immigrant narratives, for instance, are most anxious on "colored" immigrants. Their threat is of darkening the nation, which extends to the point of a global darkening since the nation in this state has achieved global hegemony. The theme of implosion means, then, that as antiblackness and anti-indigenousness (witness the reality of the Palestinian people in the Israeli-Palestinian "peace" agreements) spreads, such people are being forced, increasingly, into the belly of the beast. Borders of time and space become increasingly, then, the project of policing within, of treating, in more intensified fashion, these superfluous existents as cancerous. The irony is that statecraft can also be called political science, and political science could be called the science of the *polis*, which—properly pronounced with an elongated "i"—signifies the times.

By Way of Another Conclusion

Well, things look grim. I am not, however, a pessimist, so I should like to offer some hope. It is clear that our role, the role of theorists, is to do our best to identify not only the aetiology of the problem but also alternative ways of responding to it. It is clear that the nation-state status of the U.S. is such that its logic may not be the same as the countries over which it has control (which is, in effect, nearly all other countries). The nature of its expansion into the framework of being itself—of time and space, of temporal and quantitative boundaries—requires complex modes of resistance as well as well-founded and sundry techniques from past struggles. The pragmatic Leninist question of what can be done now requires action on more levels of social life than has been heretofore imagined.

Words and Incantations

Invocations and Evocations of a Wayward Traveler

Words. Defined as meaningful phonemes. Utterances. Incantations. From the Latin, *incantare*. Cant, as in *canter*, from *caner*, to sing. Singing magic has fallen into ill repute. To be cant is to be perfunctory and speak untruths.

Yet there is close relation between cant and incantation. Incantation calls for magical words. With incantation, we evoke, call forth, and sometimes *invoke*—bring forth, summon, or conjure—special forces. We sing—and often chant—magical words.

Intellectuals have a peculiar relationship with words. Unlike academics, whose relation to words tends to be that of technicians, the intellectual *lives* through the world of words. Words paint realities. They dance, tiptoe, from line to line, paragraph to paragraph. They sing, as does the cantor, and bring forth worlds, at times, of wonder. For the intellectual, recollection of realizing the world of words is much like remembering birth. One has not, in a way, *lived* prior to such memory.

Not all intellectuals support the idea of such a transcendental reality as a remembering before knowing. By *transcendental reality*, I mean the world by which and through which meaning is, in a word, "meaningful." Today, it is often put linguistically. One cannot *mean* anything outside of a language, and by *a language* is meant—rather circularly—any meaningful or sensical structure.

Of course, we can be creative about what such a claim signifies. A painting, for instance, is meaningful. I recently observed even the meaning behind the logic of cab driving—how cab drivers each "read" traffic so differently from common drivers. They do so almost poetically. It was early evening; I was on First Avenue in New York City, and traffic was gradually congesting. When the traffic lights turned green, every cab's turn signals immediately indicated a merge into the same, less congested, lane; those who didn't make the openings immediately switched to backup plans for the most effective route. If a civil engineer could but gain a glimpse of such vision, what would become of traffic in overcrowded cities?

Transcendental reality is timeless. To enter it demands a little audacity, even though much of the mundane circulates among us transcendentally.

Writing takes on that extraordinary hubris of making ideas transcend the self. Even diaries aren't written in "private languages."

"God," I once said, "good writing is almost as good as sex." But a friend who knew a little more about writing corrected me.

"No," she urged, "sex is *almost* as good as writing."

The intellectual has a love affair with writing. The relationship is at first sadomasochistic. It is as if writing scratched through the surface of being and lashed against the flesh of language. Such an insight places the budding writer in a situation of anguish and compromise.

"Should I go on?" he often wonders and would, upon reflection, wonder even more after encountering the following *diapsalmatum* on the poet, from Søren Kierkegaard's *Either/Or*:

> What is a poet? An unhappy man who in his heart harbors a deep anguish, but whose lips are so fashioned that the moans and cries which pass over them are transformed into ravishing music. His fate is like that of the unfortunate victims whom the tyrant Phalaris

imprisoned in a brazen bull, and slowly tortured over a steady fire; their cries could not reach the tyrant's ears so as to strike terror into his heart; when they reached his ears they sounded like sweet music. And men crowd about the poet and say to him, "Sing for us soon again"—which is as much as to say, "may new sufferings torment your soul, but may your lips be fashioned as before; for the cries would only distress us, but the music, the music, is delightful." And the critics come forward and say, "That is perfectly done—just as it should be, according to the rules of aesthetics." Now it is understood that a critic resembles a poet to a hair; he only lacks the anguish in his heart and the music upon his lips. I tell you, I would rather be a swineherd, understood by the swine, than a poet misunderstood by men (vol. I, p. 19).

In the world of speech, one speaks but often does not know why. Words float and fade away like steam from a kettle. Our effort to retain them—memory—belies the point of writing, for what is memory but inscriptions on our inner lives? In memory we see traces, ironically, of writing, and although not all intellectuals wrote on paper or stone, nearly all have inscribed themselves on the collective memory of their community, whether that community be as small as a village or as large as a nation.

Like play, writing affords a moment's recognition of agency. We needn't always inscribe words as they have been traditionally handed down. Our age, for instance, is perhaps the age of the neologism. Such is the case with the infamous academic discourse of "postmodernese." Yet there are efforts beyond ivory towers. In hip-hop culture, the morphology of words reigns over the empire of orthography; in Rastafarian culture, words are never simply words. I recall writing a letter to an incarcerated uncle, in which I opened with a simple "hello" and encouragement of "understanding" his situation. A devout Rastafarian, he immediately wrote me back, cautioning me to avoid references to "hell" and "lo," the latter of which, for him, implies "low," invoking images of "hell" and "below." In similar kind, a Rastafarian never "understands"; he "overstands."

I used to think that these semantical games were silly until I pondered the world of fictive memory several years ago in the form of a short story whose title became the name of one of my books. I had thought of including the short story, "Her Majesty's Other Children," in *Her Majesty's Other Children*, but, frankly, I later came upon the opinion that the story was not very good, so I excluded it. Today, however, I wonder, perhaps as all writers wonder, if I may have had ulterior motives; perhaps, in spite of the personal character of the book, the story was too personal.

I wrote the story as fiction, which is to say that, at that time, it was easier to write truth as fiction than fiction as truth. Little did I realize then that the story was more truthful about an intellectual's world, since it explored, as so many intellectuals explored, in one form or another, the complex relation intellectuals have with words. The story is long, so I'll include just an excerpt. By way of context, the protagonist is a little boy in a Jamaican colonial Catholic school. He speaks "perfect English," which is to say that he speaks the Queens English as cultivated under the watchful eye of his great-grandfather. Anxiety emerges among the children during the visit of a colonial dentist. At first delighted by such a gracious act of the British colonial government, their enthusiasm has waned as child after child returns from the dentist's office with a mutilated mouth. So the protagonist declares:

> I didn't want to go to that butcher. I begged my teacher to examine my teeth, hoping to show her how clean and healthy they were. It didn't work. She told me that was the dentist's job, that he would take care of me just fine.
>
> *Just fine* indeed! I urged, until she finally got annoyed and threatened me to sit or receive three strokes on the backside from her cane.
>
> I pressed on anyway, thinking, *Hell, better the cane than the pliers.*
>
> She gave me the cane.
>
> The sting made me regret my choice: I still had to go to the dentist—and then with a stinging backside!

Despite my efforts, I eventually found myself on line outside the cold little room known as "the Medical Room." We received vaccinations there for diseases and bandages when we got hurt.

Six boys were ahead of me. For a while, none of us said a thing. We were like prisoners waiting for execution—tortured slowly by the thought of each victim entering the horrid chamber and the cruel wait for his return. Finally, someone spoke.

"*Mi na scared,*" came a tough, though trembling, voice six seats ahead.

The others also decided to show they weren't scared. I didn't bother.

"Look at 'im," added the boy, pointing his index finger at me. "*Him tough, y' kno'. Mi did si some boys dem come a fight 'im one time in di yaad. Him na cry. Even when dem a step an' a kick him 'pon 'im head an' him face—stomp him down wit' all dem might!—him na cry. Him just a lay deh—a kicking up at dem. Come so—*"

He demonstrated, kicking into the air at an invisible group of attackers. A silly sight. But the others took his story as proof of my courage and strength. They didn't know that it was nothing but show. I had thought a teacher would come to my rescue. Instead, I was forced to defend myself, though without much success. I was frightened—so frightened that I didn't feel the pain as they stomped my face while my pants became drenched with urine. I felt it afterward, though, as my jaws swelled and my eyelids became thin slits between lumps and bruises.

Was that it? I thought. *Was it the pain I feared? Was it that?* I thought about my friends, Winston, Austin, and Carlton, about how their mouths were ripped apart. All the pain, how ugly their mouths looked. So much was happening so quickly. The adults used to call me "chatter-box," claiming I spoke too old for my age. Was that it? *Am I to be punished?* I silently asked myself.

I began to pray—no, not on my knees, but inside. I didn't want to have broken teeth, to have a torn or punctured tongue—to *suffer.*

I imagined myself in the dentist's office. He asked me my name. I saw myself looking at the list of names and only two were left. An idea sprung up.

"*Charley,*" I heard myself say.

In that world of imagination, he turned and looked meanly at me. Then he grabbed me, lifting me against his face, my skinny feet dangling over the shiny floor like a minuet.

"'*Charley'? You bloody little liar!*" he yelled and grabbed his pliers—their jaws opened wide—and shouted, "For that, I'm going to rip out all of your filthy little teeth!"

A loud scream broke the fantasy. I looked around. I was still in my seat, waiting, trembling in my own arms. From the medical room came bawling followed by a quick slap. And silence. Horrible, oppressive silence. I realized that the boy who told the others about me had already gone in, that it was his scream, that he was soon to come out.

The boy opened the door. Trembling, he looked at us, holding his jaw, ashamed of his tears yet seeming to want sympathy.

Our eyes only showed terror—sympathy for ourselves.

He quickly darted away, his dripping mouth leaving a trail of red spots on the shiny floor.

Each boy let out a loud cry from within the room—especially when the pliers clamped his tooth like a hungry boa constrictor over an unfortunate mouse.

One of them was extremely difficult; the dentist made three attempts at getting the tooth, struggling as he pulled, or broke, it out. The child screamed until the pliers clanged against the floor.

It was over. The boy ran out of the room.

I sat there with my eyes fastened to the door. Suddenly nothing in the world seemed to exist beyond that door and me. It looked like the mouth of a huge, hungry monster—one with a special appetite for kids.

I started to take off, but the Mother Superior was at the exit. She smiled—the only time I ever saw her do so.

I could run, I thought. But that would have meant a whipping.

My teeth are fine, I urged; *they're fine.* So he would leave me alone; he would let me leave, because they only take out bad teeth, I assured myself; *they only take out the bad ones. . . .*

I held my breath, got up, and walked as bravely as I could into the room. The door creaked slowly to a close when I let go of the knob.

The dentist seemed like a pink giant with a white, curly top. He asked me my name. I thought about lying. I looked at his pliers. I told him my real name. He told me to sit in the chair. I looked at it. Made of white-painted steel around red leather, it looked like a barber's chair—with the effect of an electric one. I hated barbers too; they always cut my so-called "coarse black hair" with a vengeance.

After he filled out some papers, the dentist asked me to open my mouth. I slowly did so, and he walked over to me and put his rough fingers into my mouth as his big pink face moved close to mine, looking in. I wriggled my nose, hoping there wasn't any embarrassing snot looking back at him. His glasses reflected light against my eyes. He seemed to have found what he was looking for, for he walked over to a steel tray on which rested a lot of tools, medicines, and cotton, where he then poured some brown liquid out of a dark-brown bottle onto a huge cotton ball, walked back over to me, and ordered, "Sniff this."

I didn't know what to do, what was happening, while he pushed the cotton against my nose, frightening me, making me inhale. I opened my mouth in an attempt to take in some air.

That's when I felt it.

It clamped one of my lower right molars.

No—no—no! I thought—No!

It ripped and ripped. I tried to grab his wrenching hands, but I was too slow. It was over. I felt myself drowning from within. He turned and gave me some cotton, saying,

"Here. Put this on the spot. It will stop the bleeding." He smiled at me, warmly.

I looked at his hand and, with trembling fingers, meekly took the cotton and put it into my quivering mouth, onto the spot, onto the vacant gum. I sniffled, which made me realize that I had cried, the memory of my crying out searing from the past into the present. My senses came back and I realized the trail of salty tears down my puffed cheeks, the pain in my mouth, the alcohol smell all around, some yucky other smell, the sunlight through the window, the pile of teeth, cotton, and blood in the waste basket by the tray.

"You may leave now," he told me, no longer sporting his warm smile.

I got up and walked slowly out of his office, leaving my trail of red spots along the floor, the last patient of his mission.

When we were dismissed from school that day, my friends Austin, Carlton, Winston, and I came upon each other in the main yard.

"*How yu feel?*" asked Winston.

I still held my jaw. "Bad," I said. A trickle of bloody saliva got away.

"*How many teet'im tek out?*"

"One." I wiped my chin and mouth, staining the back of my hand and forearm.

"*One? Yu lucki,*" he said. "*Him tek out three a mine. It's just him break di last one. Yu teet'* . . . *dem was good, den?*"

"Good," I said, releasing most of the blood-filled saliva and cotton from my mouth. "My teeth were *real* good. . . ."

"*Did yu cry?*" asked Austin.

I thought for a moment, looking into all my friends' eager eyes, where, for the first time, I began to see my own.

"Nuh," I said. "*Mi na cry.* . . ."

What can we make of words, of reason conveyed by words, when the speaker *is* the invalidity of his words? I have seen this question unsettle many anticolonial writers. It is, perhaps, such intellectuals' fundamental source of anxiety.

There are so many intellectuals who struggle with words, with reading them and learning how to write them. In my youth, I never saw words purely in terms of reading. I knew I wanted to write. Jean-Paul Sartre, in his brilliant autobiography *The Words*, articulated this point beautifully by structuring his text into *reading* and *writing* and, ironically, ending it in childhood before puberty. He exemplified the many readings of childhood, of child development, through the existential psychoanalytical significance of developing a project from the moment one first decides to fake who one is. Unlike most writers who saw truth and innocence in the eyes and mouths of children, Sartre knew very well that most children are phonies. As

Sigmund Freud once observed, they possess but one wish: to be adults. But as we all know, adults—save, at times, the elderly—have an annoying habit of getting in the way. Sartre announced, with near perverse pleasure, that his father died before he was a year old and thus relieved him of the Oedipus complex: "The death of Jean Baptiste [Sartre]," he writes, "was the big event of my life: it sent my mother back to her chains and gave me freedom." He adds, "There is no good father, that's the rule. Don't lay blame on men but on the bond of paternity, which is rotten. To beget children, nothing better; to *have* them, what iniquity! Had my father lived, he would have lain on me at full length and would have crushed me. As luck had it, he died young. . . . I left behind me a young man who did not have time to be my father and who could now be my son. Was it a good thing or a bad? I don't know. But I readily subscribe to the verdict of an eminent psychoanalyst: I have no Superego" (p. 181).

Yet Sartre's complex Oedipus complex was hardly vanquished, as the autobiography demonstrates, since his grandfather brought the Father back through an iconography of God:

There remained the patriarch. He so resembled God the Father that he was often taken for him. One day he entered a church by way of the vestry. The priest was threatening the infirm of purpose with the lightning of heaven: "God is here! He sees you!" Suddenly the faithful perceived beneath the pulpit a tall, bearded old man who was looking at them. They fled. At other times, my grandfather would say that they had flung themselves at his knees. . . . I appeared at the end of his long life; his beard had turned white, tobacco had yellowed it; and fatherhood no longer amused him. Had he begotten me, however, I think he would have been unable to keep from oppressing me, out of habit. My luck was to belong to a dead man. A dead man had paid out the few drops of sperm that are the usual cost of a child; I was a fief of the sun, my grandfather could enjoy me without possessing me (pp. 22–3).

Sartre's depiction of his grandfather's divine exterior reminds me of a story related to me by an anti-racism activist from Connecticut.

He was a bearded African American man of Palestinian descent, and his activist work focused primarily on black youth groups. His story was about one of those sadistic inflictions on justifiedly suspicious souls: a "retreat." In this case, it was a retreat for young activists. The plan was for them to spend a few days sharing ideas in the woods, inhabiting cabins, and "bonding." Yet instead of cabins, he and his colleagues found themselves in shacks, and as luck would have it—although it was early fall—the temperature dropped during the first night to 20 degrees Fahrenheit. So there they were, freezing in shacks without heaters. Tired of shivering in his cold bunk, my friend decided to take a night walk, wrapped in his blanket, which only exposed his face since his head and ears were cold. As it turned out, there was also a Christian group on retreat. They were sitting round a campfire by the lake, which by now was covered by mist under the moonlight. Spotting the warm fire, my friend walked out to join the happy Christians, who turned around and saw this black, blanket-covered, bearded Semite approaching them out of the misty darkness. They fled.

One could but imagine their thought: *Good God, Jesus really is black!*

By the time Sartre wrote *Being and Nothingness*, the Oedipus complex took on many rituals of patricide in the world of paper and ink. God, Sartre demonstrated, was an impossible desire, which rendered the Father dead by virtue of the logic of logic itself: the law of noncontradiction—an Aristotelian Father—was evoked as a father killing a father in the name of the Father. Sartre took things a step further and then violated that law by invoking the contradictory self. By demonstrating that one cannot equal oneself, he achieved, at least in theory, a fait accompli.

Ironically, in French thought, Sartre became a father to be slaughtered as well. French writers such as Jacques Derrida and Michel Foucault were, like Gaia's children, willing to make him the Ouranus whose testicles were thrown to the sea and eventually produced Aphrodite. Derrida, in "Plato's Pharmacy," evokes the father's memories and invokes writing as a patricidal offspring of language. It is no wonder that psychoanalysis and deconstruction made love in the world of literary theory. Every element of psychoanalysis gained its semiotic form in deconstruction, straight down to the unconscious that—in deconstruction—became erased/repressed words whose traces/symptoms often remained but sometimes left, in Derrida's words from "Différance," "without a trace."

Yet writing is something so much more than psychoanalytical motifs and performances of textual play. Sartre was onto something, I think, when he thought about the sense of being *called* to write, the sense of almost concluding that one *must* write. There are those moments of rapture in writing, those moments of losing the soul in a realm so timeless that one, literally, forgets time itself. It is at times orgasmic, but often, very often, spiritual and magical. There is something transcendent, in addition to being transcendental, about writing. It is beautiful; and to *be* a writer is to suffer beautifully.

An odd thing about reflecting on where one is is that it leads one to trace oneself back from the present into an origin that points to it. One becomes what one was always meant to be. The past becomes a highway of signs pointing to the present—there, a sign of what was to come; a mother's entry into a childhood recordbook; early speech, early reading and writing. . . .

I grew up in a world in which a five-year-old could take a public bus to school in a neighboring town on his own. It was a world of colonial metal plates, khaki uniforms, and no pressure to become anything historical. I didn't know what a college was until I entered high school. My image of people who became physicians, attorneys, and scientists was that they simply apprenticed and worked at it. I lacked the understanding of training, which thus led me to an entirely unorthodox education.

I was hated by the world of formal education. Although I was considered a "gifted" child, I was also feared. Because of this, it has been easy for me to identify with outcasts. We are among those who society often wishes would simply disappear, not so much because of the conventional prejudices of race, class, ethnicity, or sexual orientation, but because of our temporal displacement and violation of convention through reiteration of, as Immanuel Kant observed in his discussion of the sublime in his *Critique of Judgment*, "nature." Our eyes, perhaps, said too much; they betrayed, to some, a vision of society's limit, and their mortality. There is no calamity to narcissism worse than a petty reflection.

Writing is a magical affair. The modern era has been marked by an effort to vanquish magic. This effort is often hidden by pretense of a search for scientific rigor. In the twentieth century, it is often characterized by philosophers as the elimination of metaphysics.

I have never trusted antimetaphysics, science's Oedipus complex. At its core is a revolt against the humanity of human beings through a desire to be ahistorical and, hence, to have been born without a past and live without the imagination of a future. Nearly all that is interesting about us cannot be reduced to physics, and metaphysics, we should recall, simply means "beyond physics," as Maurice Merleau-Ponty reminds us in his important essay, "The Metaphysical in Man," in *Sense and Non-Sense*.

Writing—*genuine writing*—is magical. This is something I have always known.

My love affair with writing began in early childhood. I hated sports, but I loved drawing, music, and science. Drawing for me was a world of wonder. I drew many pictures that eventually faded into words and reemerged as worlds. Worlds eventually took many forms of expression. I discovered I had an aptitude for music through banging out rhythms on makeshift drums. Music, for instance, was a world that danced through my mind and caressed my soul with such ecstacy that I often play drums and the piano, to this day, with my eyes shut.

Science for me was a creative world. It was a world of madness and joy, a world of experiments that sparked excitement when they worked, a world in which I experienced some accolades vicariously through giving my experiments to one of my brothers, who would occasionally win first prize in a science fair. A gem was an ecological system of bees, flowers, and soil—carbon dioxide from bees to plants, oxygen from plants to bees. Beautiful. Another gem was a curiosity, in the seventh grade, regarding the physiological problems raised by the heart's pumping a flow of blood through arteries to capillaries and then back to veins. Could not a slap on the back disturb this process? The science teacher was impressed;

he asked me to write my theory down, and so I did. But some things didn't connect, so I explained more. And more. And more. Thirty-five pages later, I had a rough version, which I handed to him. Three days later, he handed it back to me and said, "Not bad, but the body doesn't work that way." He offered nothing more.

You see, I was bused in to the school I attended. I didn't look the part of a science nerd. It was the 1970s. I had grown considerably for a twelve-year-old. Skinny and tall for my age, with an Afro so big that people had to tilt to the side to make room as I passed by, I suspect that my looks—and oh, yes, my skin color—didn't quite fit the profile. The school's assistant principal told me, actually some years later, that the science teacher had shared the paper with the other teachers and remarked that it was a waste of time to invest energy in kids like me. The teachers had instead invested energy in a nerdy white kid who played the clarinet. He was routed to summer training camps in science and music and was tracked to the Bronx High School of Science—one of New York's public schools that is a feeder to the nation's first-tier colleges and universities. I learned a lesson about liberal racism back then. It's a lesson that I have continued to see reassert itself repeatedly—in many facets of my education and professional life. Frantz Fanon's insight continues: reason has a habit of walking out the door whenever a person of color walks in.

Not all of my stories are bad. If they were so, I wouldn't be in a position to tell them, would I? I could tell stories of many travels, geographic and intellectual. The geographic travels have been considerable, especially since presses carry one's words from country to country. But the world of writing is by itself also a journey. Somewhere in childhood, I had those early experiences of taking flight into a world opened up by pen and ink. For a time, I didn't go to school at all because of the stinginess—or perhaps plain old ill will—of my paternal grandfather, with whom I stayed for two years in Jamaica. My "waywardness" took strange form during those years: during errands to the store, I managed to slip a book or two into my trousers and muster enough of a poker face to make my way home with the booty. Eventually, my tiny bed had piles of books and papers—scribblings, drawings, writings, explorations. My wonderful pile continued to grow until one day, for a reason that is perhaps as fairy tale as the world of writing itself, I decided I *had to* have a hardcover adaptation of *Sleeping Beauty*, so I stuffed a copy down my trousers. The shopkeeper spotted the bulge in the seat of my pants as I was leaving the store and called me over. "*Gotcha!*" he yelled, grabbing my scrawny little hand. He let me sweat for a while until he threw me out of the store, warning me never to return. So, from that point onward, I had to walk an extra seven or eight blocks to the next store when sent on errands. My periodic delays enabled my grandfather to search my room more thoroughly; one day, while returning from an errand, I noticed that the garbage was burning earlier than usual.

There are moments for which explanations of *how* one knows would never make sense for those who always demand proof. I *knew* what was happening as I saw the smoke float ominously into the air. What was left of my wonderful pile came into view as the last papers—a drawing here or there, a word here or there—withered to ashes and floated those childhood ideas into misbegotten, but clearly never forgotten, smoke.

A part of me died that day, but in a way, it was a good death. Writers, as we know, have a tendency not to let their work go. They cling to the text, as if those precious words may suffer violation by the groping, probing eyes of others. Readers are a strange breed. They may flatter, laugh with, and cherish your writing; but they could also insult you, laugh *at* you, despise you. A writer needs to let the text live on its own, to let the text take on a world of its own; a writer has to decide, at some point, to die for the sake of the work by making and defending the distinction between writer and text. Yes, a part of me died that day. My grandfather wanted to punish me for daring to attempt to transcend my situation with that partnership of ink, lead, and paper. How dare I believe that what I thought *mattered*!

From that point on, I made a habit of throwing my writings away. I wrote much, and nearly all I wrote I threw away, in spite of those moments of recognition and encouragement through my adolescence to my early adult years as a high school teacher, where I found myself in a situation of teaching so-called wayward youth. My students were those in whom the system had lost faith; they were smart-assed, rebellious, and odd. When we got together, the obvious occurred: love at first sight. I could have remained there in the high school system, with my wayward youth, indefinitely, but I began to wonder about the very meaning of *waywardness*, especially among people whose potentials were not realized.

In my study of education, I learned some constants. One of them was that education was not a goal of most institutions of higher learning; *discipline* was. I needed an undisciplined place, because I knew that I never learned to learn in ordinary ways. Fortunately, I encountered Maurice Natanson, a man in my graduate education who taught me the difference between discipline that crushes the human spirit and discipline that nurtures it. The former is based on narcissism; the latter, on love. Author of such books as *The Journeying Self*, *Anonymity*, and *The Erotic Bird*, Natanson taught and wrote out of love.

But now, I have written too much. My topic is words and incantations, evocations and invocations. I have set in motion a course of ruminations on writing and the writer. I have defended the thesis that writing—genuine writing—is, in the end, a form of incantation; to write is to perform magic. By *magic*, I mean the act of making present that which was not there before. Although many people scribble down ideas here and there, few make that transition to magic, that act of creating a world that transforms what exists. Think of Plato's Forms, William Shakespeare's Hamlet, or Frantz Fanon's evocation of the damned of the earth and his incantation of revolution. These are not mere creations of past souls because they have taken on a life in humanity's collective consciousness. There is much that can be meaningfully said on what Hamlet *thinks*, and such thoughts stand as more than curiosities; Hamlet has a history. The brilliance of Fanon's works is their evocative force: in his writings, the fingernails of the Third World scratch our soul. I was attracted to Fanon because he was a revolutionary thinker. I continue to study him because he is a writer who has created a world. But more, when we think of Albert Einstein's gift of ideas, we should bear in mind that his gift also came by way of wonder and an incantative understanding of physical reality. His formula $E = mc^2$ does, after all, have the effect of "Presto!" And the glamour of "Presto!" is ironically at the heart of the basis of language itself—grammar—both of which have similar etymologies. This glamorous magic underlies music as well. When we listen to Bob Marley's lyrics—"One Love!," "Stand up for Your Rights!," or "Redemption Song"—we encounter a vision of our shared understanding. Whatever one thinks of reggae, only the truly tasteless hate Bob Marley. I could say the same of a Charlie Parker riff, a hymn or ballad by John Coltrane, an Abbey Lincoln sung tale, or even one of J. S. Bach's many fugues.

Magic creates a world that stimulates the human creative spirit to move a step further. Great thinkers are not individuals who engage in petty squabbles about connecting dots or supposedly freeing thought of the interesting. Creative spirits are those whose incantations move us forward. Think of science fiction: many so-so writers have written about alternative worlds, but few have managed to create them. To create a world means to become so much a part of how we conceive of the world that, in effect, the creation becomes our world. We know, for instance, who extraterrestrials are. They are our future; they are us.

Incantative forces need to be renewed and expanded in our humanistic search for our humanity. Many a thinker has called upon us to create new concepts, to set afoot new humanities, to engage the human struggle for significance. That struggle need not collapse into the nightmare of a boring world.

Notes

1. A bibliography of selected works of these thinkers is provided at the end of this volume. In addition, all referenced works receive full citation here.

2. The Human Genome Project would answer Beecher's question very differently: the diversity of genes that constitute human beings. In other words, whites are simply Africans who have lightened themselves through cultural emphasis of certain genes from their black African ancestry. We'll return to this question of genetics in our discussion of Du Bois on human science.

3. For more discussion of these concepts, see chapter 4 of this volume.

4. Readers not familiar with this remarkable work and its author should consult it and Jack Lindsay's introduction to the English translation.

5. Hume's autobiography is a short statement (see bibliography). Rousseau's *Confessions* illustrates this point.

6. I do not aim to discount the value of black teenagers' autobiographical literature. My point is simply that, in addition to its aesthetic value, it is symptomatic of how race functions on the market. For an example of a black teenaged autobiography, see Latoya Hunter, *The Diary of Latoya Hunter: My First Year of Junior High School*. These observations are not meant to discount, as well, autobiographical literature of traumatic experiences of such conflicts as war or forced migration or genocide, as we find in *The Diary of Anne Frank*.

7. I am thinking here of the Oxford University Press series on nineteenth-century black women writers, generally edited by Henry Louis Gates Jr. and his foreword to that series. For discussion and critique of the ascent of the black textualist and literary critic with development of some of the themes briefly stated here, see Sandra Adell, *Double Consciousness/Double Bind*.

8. For critical discussion of Senghor, see Fanon's *Black Skin, White Masks*, chap. 5; Tsenay Serequeberhan's *The Hermeneutics of African Philosophy*; and Sandra Adell's *Double Consciousness/Double Bind*.

9. Masolo, the philosopher, supports Gates through a preference for pragmatism, which makes him suspicious of the notion of thinkers transcending their time.

10. I thank Paget Henry for this point.

11. For discussion of the existentially serious, see *Bad Faith and Antiblack Racism*, chap. 6.

12. For discussions of the demand for bodies without points of view, see *Bad Faith and Antiblack Racism*, chaps. 14–16.

13. I thank Jane Comaroff Gordon for this observation.

14. I am here delighted to report that such projects with regard to this short list of thinkers have already made their way to print. For example, see discussions of Douglass, Du Bois, and Cooper in *Existence in Black* and Frank Kirkland and Bill Lawson's *Frederick Douglass: A Critical Reader* and Anthony Bogues's *Caliban's Freedom: The Early Political Thought of C.L.R. James*. *Existence in Black* and *Caliban's Freedom* have already sparked discussion on the need to revise not only our understanding of Africana thought, but also American philosophy, philosophy of existence, and social and political philosophy. See, for example, Joseph Filonowicz's *APA Newsletter on the Black Experience* article, "Black American Philosophy as American Philosophy: Transcendentalism, Pragmatism, and Black Existentialism: An Experimental Course and Syllabus," Richard Small's "*Caliban's Freedom*: Its Significance," Brian Alleyene's "Classical Marxism, Caribbean Radicalism and the Black Atlantic Intellectual Tradition," and my review of *Caliban's Freedom* in the *APA Newsletter on Philosophy and the Black Experience*.

15. The popular versions of Sartrean existential phenomenology as asocial, psychologistic, and endorsing "radical freedom" have been contested in two of my books, *Bad Faith and Antiblack Racism* and *Fanon and the Crisis of European Man*, and in Linda Bell's *Ethics in the Midst of Violence*. In my work, I point out the distinction between existentialism and philosophy of existence. Sartre rejected existentialism (see his *Search for a Method*) but not philosophical discussions of existence. Compare, for instance, the *systematic* nature of Sartre's thought versus the *antisystematic* thought of Martin Buber and Albert Camus. Moreover, Sartre's discussion of bad faith and his critique of the bourgeoisie as an "unbound" consciousness in *Being and Nothingness* do not comport with notions of absolute freedom. For collective discussions of these issues, see the discussions of Sartre in my edited volume *Existence in Black* and co-edited volume *Fanon: A Critical Reader*.

16. *Yahweh* is the name used in the J version of Genesis—namely, Genesis 2 where the Hebred god is known also as Jehovah. My interpretation

is philosophical and far from orthodox. It is my goal here to raise the identification that a slave like Douglass would have with certain stages of the myth. For a popular discussion of the history of the various versions of Genesis, including the various Canaanite and Midianite deities that converge as the God of Abraham, see Karen Armstrong's *A History of God*.

17. Again, this is but one interpretation, a uniquely existential one, meant to be heuristic. Yahweh's possible history as a warrior god with highly partisan politics and military predilections toward obedience suggests also an interpretation in which he loves a select or elected group, given particularly the interpretations that emerge in Deuteronomy. The issue has been debated in many Judaic, Christian, and Muslim theologies. Armstrong's *A History of God* provides an introductory analysis of the debate, but for discussion in a context relevant here—namely, black theology—see Gayraud Wilmore's *African American Religious Studies*, especially the section on theology. The most forceful challenge to this theology is William R. Jones's *Is God a White Racist?* See James Cone's discussion of the impact of Jones's work in "Black Theology as Liberation Theology," in the Wilmore volume.

18. The masochist here should not be confused with the individual who is locked in a situation like a battered low-income female spouse under patriarchy. The analysis of this chapter refers to that situation as "oppression."

19. Some commentators might object to the continued use of Fanon in the study of racial matters in the United States. My discussion here isn't limited to the United States, but even if it were, Fanon's discussions in *Black Skin, White Masks* pertained to New World black populations in the midst of liberal humanism. And more, Fanon's subsequent work on colonial Africa relates well to indigenous populations in the U.S. when we remember that the U.S. was founded on conquest of the indigenous populations of North America and subsequent genocidal practices that nearly eliminated the entire population by the end of the nineteenth century. New World blacks relate to African blacks on the basis of "race" and cultural retentions that have been fused with other cultures in the New World, but Native Americans relate to Africans on the basis of their common history of conquest by European nations.

20. See Tukufu Zuberi for a wonderful analysis of this fallacy in his "Social Statistics and Race: Problems in Population Analysis." It is a fallacy that receives much attention in my *Bad Faith and Antiblack Racism*.

21. For a stinging critique, see H. P. Rickman "Deconstruction: The Unacceptable Face of Hermeneutics."

22. See the fourth chapter, "Sex, Race, and Matrices of Desire in an Antiblack World." See the fourth chapter of my book *Her Majesty's Other Children*.

23. For discussion, see, for example, Stanley O. Gaines Jr., "Refuting Hereditarian Claims about IQ and Race," Daniel Wideman, "The 'African Origin' of AIDS: De-Constructing Biomedical Discourse." and for an account of some 1990s' "stars" of racist science and the funding apparatuses that support them, see Adam Miller's "Academia's Dirty Secret: Professors of Hate."

24. The existential and ethical significance of racism is where Appiah misses the point. In his Millercomm Lecture at the University of Illinois-Urbana (March 2, 1995), Appiah persistently compared the fiction of racial identity with the fiction of witches. Although his claim that one doesn't have to believe in witches to defend people accused of being witches is valid, it is nevertheless a bad analogy. For if witches did exist (in the form, at least, that Appiah conceives of them), the general community responses may be appropriate, since their practices may violate certain community norms against infanticide and a host of other human violations that may occur in some forms of witchcraft. But if races exist, that wouldn't change the moral impropriety of the general community response. A case in point would be extraterrestrials. In such a case, there is no notion of intraspecies' connection. Would that change one bit the question of treating extraterrestrials with moral respect? Shouldn't we then fight against antiextraterrestrial racism?

25. For recent discussion, see Renée T. White, *Putting Risk into Perspective: Black Teenage Lives in the Era of AIDS*.

26. For Heidegger's view, see *"The Question Concerning Technology" and Other Essays*.

27. For some of Zack's views on race and problems of philosophy of language, see her article, "Race and Philosophical Meaning."

28. For critical discussion of these dimensions of liberalism, see Robert Paul Wolff, Barrington Moore Jr., and Herbert Marcuse, *A Critique of Pure Tolerance*. See also *Bad Faith and Antiblack Racism*, Part II.

29. In *Existence in Black*, pp. 91–98.

30. By *worship* I mean a practice or ritual the purpose of which is to encourage the presence of God or a similarly revered figure. I use the word *practice* in the spirit of John Rawls's instructive essay, "Two Conceptions of Rules." Rawls writes, "I use the word 'practice' throughout as a sort of technical term meaning any form of activity specified by a system of

rules which defines offices, roles, moves, penalties, defenses, and so on, and which gives the activity its structure. As examples one may think of games and rituals, trials and parliaments" (p. 20, n1).

31. In the original version of this chapter, I used the term *authenticity*. I have since been a critic of the notion of authenticity. It is my suspicion that it is a term that leads nowhere. Thus, in this version, I've abandoned it entirely.

32. Leonard Harris noted to me on an early draft of this chapter that this consideration works if and only if God is regarded, at least symbolically, as homo sapient. I here assume anthropomorphic imagery primarily because such is the symbolism of the Jewish, Christian, and Muslim heritage in which I am making these investigations.

33. For discussion of the use of these proverbs in theoretical work, see Kwame Gyekye's *An Essay on African Philosophy*. The strongest proponent of this approach was the late Odera Oruka; see his "Sagacity in African Philosophy."

34. The influence of this passage on black liberation thought is manifold. Rastafarianism, for instance, drew its support from this passage. For discussion, see Barry Chevannes's *Rastafari*.

35. If there is any doubt, I encourage the reader to consult the chapter entitled, "Love," in Tzevan Todorov's *Conquest of the Americas*, and William R. Jones's *Is God a White Racist?* See also Hellen Ellerbe's *The Dark Side of Christian History*.

36. Young appropriately responds to Crummell's argument by citing James's *Black Jacobins*, where James presents a detailed account of the cruelty inflicted by their masters upon slaves. What prevented slavery from being worse were the slaves themselves, and those resources of resistance came from aspects of their "pagan" traditions that survived since many of them were not Christian but, for example, Yoruban or Akan.

37. Similar criticism is held by Roy Morrison, II, in his survey article on Black Theology, "Self Transformation in American Blacks: The Harlem Renaissance and Black Theology."

38. There is another reading of Herder that could be advanced, where Herder's focus is not racial nor ethnic but linguistic. His position was that language expressed a community's way of seeing the world, and to learn that language is to have access to that perspective. We are on familiar terrain here, as we saw in our discussion of Crummell, but with a twist: Herder's point was not to advocate a particular language over others; in learning, say, Kiswahili, one learns a great deal about, say, Bantu conceptual schemes, although that does not mean that one would know the be-

liefs of every single native speaker of Kiswahili. For an example of this alternative reading of Herder (and Du Boisian double consciousness, which is Anderson's quarry here), see Earnest Allen Jr., "On the Reading of Riddles" (pp. 49–68).

39. James Cone's and William R. Jones's fame as teachers is legendary. Cone's work at Union Theological Seminary has ushered more progressive scholars into the professional life of the mind than any scholar in religious and theological studies, and Jones developed a doctoral program in Criminology at Florida State University at Tallahassee that has produced more black graduates than any other program in the nation.

40. And for a critique of the emergence of the elite critic in African American thought, see Joy James's *Transcending the Talented Tenth*. For discussion of conservatism and political nihilism in a postmodern age, see chapter 5 of my *Her Majesty's Other Children*.

41. The influential list of critics in *Beyond Ontological Blackness*, from Baker and Gates to hooks and Dyson, consists of individuals who identify themselves as liberals, neoliberals, Marxists, revolutionary feminists, womanists, and more.

42. For criticisms of utilizing Nietzsche in the interest of black existentialism, see William Preston's provocative essay, "Nietzsche on Blacks."

43. For Young, it is a rejection of demonology in the form of a false salvation.

Works Consulted

Achebe, Chinuaho. 1959. *Things Fall Apart*. New York: Fawcett Cress/Ballantine.

Adell, Sandra. 1994. *Double-Consciousness/Double Bind: Theoretical Issues in Twentieth-Century Black Literature*. Urbana and Chicago: University of Illinois Press.

Ahmad, Aijaz. 1992. *In Theory: Classes, Nations, Literatures*. London and New York: Verso.

Allen, Earnest. 1997. "On the Reading of Riddles: Rethinking Du Boisian 'Double Consciousness.'" In *Existence in Black*, pp. 49–68. (See Gordon 1997a.)

Allen, Norman, ed. 1991. *African-American Humanism: An Anthology*. Buffalo, NY: Prometheus Books.

Alleyne, Brian W. 1998. "Classical Marxism, Caribbean Radicalism and the Black Atlantic Intellectual Tradition," *Small Axe* 3 (March): 157–169.

Anderson, Victor. 1995. *Beyond Ontological Blackness: An Essay on African American Religious and Cultural Criticism*. New York: Continuum.

Anzaldúa, Gloria. 1987. *Borderlands: The New Mestiza-La Frontera*. San Francisco: Spinsters/Aunt Late.

Appiah, Kwame Anthony. 1990. "Racisms." In *Anatomy of Racism*. (See Goldberg 1990.) Pp. 3–17.

———. 1992. *In My Father's House: Africa in the Philosophy of Culture*. New York: Oxford University Press.

———. 1998. "The Illusion of Race." In *African Philosophy*, pp 275–290. (See Eze 1998.)

Appiah, Kwame Anthony, and Amy Gutmann. 1996. *Color Conscious: The Political Morality of Race*. Princeton, NJ: Princeton University Press.

Aptheker, Herbert, 1963. *American Negro Slave Revolts*. New York: International Publishers.

Apuleius, Lucius. 1971. *The Golden Ass*. Trans. with an intro. by Jack L. Lindsay. Bloomington: Indiana University Press.

Arendt, Hannah. 1958. *The Human Condition*. Chicago: The University of Chicago Press.

———. 1969. *On Violence*. New York: Harcourt Brace Jovanovich.

Aristotle. 1941. *The Basic Works of Aristotle*. Ed. with an intro. by Richard McKeon. New York: Random House.

Armstrong, Karen. 1993. *A History of God: The 4000-Year Quest of Judaism, Christianity, and Islam*. New York: Knopf.

Asante, Molefi K. 1988. *Afrocentricity*. Trenton, NJ: Africa World.

Augustine, St. 1950. *The City of God*. Trans. Marcus Doas, with an intro. by Thomas Merton. New York: Modern Library.

Austin, Allan S. 1997. *African Muslims in Antebellum America: Transatlantic Stories of Spiritual Struggles*. New York: Routledge.

Austin, J. L. 1961. *Philosophical Papers*. Oxford: Oxford University Press.

Azevedo, Aluísio. 1990. *Mulatto*. Trans. Murray Grameme MacNicoll; ed. Daphne Patai; intro. by Daphne Patai and Murray Grameme MacNicoll. Austin: University of Texas Press.

Azevedo, Mario, ed. 1998. *Africana Studies: A Survey of Africa and the African Diaspora*. Durham: Carolina Academic Press.

Baker, Jr., Houston. 1973. *Long Black Song: Essays in Black American Literature and Culture*. Charlottesville: University Press of Virginia: 1998.

————. *Afro-American Poetics: Revisions of Harlem and the Black Aesthetic*. Madison: University of Wisconsin Press.

Baldwin, James. 1962. *The Fire Next Time*. New York: Dell.

————. 1983. *Notes of a Native Son*. Boston: Beacon Press.

Baltazar, Eulalio. 1973. *The Dark Center: A Process Theology of Blackness*. New York: Paulist Press.

Barnes, Hazel. 1967. *An Existentialist Ethics*. New York: Vintage.

Barrett, William. 1962. *Irrational Man: A Study in Existential Philosophy*. Garden City, NY: Doubleday/Anchor Books.

Bartky, Sandra Lee. 1990. *Femininity and Domination: Studies in the Phenomenology of Oppression*. New York and London: Routledge.

Batstone, David, Eduardo Mendieta, Lois Ann Lorentzen, Dwight N. Hopkins, eds. 1997. *Liberation Theologies, Postmodernity, and the Americas*. New York and London: Routledge.

Baudrillard, Jean. 1979. *Seduction*. Trans. Brian Singer. New York: St. Martin's Press.

Beauvoir, Simone de. 1947. *Pour une morale de l'ambiguïté*. Paris: Gallimard.

————. 1948. *The Ethics of Ambiguity*. Trans. Bernard Frechtman. Secaucus, NJ: Citadel Press, 1948.

————. 1949. *Le deuxième sexe*. Paris: Gallimard.

Begley, Sharon. 1995. "Three Is Not Enough: Surprising New Lessons from the Controversial Science of Race," *Newsweek* (February 13): 67–69.

Bell, Bernard, Emily Grosholz, and James Stewart, eds. 1996. *The Critique of Custom: W. E. B. Du bois and Philosophical Questions*. New York: Routledge.

Bell, Derrick. 1992. *Faces at the Bottom of the Well: The Permanence of Racism*. New York: Basic Books.

Bell, Linda. 1993. *Rethinking Ethics in the Midst of Violence*. Boston: Rowman & Littlefield.

Bergner, Gwen. 1995. "Who Is That Masked Woman? or, The Role of Gender in Fanon's Black Skin,White Masks." Publications of the Modern Language Association of America 110, no. 1 (January): 75–88.

Berkeley Faculty against Proposition 187 and the California [Anti] Civil Rights Initiative.

Bernal, Martin. 1987. Black Athena: The Afroasiatic Roots of Classical Civilization. New Brunswick: Rutgers University Press.

Bhabha, Homi. 1994. The Location of Culture. London: Routledge.

Birt, Robert. 1977–1978. "An Examination of James Cone's Concept of God and Its Role in Black Liberation," The Philosophical Forum IX, nos. 2–3 (Winter-Spring): 339–350.

————. 1997. "Existence, Identity, and Liberation." In Existence in Black. (See Gordon 1997a.) Pp. 203–214.

Blumenberg, Hans. 1985. The Legitimacy of the Modern Age. Trans. by Robert M. Wallace. Cambridge: Massachusetts Institute of Technology Press.

Blyden, Edward. 1908. African Life and Customs. London: C.M. Phillips.

Bogues, Anthony. 1997. Caliban's Freedom: The Early Political Thought of C.L.R. James. London and Chicago: Pluto Press.

————. 1998. "C. L. R. James, Black Radicalism, and Critical Theory: A Response." Small Axe 3 (March):170–74.

Bowman, James E. Forthcoming (2000). "Anthropology of African Americans: From Bones to the Human Genome." Annals of the American Academy of Social and Political Science.

Boxill, Bernard. 1977–1978. "Du Bois and Fanon on Culture," The Philosophical Forum IX, nos. 2–3 (Winter-Spring): 326–338.

————. 1997. "The Fight with Covey." In Existence in Black, pp. 273–290. (See Gordon, 1997a.)

Butler, Broadus. 1983. "Frederick Douglass: The Black Philosopher in the United States: A Commentary." In Philosophy Born of Struggle, pp. 1–10. (See Harris 1983.)

Bracey, Jr., John, August Meier, and Elliott Rudwick, eds. 1971. The Black Sociologists:The First Half Century. Belmont, CA: Wadsworth.

Brandon, George. 1993. Santeria in Africa and the New World:The Dead Sell Memories. Bloomington: Indiana University Press.

Brotz, Howard M. 1970. The Black Jews of Harlem: Negro Nationalism and the Dilemmas of Negro Leadership. New York: Schocken.

Brown v. Board of Education of Topeka Kansas. 1954. 347 U.S. Supreme Court 483.

Brown, Karen McCarthy. 1991. Mama Lola: A Vodou Priestess in Brooklyn. Berkeley: University of California Press.

———. 1997. "Systematic Remembering, Systematic Forgetting: Ogou in Haiti." In *African-American Religion*, pp. 433–461. (See Fulop and Raboteau.)

Buber, Martin. 1948. *Das Problem des Menschen*. Heidelberg: Verlag Lambert Schneider.

———. 1958. *I and Thou*. Trans. Ronald Gregor Smith. New York: Scribner's Sons, Collier Books.

———. 1965. *Between Man and Man*. Trans. Ronald Gregor Smith; intro. by Maurice Friedman. New York: Collier Books.

Bulhan, Hussein Abdilahi. 1985. *Frantz Fanon and the Psychology of Oppression*. New York: Plenum Press.

Butler, Judith. 1987. *Subjects of Desire: Hegelian Reflections in Twentieth-Century France*. New York: Columbia University Press.

———. 1990. *Gender Trouble: Feminism and the Subversion of Identity*. New York: Routledge.

———. 1993. *Bodies That Matter: On the Discursive Limits of "Sex."* New York: Routledge.

Cabral, Amilcar. 1969. *Revolution in Guinea: Selected Texts*. Trans. and ed. Richard Handyside. New York: Monthly Review Press.

Callari, Antonio, Stephen Cullenberg, and Carole Biewener, eds. 1995. *Marxism in the Postmodern Age: Confronting the New World Order*. New York and London: Guilford Press.

Callinicos, Alex. 1989. *Against Postmodernism: A Marxist Critique*. Oxford, UK: Blackwell/ Polity.

Camus, Albert. 1955. *"The Myth of Sisyphus" and Other Essays*. Trans. Justin O'Brien. New York: Vintage Books.

———. 1956. *The Rebel: An Essay on Man in Revolt*. Trans. Anthony Bower; foreword by Sir Herbert Read. New York: Vintage.

———. 1960. *Resistance, Rebellion, and Death*. Trans. with an intro. by Justin O'Brien. New York: Vintage.

Canetti, Elias. 1984. *Crowds and Power*. Trans. Carol Stewart. New York: Farrar Straus Giroux.

Cannon, Katie Geneva. 1995. *Katie's Canon: Womanism and the Soul of the Black Community*. Foreword by Sara Lawrence-Lightfoot. New York: Continuum.

Casey, Edward. 1976. *Imagination: A Phenomenological Study*. Bloomington: Indiana University Press.

———. 1993. *Getting into Place: Toward a Renewed Understanding of the Place-World*. Bloomington: Indiana University Press.

Cassires, Ernst. 1944. *An Essay on Man*. New Haven: Yale University Press.

———. 1981. *Kant's Life and Thought*. Trans. James Haden; intro. by Stephan Körner. New Haven, CT: Yale University Press.

Catalano, Joseph. 1980. *A Commentary on Jean-Paul Sartre's "Being and Nothingness."* Chicago: University of Chicago Press.

———. 1986. *A Commentary on Jean-Paul Sartre's "Critique of Dialectical Reason," Volume 1, "Theory of Practical Ensembles."* Chicago: University of Chicago Press.

———. 1996. *"Good Faith" and Other Essays*. Foreword by William C. McBride. Lanhomi: Rowman and Littlefield.

Caute, David. 1970. *Frantz Fanon*. New York: Viking Press.

Cavall-Sforza, Luigi Luca, Paolo Menozzi, and Albert Piazza. 1994. *The History and Geography of Human Genes*. Princeton, NJ: Princeton University.

Cavendish, Richard. 1987. *A History of Magic*. London: Arkana.

Césaire, Aimé. 1960. *Cahier d'un retour au pays natal*. 2nd ed. Pref. de Petar Guberina. Paris: Présence africaine.

Charmé, Stuart. 1991. *Vulgarity and Authenticity: Dimensions of Otherness in the World of Jean-Paul Sartre*. Amherst, MA: University of Massachusetts Press.

Chevannes, Barry. 1994. *Rastafari: Roots and Ideology*. Syracuse: Syracuse University Press.

———, ed. 1998. *Rastafari and Other African-Caribbean Worldviews*. New Brunswick, NJ: Rutgers University Press.

Cioran, E. M. 1998. *The Temptation to Exist*. Trans. Richard Howard, with an intro. by Susan Sontag. Chicago: University of Chicago Press.

Collins, Patricia Hill. 1990. *Black Feminist Thought: Knowledge, Consciousness, and the Politics of Empowerment*. New York: Routledge.

Comaroff, Jean. 1985. *Body Power, Spirit of Resistance: The Culture and History of a South African People*. Chicago: University of Chicago Press.

Comaroff, Jean and John Comaroff. 1991. *Of Revelation and Revolution: Christianity, Colonialism, and Consciousness in South Africa*. Chicago: University of Chicago Press.

———. 1997. *Of Revelation and Revolution: The Dialectics of Modernity on a South African Frontier*. Chicago: University of Chicago Press.

Comer, James, and Alvin Poussaint. 1975. *Black Childcare: How to Bring up a Black Child in America*. New York: Pocketbooks.

Cone, James. 1969. *Black Theology and Black Power*. New York: Seabury.

———. 1970. *A Black Theology of Liberation*. Philadelphia: J. B. Lippencott.

———. 1975. *God of the Oppressed*. New York: Seabury.

———. 1989. "Black Theology as Liberation Theology." In *African American Religious Studies*, pp. 177–207. (See Wilmore.)

Conyers, Jr., James L., ed. 1997. *Africana Studies: A Disciplinary Quest for Both Theory and Method.* Jefferson, N.C.: McFarland and Company.

Cooper, Anna Julia. 1988. *A Voice from the South.* Intro. by Mary Helen Washington; foreword by Henry Louis Gates Jr. New York: Oxford University Press.

———. 1998. *The Voice of Anna Julia Cooper: Including "A Voice from the South" and Other Important Essays, Papers, and Letters."* Ed. Charles Lemert and Esme Bhan. Lanham, MD: Rowman & Littlefield.

Copeland, M. Shawn. 1996. "The Exercise of Black Theology in the United States." *Journal of Hispanic/Latino Theology* 3, no. 3 (February): 5–15.

Cornell, Drucilla. 1992. *Philosophy of the Limit.* New York: Routledge.

Crowell, Steven, ed. 1995. *The Prism of the Self: Essays in Honor of Maurice Natanson.* Dordrecht, Netherlands: Kluwer Academic Publishers.

Cruse, Harold. 1984. *The Crisis of the Negro Intellectual: A Historical Analysis of the Failure of Black Leadership.* New York: Quill.

Davis, Angela Y. 1983a. *Women, Race, and Class.* New York: Vintage.

———. 1988. *Angela Davis: An Autobiography.* New York: International Publishers.

———. 1998. "Unfinished Lecture on Liberation—II." In *Angela Davis: A Primary Reader.* Ed. with an intro. by Joy Ann James. Oxford, UK: Blackwell. Pp. 53–60.

Davis, Angela Y., Ruchell Magee, the Soledad Brothers, and Other Political Prisoners. 1971. *If They Come in the Morning: Voices of Resistance.* Foreword by Julian Bond. New York: New American Library.

Davis, Benjamin J. 1969. *Communist Congressman from Harlem: Autobiographical Notes Written in a Federal Penitentiary.* New York: International Publishers.

Davis, Horace. 1978. *Toward a Marxist Theory of Nationalism.* New York: Monthly Review Press.

Debray, Régis. 1967. *Revolution in the Revolution?* New York: Grove Press.

Derrida, Jacques. 1982. *The Margins of Philosophy.* Trans. with additional Notes by Alan Bass. Chicago: University of Chicago Press.

———. 1988. *Limited Inc.* Ed. Gerald Graff. Evanston, IL: Northwestern University Press.

———. 1991. *A Derrida Reader: Between the Lines,* ed. by Peggy Kamuf. New York: Columbia University Press.

———. 1994. *Specters of Marx: The State of the Debt, the Working of Mourning, and the New International.* Trans. Peggy Kamuf; intro. by Bernd Magnus and Stephen Cullenberg. New York: Routledge.

Descartes, René. 1952. *Descartes' Philosophical Writings.* Trans. and ed. Norman Kemp Smith. London: MacMillan.

Dewey, John. 1938. *Logic: The Theory of Inquiry.* New York: Henry Holt.

Diawara, Manthia, ed. 1993. *Black American Cinema.* New York: Routledge.

———. 1994. "Malcolm X and the Black Public Sphere: Conversionists versus Culturalists." *Public Culture* 7, no. 1: 35–48.

———. 1998. *In Search of Africa.* Cambridge, MA: Harvard University Press.

Doane, Mary Ann. 1991. *Femmes Fatales.* New York: Routledge.

Dostoyevsky, Fyodor. 1968. *Great Short Works of Fyodor Dostoyevsky.* Ed. with an intro. by Ronald Hingley. New York: Perennial Classic, Harper & Row.

Douglass, Frederick. 1950. *The Life and Writings of Frederick Douglass,* vols. 1–5. Ed. by P. Foner. New York: International Publishers.

———. 1962. *The Life and Times of Frederick Douglass: The Complete Autobiography.* Intro. by R.W. Logan. New York: Crowell-Collier.

———. 1968. *Narrative of the Life of Frederick Douglass, an American Slave, Written by Himself.* New York: New American Library.

———. 1987. *My Bondage, My Freedom.* Ed. with an intro. by William L. Andrews. Urbana: University of Illinois Press.

Du Bois, W. E. B. 1898. "The Study of the Negro Problem." *Annals of the American Academy of Political and Social Science* XI (January): 1–23.

———. [1898].1998. "On the Conservation of the Races." In *African Philosophy: An Anthology,* pp. 269–274. (See Eze 1998.)

———. 1899. *The Philadelphia Negro: A Social Study.* Philadelphia: University of Pennsylvania Press.

———. 1920. *Darkwater: Voices from within the Veil.* New York: Harcourt, Brace and Howe.

———. [1903]. 1982. *The Souls of Black Folk.* Intros. by Dr. Nathan Hare and Alvin Poussaint, M.D. Revised and updated bibliography. New York: New American Library.

———. [1935]. 1992. *Black Reconstruction in America, 1860–1880.* New York: Atheneum.

———. 1947. *The World and Africa: An Inquiry into the Part which Africa Has Played in History.* New York: International Publishers, 1996.

———. 1968. *The Autobiography of W.E.B. Du Bois: A Soliloquy on Viewing My Life from the Last Decade of Its First Century.* Ed. Herbert Aptheker. New York: International Publishers.

Dussel, Enrique. 1996. *The Underside of Modernity: Apel, Ricoeur, Rorty, Taylor, and the Philosophy of Liberation.* Trans. and ed. with an intro. by Eduardo Mendieta. New York: Prometheus Books/Humanity Books.

Duster, Troy. 1994. "Human Genetics, Evolutionary Theory, and Social Stratification." In *The Genetic Frontier: Ethics, Law, and Policy,* ed. by Mark S.

Frankel and Albert H. Teich. Washinton, D.C.: American Association for the Advancement of Science. Pp. 13–153.

Dworkin, Ronald. 1986. *Law's Empire*. Cambridge, MA: Harvard University Press.

Dyson, Michael Eric. 1996. *Race Rules: Navigating the Color Line*. Reading, MA: Addison-Wesley.

Ellerbe, Hellen. 1995. *The Dark Side of Christian History*. San Rafael, CA: Morningstar Books.

Ellison, Ralph. 1972. *Shadow and Act*. New York: Vintage Edition.

———. 1987. *Going into the Territory*. New York: Vintage.

———. 1990. *Invisible Man*. New York: Vintage.

Embree, Lester. 1997. "American Ethnophobia. E.g., Irish-American, in Phenomenological Perspective." *Human Studies* 20: 1–16.

Euripides. 1995. *Euripides*, Volume I, *"Alcestis," Translated by Richmond Lattimore, "The Medea," Translated by Max Warner, "The Heracleidae," Translated by Ralph Gladstone, "Hippoloytus," Translated by David Grene*. Intro. by Richard Lattimore; ed. by David Grene and Richmond Lattimore. Chicago and London: University of Chicago Press.

Eze, Emmanuel Chukwudi, ed. 1998. *African Philosophy: An Anthology*. Oxford, UK: Blackwell.

Fanon, Frantz. 1952. *Peau noire, masques blancs*. Paris: Editions de Seuil.

———. 1961. *Les damnés de la Terre*. Préface de Jean-Paul Sartre, présentation de Gérard Chaliand. Paris: François Maspero éditeur S.A.R.L.; Paris: Éditions Gallimard, 1991.

———. 1963. *The Wretched of the Earth*. Preface by Jean-Paul Sartre; trans. Constance Farrington. New York: Grove Press.

———. 1967a. *Black Skin, White Masks*. Trans. Charles Lam Markmann. New York: Grove Press.

———. 1967b. *Toward the African Revolution*. Trans. Haakon Chevalier. New York: Grove Press.

———. 1968. *Sociologie d'une révolution*. Paris: François Maspero. [Originally, *L'An V de la révolution algerienne*. Paris: Maspero, 1959.]

———. 1979. *Pour la révolution africaine: écrits politiques*. Paris: François Maspero.

Figes, Eva. 1976. *Tragedy and Social Evolution*. New York: Persea Books.

Filonowicz, Joseph. 1998. "Black American Philosophy as American Philosophy: Transcendentalism, Pragmatism, and Black Existentialism: An Experimental Course and Syllabus," *APA Newsletter on Philosophy and the Black Experience* 97, no. 2 (spring): 30–38.

Finkelstein, Norman G. 1998. "Oslo: The Last Stage of Conquest," *Radical Philosophy Review* 1, no. 2: 133–140.

Fortes, M. 1959. *Oedipus and Job in West African Religion*. New York: Cambridge University Press.

Foucault, Michel. 1967. *Nietzsche*. Paris: Minuit.

———. 1972. *The Archaeology of Knowledge and the Discourse on Language*. Trans. A. M. Sheridan Smith. New York: Pantheon Books.

———. 1979. *Discipline and Punish*. Trans. Alan Sheridan. New York: Vintage.

———. 1980. *Power/Knowledge*. Trans. C. Gordon, L. Marshall, J. Mehpam, and K. Soper; ed. C. Gordon. New York: Pantheon Books.

———. 1994. *The Order of Things: An Archaeology of the Human Sciences*. New York: Vintage Books.

———. 1995. "Technologies of the Self." In *Technologies of the Self*, ed. Luther H. Martin, Huck Gutman, and Patrick H. Hutton. Amherst: University of Massachusetts Press.

Frank, Anne. 1989. *The Diary of Anne Frank: The Critical Edition*. Ed. David Barnouw and Gerrold van der Stroom; trans. by Arnold J. Pomerans and B. M. Mooyaart. New York: Doubleday.

Frankel, Mark S., and Albert H. Teich, eds. 1994. *The Genetic Frontier: Ethics, Law, and Policy*. Washington, D.C.: American Association for the Advancement of Science.

Frankenberg, Ruth. 1993. *The Social Construction of Whiteness: White Women, Race Matters*. Minneapolis: University of Minnesota Press.

Frazier, E. Franklin. 1939. *The Negro Family in the United States*. Chicago: University of Chicago Press.

———. 1955 *Bourgeoisie noire*. Paris: Librairie Plon.

———. 1957. *The Black Bourgeoisie*. Glencoe, IL: The Free Press.

Fredrickson, George M. 1995. *Black Liberation: A Comparativer History of Black Ideologies in the United States and South Africa*. New York: Oxford University Press.

Freire, Paulo. 1990. *Pedagogy of the Oppressed*. New York: Continuum.

Freud, Sigmund. 1961. *Civilization and Its Discontents*. Trans. and ed. James Strachey. New York: Norton.

———. 1963. *Character and Culture*. Ed. Philip Rieff. New York: Collier Books.

———. 1969. *An Outline of Psycho-Analysis*. Revised edition. Trans. James Strachey. New York: Norton.

Friedman, Maurice, ed. 1991. *The Worlds of Existentialism: A Critical Reader*. Atlantic Highlands, NJ: Humanities Press.

Fromm, Erich. 1969. *Escape from Freedom*. New York: Avon Books.

Fulop, Timothy E., and Albert J. Raboteau, eds. 1997. *African-American Religion: Interpretive Essays in History and Culture*. New York: Routledge.

Gaines, Jr., Stanley O. 1996. "Refuting Hereditarian Claims about IQ and Race: W.E.B. Du Bois, Academic Racism, and The Bell Curve." In *Black Texts and Black Textuality*. (See Gordon and White, forthcoming.)

Garvey, Marcus. Not dated. *Selected Utterances of Marcus Garvey*. Kingston, JA: Sons of Garvey Press Association.

Gates, Jr., Henry Louis, ed. 1986. *"Race," Writing and Difference*. Chicago: University of Chicago Press.

——. 1991. "Critical Fanonism." *Critical Inquiry* 17: 457–478.

Gayle, Addison, ed. 1971. *The Black Aesthetic*. Garden City, NY: Doubleday.

Gendzier, Irene. 1973. *Frantz Fanon: A Critical Study*. New York: Pantheon Books.

Gilligan, Carole. 1985. *In a Different Voice: Psychological Theory and Women's Development*. Cambridge, MA: Harvard University Press.

Gilroy, Paul. 1993. *The Black Atlantic: Modernity and Double Consciousness*. Cambridge, MA: Harvard University Press.

Glissant, Edouard. 1981. *Le Discours Antillais*. Paris: Les Editions du Seuil.

——. 1989. *Caribbean Discourse: Selected Essays*. Trans. with an intro. by J. Michael Dash. Charlottesville: University of Virginia Press and Caraf Books.

Gödel, Kurt. 1931. "Über formal unentscheidbare Sätze der Principia Mathematica und verwandter Systeme I," *Monatshefte für Mathematik und Physik* 38: 173–198.

Goldberg, David Theo, ed. 1990. *Anatomy of Racism*. Minneapolis: University of Minnesota Press.

——. 1993. *Racist Culture: Philosophy and the Politics of Meaning*. Oxford, UK: Blackwell.

——. 1997. *Racial Subjects*. New York: Routledge.

Gooding-Williams, Robert, ed. 1993. *Reading Rodney King, Reading Urban Uprising*. New York: Routledge.

Gordon, Lewis R. 1989. "Her Majesty's Other Children," *The Yale Observer* 2, no. 2 (26 October): 8–9, 22–23.

——. 1995a. *Bad Faith and Antiblack Racism*. Atlantic Highlands, NJ: Humanities Press.

——. 1995b. *Fanon and the Crisis of European Man: An Essay on Philosophy and the Human Sciences*. New York: Routledge.

——. 1995c. "Review of Thomas C. Anderson's Sartre's Two Ethics," *Canadian Philosophical Review* (April): 73–77.

————, ed. 1997a. *Existence in Black: An Anthology of Black Existential Philosophy*. New York: Routledge.

————. 1997b. *Her Majesty's Other Children: Sketches of Racism from a Neocolonial Age*. Lanham, MD: Rowman & Littlefield.

————. 1998. "African-American Philosophy: Philosophy, Politics, and Pedagogy," *Journal of the Philosophy of Education Society*: 39–46.

————. 1999a. "Philosophy of Existence," pp. 103–114. *The Edinburgh Encyclopedia of Continental Philosophy*. General editor, Simon Glendenning. Edinburgh: Edinburgh University Press.

————. 1999b. "Philosophy of Existence, Religion, and Theology: Faith and Existence," pp. 141–151. *The Edinburgh Encyclopedia of Continental Philosophy*.

Gordon, Lewis R., and Renée T. White, eds. Forthcoming. *Black Texts and Textuality: Constructing and De-Constructing Blackness*. Lanham, MD: Rowman & Littlefield.

Gordon, Lewis R., T. Denan Sharpley-Whiting, and Renée T. White, eds. 1996. *Fanon: A Critical Reader*. Oxford, UK: Blackwell.

Gossett, Thomas F. 1965. *Race: The History of an Idea in America, 1900–1930*. Baton Rouge: Louisiana State University Press.

Gramsci, Antonio. 1971. *Selections from the "Prison Notebooks" of Antonio Gramsci*. Trans. and ed. Quintin Hoare and Geoffrey Nowell Smith. New York: International Publishers.

Grant, Jacquelyn. 1989. *White Women's Christ and Black Women's Jesus*. Atlanta: Scholars Press.

Gutierrez, Gustabo. 1983. *The Power of the Poor in History*. Maryknoll, NY: Orbis Books.

Gutman, Herbert G. 1976. *The Black Family in Slavery and Freedom 1750–1925*. New York: Vintage.

Guy-Sheftall, Beverly, ed. 1995. *Words of Fire: An Anthology of African-American Feminist Thought*. New York: New Press.

Gyekye, Kwame. 1995. *An Essay on African Philosophical Thought: The Akan Conceptual Scheme*. Revised edition. Philadelphia: Temple University Press.

Habermas, Jürgen. 1971. *Knowledge and Human Interests*. Trans. Jeremy J. Shapiro. Boston: Beacon Press.

————. 1973. *Legitimation Crisis*. Trans. Thomas McCarthy. Boston: Beacon Press.

————. 1983. *Philosophical Profiles*. Trans. Frederick G. Lawrence. Cambridge: Massachusetts Institute of Technology Press.

Hack, Susan. 1978. *Philosophy of Logics*. New York: Cambridge University Press.

Hansberry, Lorraine. 1994. "Les Blancs": The Collected Plays by Lorraine Hansberry. Ed. with critical backgrounds by Robert Nemiroff, foreword by Jewell Handy Gresham Nemiroff, and intro. by Margaret B. Wilkerson. New York: Vintage.

Hansen, Emmanuel. 1977. Frantz Fanon: Social and Political Thought. Columbus: Ohio State University Press.

Harris, Joseph E. 1972. Africans and Their History. New York: Mentor Books.

Harris, Leonard, ed. 1983. Philosophy Born of Struggle: Anthology of Afro-American Philosophy from 1917. Dubuque, IA: Kendall/Hunt.

————. 1994–1995. "The Status of Blacks in Academic Philosophy." The Journal of Blacks in Higher Education (Winter): 116.

Harris, Wilson. 1999. Selected Essays of Wilson Harris: The Unfinished Genesis of the Imagination, ed. with an intro. by Andrew Bundy. London: Routledge.

Hayes III, Floyd. 1996. "Fanon, African-Americans, and Resentment." In Frantz Fanon: A Critical Reader, pp. 11–24. (See Gordon et al, 1996.)

Hayes, Paul. 1973. Fascism. New York: The Free Press, 1973.

Hegel, G. F. W. 1956. Philosophy of History. Trans. with an intro. by J. Sibree; preface by Charles Hegel; new intro. by C. J. Friedrich. New York: Dover.

————. 1967. Philosophy of Right. Trans. with notes by T. M. Knox. Oxford: Clarendon Press.

————. 1977. Phenomenology of Spirit. Trans. A. V. Miller, with analysis of the text and foreword by J. N. Findlay. New York: Oxford University Press.

Heidegger, Martin. 1962. Being and Time. Trans. John Macquarrie and Edward Robinson. New York: Harper & Row.

————. 1977a. "The Question Concerning Technology" and Other Essays. Trans. William Lovitt. New York: Harper & Row.

————. 1977b. Martin Heidegger: Basic Writings from "Being and Time" (1928) to "The Task of Thinking" (1964). Ed. with an intro. by David F. Krell. San Francisco: HarperSanFrancisco.

Henry, Paget. 1997. "Rastafarianism and the Reality of Dread." In Existence in Black, pp. 157–164. (See Gordon 1997a.)

————. 2000. Caliban's Reason: Introducing in Afro-Caribbean Philosophy. New York: Routledge.

Henry, Paget, and Paul Buhle, eds. 1992a. C. L. R. James's Caribbean. Durham, NC: Duke University Press.

————. 1992b. "Caliban as Deconstructionist." In C. L. R. James's Caribbean, pp. 111–142.

Hernton, Calvin. 1965. *Sex and Racism in America*. New York: Grove Press.

Hesiod. 1973. *Hesiod, "Theogony," "Works and Days," Theognis, "Elegies."* Trans. with an intro. by Dorothea Wender. New York: Penguin Books.

Hockenos, Paul. 1993. *Free to Hate: The Rise of the Right in Post-Communist Eastern Europe*. New York: Routledge.

Holloway, Victoria. 1991. "President's Message." *The Drum: The SNMA-Yale Chapter Newsletter* (October): 1.

Holy Bible, King James Version. 1985. Grand Rapids, MI: Zondervan Bible Publishers.

hooks, bell. 1981. *"Ain't I a Woman?": Black Women and Feminism*. Boston: South End Press.

———. 1984. *Feminist Theory from Margins to Center*. Boston: South End Press.

———. 1990. *Yearning: Race, Gender, and Cultural Politics*. Boston: South End Press.

———, with Cornel West. 1991. *Breaking Bread: Insurgent Black Intellectual Life*. Boston: South End Press.

———. 1992. *Black Looks: Race and Representation*. Boston: South End Press.

———. 1994a. *Outlaw Culture: Resisting Representations*. New York: Routledge.

———. 1994b. *Teaching to Transgress: Education as the Practice of Freedom*. New York: Routledge.

Hord, Lee (Mzee Lasana Okpara), and Johnathan Scott Lee, eds. 1995. *I Am Because We Are: Readings in Black Philosophy*. Amherst: University of Massachusetts Press.

Horne, Gerald. February 1994. "On the Criminalization of a Race." *Political Affairs* 73, no. 2: 26–30.

Hountondji, Paulin. 1983. *African Philosophy: Myth and Reality*. Trans. Henri Evans and Jonathan Rée; Intro. by Abiola Irele. London: Hutchinson University Library for Africa.

Hughes, Robert. 1986. *The Fatal Shore: The Epic of Australia's Founding*. New York: Vintage.

Hume, David. 1927. *"An Enquiry Concerning Human Understanding"; and Selections from "A Treatise of Human Nature,"* with Hume's Autobiography and a Letter from Adam Smith. Chicago: Open Court.

Hunter, Latoya. 1992. *The Diary of Latoya Hunter: My First Year of Junior High School*. New York: Vintage.

Huntington, Patricia. 1996. "Fragmentation, Race, and Gender: Building Solidarity in the Postmodern Era." In *Existence in Black*, pp. 185–202. (See Gordon 1997a.)

———. 1998. *Ecstatic Subjects, Utopia, and Recognition*. Albany, NY: State University of New York Press.

Husserl, Edmund. 1960. *Cartesian Meditations: An Introduction to Phenomenology.* Trans. Dorion Cairns. Dordrecht: Martinus Nijhoff.

———. 1965. *Phenomenology and the Crisis of Philosophy.* Trans. Quentin Lauer. New York: Harper Torchbooks.

———. 1970. *The Crisis of European Sciences and Transcendental Phenomenology: An Introduction to Phenomenological Philosophy.* Trans. with an intro. by David Carr. Evanston: Northwestern University Press.

———. 1989. *Ideas Pertaining to a Pure Phenomenology and a Phenomenological Philosophy,* vols. 1–3. Trans. by R. Rojcewicz and A. Schuwer. Dordrecht, Netherlands: Kluwer.

Jackson, Fatimah. 1997a. "Concerns and Priorities in Genetic Studies: Insights from Recent African American Biohistory," *Seton Hall Law Review* 27, no. 3: 951–97.

———. 1997b. "Correlation of Geographic Patterns of Ecological Diversity and Ethnic Variation in Africa: Implications for Identifying Gene X Environment Interactions and Patterns of Human Genetic Heterogeneity," *American Journal of Human Biology* 9, no. 1: 129.

———. 1997c. "Taxonomic Implications of the Human Genome Project (HGP)," *American Journal of Human Biology* 9, no. 1: 130.

———. 1998. "Scientific Limitations and Ethical Ramifications of a Non-Representative Human Genome Project: African American Responses," *Science and Engineering Ethics* 4: 155–70.

———. Forthcoming (2000). "The Mismasure and Non-Measure of African Peoples: A Reoccurring Anthropological Limitation." *Annals of the American Academy of Social and Political Science.*

Jackson, Bruce. 1997. "The Other Kind of Doctor: Conjure and Magic in Black American Folk Medicine." In *African-American Religion,* pp. 415–431. (See Fulop and Raboteau, 1997.)

Jacoby, Russel. 1987. *The Last Intellectuals: American Culture in the Age of Academe.* New York: Basic Books.

James, C. L. R. 1982. 1989. *The Black Jacobins: Toussaint L'Ouverture and the San Domingo Revolution.* 2nd Edition, revised. New York: Vintage.

———. 1993. *The C. L. R. James Reader.* Ed. with intro. by Anna Grimshaw. Oxford, UK: Blackwell.

———. 1995. *A History of Pan-African Revolt.* Intro. by Robin D. G. Kelley. Chicago: Charles H. Kerr Publishing Co.

James, Joy Ann. Fall 1994. "Ella Baker, 'Black Women's Work,' and Activist Intellectuals." *The Black Scholar* 24, no. 4: 8–15.

———. 1996. *Resisting State Violence*. Foreword by Angela Y. Davis. Minneapolis and London: University of Minnesota Press.

———. 1997a. *Transcending the Talented Tenth: Black Leaders and American Intellectualism*. Foreword by Lewis R. Gordon. New York and London: Routledge.

———. 1997b. "Black Feminism: Liberation Limbos and Existence in Gray." In *Existence in Black*, pp. 215–224. (See Gordon 1997a.)

———. 1999. *Shadowboxing: Representations of Black Feminist Politics*. New York: St. Martin's Press.

James, Joy Ann, and Ruth Farmer, eds. 1992. *Spirit, Space, and Survival: African American Women in (White) Academe*. Foreword by Angela Y. Davis. New York and London: Routledge.

Jameson, Fredric. 1971. *Marxism and Form: Twentieth-Century Dialectical Theories of Literature*. Princeton: Princeton University Press.

———. 1991. *Postmodernism, or, The Cultural Logic of Late Capitalism*. Durham, NC: Duke University Press.

Jaspers, Karl. 1955. *Reason and Existenz: Five Lectures*. Trans. with an intro. by William Earle. New York: Noonday Press.

———. 1969–1971. *Philosophy*, 3 vols. Trans. E. B. Ashton. Chicago: University of Chicago Press.

Jaynes, Gerald, and Robin Williams, eds. 1989. *A Common Destiny: Blacks and American Society*. Washington, D.C.: National Academy Press.

Jinadu, Adele L. 1986. *Fanon: In Search of the African Revolution*. London: KPI/Routledge & Kegan Paul.

Jones, Leroi. 1963. *Blues People: The Negro Experience in White America and the Music that Developed from It*. New York: William Morrow.

Jones, William R. 1967. "Sartre's Critical Methodology." Ph.D. diss., religious studies, Brown University.

———. 1973–1979. "Crisis in Philosophy: The Black Presence," *Proceedings and Addresses of the American Philosophical Association* XLVII.

———. 1977–1978. "The Legitimacy and Necessity of Black Philosophy: Some Preliminary Considerations," *The Philosophical Forum* IX, nos. 2–3 (Winter-Spring): 149–160.

———. 1983. "Liberation Strategies in Black Theology: Mao, Martin, or Malcolm?" In *Philosophy Born of Struggle*, pp. 229-241. (See Harris 1983.)

———. 1998. *Is God a White Racist?: A Preamble to Black Theology*. Boston: Beacon Press.

Julien, Isaac. 1996. *Frantz Fanon: "Black Skin, White Mask."* Produced by Mark Nash. London: Normal Films.

Kant, Immanuel. 1959. *Foundations of the Metaphysics of Morals.* Trans. with intro. by Lewis White Beck. Indianapolis: Bobbs-Merrill.

———. 1965. *Critique of Pure Reason (Unabridged Edition).* Trans. Norman Kemp Smith. New York: St. Martin's Press.

———. 1970. *Kant's Political Writings.* Trans. H. B. Nisbet; ed. with an intro. and notes by Hans Reiss. London: Cambridge University Press.

———. 1987. *Critique of Judgment (Including the First Introduction).* Trans. with intro. by Werner S. Pluhar; foreword by Mary J. Gregor. Indianapolis: Hackett.

Katz, William L. 1986. *Black Indians: A Hidden Heritage.* New York: Atheneum.

Kierkegaard, Søren. 1959a. *Either/Or,* vol. 1. Trans. David F. Swenson and Lillian Marvin Swenson; revisions and foreword by Howard A. Johnson. Princeton, NJ: Princeton University Press.

———. 1959b. *Either/Or,* vol. 2. Trans. Walter Lowrie; revisions and foreword by Howard A. Johnson. Princeton, NJ: Princeton University Press.

———. 1962. *Works of Love: Some Christian Reflections in the Form of Discourses.* Trans. Howard V. Hong and Edna H. Hong. New York: Harper & Row.

———. 1968. *Concluding Unscientific Postscript.* Trans. David F. Swenson and Walter Lowrie. Princeton, NJ: Princeton University Press.

———. 1980a. *Kierkegaard's Writings, VIII, The Concept of Anxiety: A Simply Psychologically Orienting Deliberation on the Dogmatic Issue of Hereditary Sin.* Trans. and ed. with intro. and notes by Reidar Thompte and Albert Anderson. Princeton, NJ: Princeton University Press.

———. 1980b. *Kierkegaard's Writings, XIX, The Sickness unto Death: A Christian psychological Exposition for Upbuilding and Awakening,* ed. and trans. by Howard V. Hong and Edna H. Hong wit intro. and notes. Princeton: Princeton University Press.

———. 1983. *Kierkegaard's Writings, VII, "Fear and Trembling" and "Repetition."* Trans. and ed. with Introduction and notes by Howard V. Hong and Edna H. Hong. Princeton, NJ: Princeton University Press.

King, Jr., Martin Luther. 1996. *A Testament of Hope: The Essential Writings and Speeches of Martin Luther King, Jr.,* ed. by James Washington. New York: Harper Collins.

Kirkland, Frank M. 1992–1993. "Modernity and Intellectual Life in Black." *Philosophical Forum* XXIV, no. 1–3: 136–163.

Klein, Joe. 1995. "The End of Affirmative Action," *Newsweek* (February 13): 36–37.

Krondorfer, Björn, ed. 1995. *Men's Bodies, Men's Gods: Male Identities in a (Post-) Christian Culture.* New York: New York University Press.

Kohat, Heinz. 1998. "Thoughts on Narcissism and Narcissistic Rage." In *Self-Psychology and the Humanities: Reflections on a New Psychoanalytical Approach*, ed. by C.B. Strozier. New York: W.W. Norton.

Lacan, Jacques. 1977. *Écrits: A Selection*. Trans. Alan Sheridan. New York: Norton.

Lawson, Bill. 1997. "On Disappointment in the Black Context." In *Existence in Black*, pp. 149–156. (See Gordon 1997a.)

Lawson, Bill, and Frank Kirland, eds. 1999. *Frederick Douglass: A Critical Reader*. Oxford, UK: Blackwell.

Leder, Drew. 1990. *The Absent Body*. Chicago: University of Chicago Press.

Lenin, V. I. 1969. *What Is to Be Done?: Burning Questions of Our Movement*. Trans. Joe Fineberg and George Hanna. New York: International Publishers.

Levinas, Emmanuel. 1989. *The Levinas Reader*, ed. by Seán Hand. Oxford: Blackwell.

Lewis, C. I. 1929. *Mind and the World Order: Culture of a Theory of Knowledge*. New York: Dover.

Lewis, David L. 1993. *W.E.B. Du Bois: Biography of a Race*. New York: Henry Holt.

Lewis, Rupert. 1988. *Marcus Garvey: Anti-Colonial Champion*. Trenton, NJ: Africa World Press.

———. 1998. *Walter Rodney's Intellectual and Political Thought*. Kingston: The University Press of the West Indies.

Lincoln, Abbey. 1961. *Straight Ahead*. CCD 79015. New York: BMI and Columbia Records CCD79015.

Lincoln, C. Eric. 1973. *The Black Muslims in America*. Revised edition. Boston: Beacon Press.

Locke, Alain. 1983. "The New Negro." In *Philosophy Born of Struggle*, pp. 242–251. (See Harris 1983.)

———. 1989. *The Philosophy of Alain Locke: Harlem Renaissance and Beyond*. Ed. with intro. and interpretation by Leonard Harris. Philadelphia: Temple University Press.

Long, Charles. 1997. "Perspectives for a Study of African-American Religion in the United States," in *African-American Religion*, pp. 21–35. (See Fulop and Raboteau 1997.)

Lorde, Audre. 1984. *Sister Outsider*. Trumansburgh, NY: Crossing Press.

Lott, Tommy L. 1992–1993. "Du Bois on the Invention of Race," *Philosophical Forum* 24, nos. 1–3 (fall-spring): 166–187.

———, ed. 1998. *Subjugation and Bondage: Critical Essays on Slavery abd Social Philosophy*. London: Rowman and Littlefield.

———. 1999. *The Invention of Race: Black Culture and the Politics of Representation*. Malden, MA: Blackwell.

Love, Monifa A. 1998. *Freedom in the Dismal: A Novel*. Kaneohe, Hawaii: Plover Press.

Lowenthal, David. 1967. "Race and Color in the West Indies." *Daedalus* 96, no. 2 (spring): 580–626.

Löwith, Karl. 1949. *Meaning in History: The Theological Implications of the Philosophy of History*. Chicago: University of Chicago Press.

———. 1966. *Nature, History, and Existentialism, and Other Essays in the Philosophy of History*. Ed. with a critical intro. by Arnold Levinson. Evanston, IL: Northwestern University Press.

Lyotard, Jean-François. 1984. *The Postmodern Condition: A Report on Knowledge*. Trans. Geoff Bennington and Brian Massumi; foreword by Fredric Jameson. Minneapolis: University of Minnesota Press.

Madhubuti, Haki R. 1990. *Black Men: Obsolete, Single, Dangerous? The Afrikan American Family in Transition*. Chicago: Third World Press.

Major, Clarence. 1970. *Dictionary of Afro-American Slang*. New York: International Publishers.

Manganyi, Noel Chabani. 1973. *Being-Black-in-the-World*. Johannesburg: Ravan Press.

———. 1977. *Alienation and the Body in Racist Society: A Study of the Society that Invented Soweto*. New York: NOK Publishers.

Mannoni, Dominique. 1964. *Prospero and Caliban: The Psychology of Colonialization*. New York: Praeger.

Marable, Manning. 1983. *How Capitalism Underdeveloped Black America*. Boston: South End Press.

Marcuse, Herbert. 1969. *An Essay on Liberation*. Beacon Press: Boston.

———. 1972. *From Luther to Popper*. Trans. Joris De Bres. London: Verso.

Marx, Karl, and Friedrich Engels. 1978. *The Marx-Engels Reader*. 2nd edition. Ed. Robert C. Tucker. New York: Norton.

Masolo, D. A. 1994. *African Philosophy in Search of Identity*. Bloomington: Indiana University Press; London: Edinburgh University Press.

———. 1998. "Sartre Fifty Years Later: A Review of Lewis Gordon's *Fanon and the Crisis of European Man*." *APA Newsletter on Philosophy and the Black Experience* 97, no. 2 (spring): 24–29.

Massey, Douglas S., and Nancy A. Dentin. 1993. *American Apartheid: Segregation and the Making of the Underclass*. Cambridge, MA: Harvard University Press.

Matuštík, Martin. 1993. *Postnational Identity: Critical Theory and Existential Philosophy in Habermas, Kierkegaard, and Havel*. New York and London: Guilford Press.

———. 1998. *Specters of Liberation: Great Refusals in the New World Order*. Albany: State University of New York Press.

Mbiti, John. 1970. *African Religions and Philosophy*. Garden City, NY: Anchor Books.

McBride, William L. 1991. *Sartre's Political Theory*. Bloomington: Indiana University Press.

———. 1998. "Radicalism as the Lucid Awareness of Radicalized Evil: A Second Look at Manichaeisms," *Radical Philosophy Review* 1, no. 1: 35–39.

McGary, Howard. 1998. *Race and Social Justice*. Oxford, UK: Blackwell Publishers.

McGary, Howard, and William Lawson. 1993. *Between Slavery and Freedom*. Bloomington: Indiana University Press.

McIntyre, Charshee C.L. 1993. *Criminalizing a Race: Free Blacks During Slavery*. New York: Kayode.

Melton, J. Gordon. 1999. *The Vampire Book: The Encyclopedia of the Undead*. 2nd edition. Foreword by Martin V. Ricardo; preface and intro. by J. Gordon Melton. Detroit and London: Visible Ink Press.

Memmi, Albert. 1968. *Dominated Man*. New York: Orion Press.

Merleau-Ponty, Maurice. 1962. *Phenomenology of Perception*. Trans. Colin Smith. Atlantic Highlands, NJ: Humanities Press; New York and London: Routledge.

———. 1964. *Sense and Non-Sense*. Trans. with a Preface by Hubert L. Dreyfus and Patricia Allen Dreyfus. Evanston, IL: Northwestern University Press.

———. 1968. *The Visible and the Invisible: Followed by Working Notes*. Ed. Claude Lefort; trans. Alphonso Lingis. Evanston, IL: Northwestern University Press.

Mill, John Stuart. 1980. *John Stuart Mill: A Selection of His Works*. Ed. with an intro. by John Robson. Indianapolis: Odyssey Press.

Miller, Adam. 1994. "Academia's Dirty Secret: Professors of Hate." *Rolling Stone* (October 20): 106–114.

Mills, Charles W. 1998a. *The Racial Contract*. Ithaca, NY: Cornell University Press.

———. 1998b. *Blackness Visible: Essays on Philosophy and Race*. Ithaca, NY: Cornell University Press.

Mintz, Sidney W., and Richard Price. 1997. "The Birth of African-American Culture." In *African-American Religion*, pp. 37–53. (See Fulop and Baboteau 1997.)

Monteiro, Anthony. 1998. "From Racialized Philosophy to Philosophy of Race," *Radical Philosophy Review* 1, no. 2: 157–174.

More, Percy Mbogo. 1995. "Universalism and Particularism in South Africa," *Dialogue and Universalism* 5, no. 4: 34–51.

Morrison, II, Roy. 1997. "Self Transformation in American Blacks: The Harlem Renaissance and Black Theology." In *Existence in Black*, pp. 37–48. (See Gordon 1997a.)

————. 1994. *Science, Theology and the Transcendental Horizon: Einstein, Kant, and Tillich*. Atlanta: Scholars Press.

Morrison, Toni. 1970. *The Bluest Eye*. New York: Holt, Rinehart, and Winston.

————. 1987. *Beloved*. New York: Knopf.

————. 1992. *Playing in the Dark*. Cambridge, MA: Harvard University Press.

Moses, Greg. 1997. *Revolution of Conscience: Martin Luther King, Jr., and the Philosophy of Nonviolence*. Foreword by Leonard Harris. New York: Guilford Press.

Moynihan, Daniel Patrick. 1965. *The Negro Family in America: A Case for National Action*. Washington, D.C.: Government Printing Office.

Mudimbe, V. Y. 1988. *The Invention of Africa*. Bloomington: Indiana University Press.

Mullin, Michael. 1994. *Africa in America: Slave Acculturation and Resistance in the American South and the British Caribbean (1736–1831)*. Urbana and Chicago: University of Illinois Press.

Murrell, Nathaniel S., William D. Spencer, and Adrian A. McFarlane, eds. 1988. *Chanting Down Babylon: The Rastafarian Reader*. Philadelphia: Temple University Press.

Nagel, Ernest, and James R. Newman. 1958. *Gödel's Proof*. New York: New York University Press.

Naison, Mark. 1985. *Communists in Harlem During the Depression*. New York: Grove Press.

Natanson, Maurice, ed. 1963. *Philosophy of the Social Sciences: A Reader*. New York: Random House.

————. 1970. *The Journeying Self: A Study in Philosophy and Social Role*. Reading, MA: Addison-Wesley.

————, ed. 1973a. *Phenomenology and the Social Sciences*, Volume 1. Evanston, IL: Northwestern University Press.

————. 1973b. *Edmund Husserl: Philosopher of Infinite Tasks*. Evanston, IL: Northwestern University Press.

————. 1986. *Anonymity: A Study in the Philosophy of Alfred Schutz*. Bloomington: Indiana University Press.

————. 1998. *The Erotic Bird: Phenomenology in Literature*. Foreword by Judith Butler. Princeton, NJ: Princeton University Press.

Niebuhr, Richard. 1963. *The Responsible Self*. New York: Harper & Row.

Nietzsche, Friedrich. 1968. *Will to Power*. Trans. Walter Kaufmann and R. J. Hollingdale. New York: Vintage.

————. 1974. *The Gay Science.* Trans. Walter Kaufmann. New York: Vintage.

Nishida, Kitāro. 1987. *Last Writings: Nothingness and the Religious Worldview.* Trans. with an intro. by David A. Dilworth. Honolulu: University of Hawaii Press.

Nishitani, Keiji. 1982. *Religion and Nothigness.* Trans. Jan Van Bragt; foreword by Winston L. King. Berkeley: University of California Press.

Nissim-Sabat, Marilyn. 1990. "Autonomy, Empathy, and Transcendence in Sophocles' Antigone: A Phenomological Perspective," *Listening: A Journal of Religion and Culture* 25, no. 3: 225–250.

————. 1997. "Globalization from Below." *The C.L.R. James Journal* 5, no. 1: 118–135.

————. 1998. "Victims No More," *Radical Philosophy Review* 1, no. 1: 17–34.

Nkrumah, Kwame. 1963. *Africa Must Unite.* New York: International Publishers.

————. 1965. *Neo-Colonialism: The Last Stages of Imperialism.* New York: International Publishers.

————. 1970. *Consciencism.* New York: Monthly Review Press.

Nzegwu, Nkiru. 1996. "Questions of Identity and Inheritance: A Critical Review of Kwame Anthony Appiah's In My Father's House." *Hypatia* 11, no. 1 (winter): 175–201.

Omi, Michael, and Howard Winant. 1994. *Racial Formations in the United States: From the 1960s to the 1990s.* 2nd ed. New York: Routledge.

O'Neill, John. 1995. *The Poverty of Postmodernism.* New York: Routledge.

Ortega y Gasset, José. 1932. *The Revolt of the Masses.* New York: W. W. Norton.

————. 1960. *What Is Philosophy?* Trans. Mildred Adams. New York: W. W. Norton.

Oruka, Odera. 1991. "Sagacity in African Philosophy." In *African Philosophy,* pp. 47–62. (See Serequeberhan 1991.)

Outlaw, Lucius. 1996. *On Race and Philosophy.* New York: Routledge.

Owens, Joseph. 1976. *Dread: The Rastafarians of Jamaica.* Kingston: Sangster.

Patterson, H. Orlando. 1982. *Slavery and Social Death: A Comparative Study.* Cambridge, MA: Harvard University Press.

————. 1986. *The Children of Sisyphus.* Harlow, UK: Longman.

————. 1991. *Freedom.* New York: Basic Books.

————. 1998. *Rituals of Blood: Consequences of Slavery in Two American Centuries.* Washinghton, D.C.: Civitas.

Patterson, William. 1971. *The Man Who Cried Genocide: An Autobiography.* New York: International Publishers.

Pico, Giovanni Della Mirandola. 1948. *Oration on the Dignity of Man.* Trans. Elizabeth L. Forbes. In *The Renaissance Philosophy of Man,* ed. Ernst Cassirer, Paul Oskar Kristeller, and John Herman Randall, Jr. Chicago: University of Chicago Press.

Pieterse, Jan Nederveen. 1992. *White on Black: Images of Africa and Blacks in Western Popular Culture.* New Haven, CT: Yale University Press.

Preston, William. 1997. "Nietzsche on Blacks." In *Existence in Black,* pp. 165–172. (See Gordon 1997a.)

Rawls, John. 1971. *A Theory of Justice.* Cambridge, MA: Harvard University Press.

———. 1955. "Two Conception of Rules." In *John Rawls: Collected Papers,* ed. by Samuel Freeman, pp. 20–46. Cambridge, MA: Harvard University Press.

Revankar, Ratna. 1971. *The Indian Constitution: A Case Study of Backward Classes.* Teaneck, NJ: Fairleigh Dickinson University Press.

Rickman, H. P. 1998. "Deconstruction: The Unacceptable Face of Hermeneutics," *Journal of the British Society for Phenomenology* 29, no. 3 (October): 299–313.

Ricoeur, Paul. 1991. *From Text to Action: Essays in Hermeneutics, II.* Trans. Kathleen Blamey and John B. Thompson. Evanston, IL: Northwestern University Press.

Riggs, Marcia. 1994. *Awake, Arise, and Act: A Womanist Call for Black Liberation.* Cleveland, OH: Pilgrim Press.

Robeson, Paul. 1958. *Here I Stand.* Boston: Beacon Press.

Robinson, Cedric. 1983. *Black Marxism: The Making of the Black Radical Tradition.* London: Zed.

———. 1993. Cedric Robinson, "The Appropriation of Frantz Fanon." *Race & Class* 35, no. 1: 79–91.

Rodney, Walter. 1974. *How Europe Underdeveloped Africa.* Washington, D.C.: Howard University Press.

Rorty, Richard. 1982. *Consequences of Pragmatism (Essays: 1972–1980).* Minneapolis: University of Minnesota Press.

———. 1989. *Contingency, Irony, and Solidarity.* New York: Cambridge University Press.

Rosenau, Pauline Marie. 1992. *Post-Modernism and the Social Sciences: Insights, Inroads, and Intrusions.* Princeton, NJ: Princeton University Press.

Rosnzweig, Paul, ed. 1965. *The Book of Proverbs: Maxims from the East and West.* New York: Philosophical Library.

Rousseau, Jean-Jacques. 1971. "Discours sur les sciences et les arts"; "Discours sur Portgine de l'inégalité parmi les hommes. Chromologie et introduction par Jacques Roger. Paris: Garneit-Flammarian.

———. 1995. "The Confessions" and "Correspondence," including the Letters to Malesherbes. Ed. Christopher Kelly, Roger D. Masters, and Peter G. Stillman; trans. Christopher Kelly. Hanover, NH: University Press of New England for Dartmouth College.

———. 1997. "The Social Contract" and Other Later Political Writings. Ed. and trans. Victor Gourevitch. Cambridge, UK, and New York: Cambridge University Press.

Royce, Josiah. 1908. The Philosophy of Loyalty. New York: Macmillan.

———. 1958. The Religious Aspect of Philosophy: A Critique of the Bases of Conduct and of Faith. New York: Harper Torchbooks. (Originally published by Houghton Mifflin in 1885.)

Said, Edward. 1979. Orientalism. New York: Vintage.

———. 1996. Representations of the Intellectual. New York: Vintage.

Santayana, George. 1955. The Sense of Beauty: Being the Outlines of Aesthetic Theory. Foreword by Philip Blair Rice. New York: Modern Library.

Sartre, Jean-Paul. 1940. L'Imaginaire: Psychologie phénomenogique de l'imagination. Paris: Gallimard.

———. 1943. L'être et le néant: essai d'ontologie phénoménologique. Paris: Galli-mard.

———. 1946. Réflexions sur la question juive. Paris: Paul Morihien.

———. 1948a. The Emotions: Outline of a Theory. Trans. Bernard Frechtman. New York: Philosophical Library.

———. 1948b. Anti-Semite and Jew. Trans. George Becker. New York: Schocken Books.

———. 1949. The Respectful Prostitute. Trans. Lionel Abel. New York: Knopf.

———. 1955. "No Exit" and Three Other Plays. Trans. Stuart Gilbert and Lionel Abel. New York: Vintage.

———. 1956. Being and Nothingness: A Phenomenological Essay on Ontology. Trans. with an intro. by Hazel Barnes. New York: Washington Square Press.

———. 1962. Imagination: A Psychological Critique. Trans. Forrest Williams. Ann Arbor: University of Michigan Press.

———. 1963. "Preface." The Wretched of the Earth. (See Fanon.)

———. 1964, unpublished. 1964 Rome Lecture Notes. Paris: Bibliothèque Nationale.

———. 1965. Nausea. Trans. Robert Baldick. New York: Penguin Books.

————. 1968. *Search for a Method*. Trans. with an intro. by Hazel Barnes. New York: Vintage.

————. 1974. "Black Presence." In *The Writings of Jean-Paul Sartre*, Vol. 2, Selected Prose. Trans. Richard McCleary; ed. Michel Contat and Michel Rybalka. Evanston: Northwestern University Press.

————. 1981. *The Words: The Autobiography of Jean-Paul Sartre*. Trans. Bernard Frechtman. New York: Vintage.

————. 1982. *Cahiers pour une morale*. Paris: Gallimard.

————. 1988a. *"What Is Literature?" and Other Essays*. Ed. with an intro. by Steven Ungar. Cambridge, MA: Harvard University Press.

————. 1988b. "Black Orpheus." trans. John MacCombie. In *"What Is Literature?" and Other Essays*. Pp. 289–330.

————. 1988c. *Transcendence of the Ego: An Existential Theory of Consciousness*. Trans. and annotated with an intro. by Forrest Williams and Robert Kirkpatrick. New York: Farrar, Straus, Giroux.

————. 1991a. *Critique of Dialectical Reason, Volume I, Theory of Practical Ensembles*. Trans. Alan Sheridan-Smith; ed. by Jonathan Rée. London and New York: Verso.

————. 1991b. "Kennedy and West Virginia," excerpt from unpublished *Morality and History*. Trans. Elizabeth A. Bowman and Robert Stone. In *Sartre, Alive!*, pp. 37–52. Detroit: Wayne State University Press. (See Ronald Aronson and Adrian van den Hoven 1991.)

————. 1991c. *The Psychology of Imagination*, Trans. Bernard Frechtman. New York: Citadel Press.

————. 1992a. *Notebooks for an Ethics*, trans. David Pellauer. Chicago: University of Chicago Press.

————. 1992b. *Critique of Dialectical Reason*, Vol. II, *The Intelligibility of History*. Trans. Quintin Hoare; ed. Arlette Elkaïm-Sartre. New York: Verso.

————. 1997. "What Jean-Paul Sartre Learned about the Black Problem: His Return from the United States in 1945 with a Comparison of 1995." Trans. and annotated by T. Denean Sharpley-Whiting. In *Existence in Black*, pp. 81–90. (See Gordon 1997a.)

Schopenhauer, Arthur. 1883. *The World as Will and Idea*, Vols. I–III. Trans. R. B. Haldane and J. Kemp. London: Kegan Paul, Trench, Trubner.

Schrag, Calvin O. 1980. *Radical Reflection and the Origin of the Human Sciences*. West Lafayette, IN: Purdue University Press.

————. 1992. *The Resources of Rationality: A Response to the Postmodern Challenge*. Bloomington: Indiana University Press.

———. 1994. *Philosophical Papers: Betwixt and Between*. Albany: State University of New York Press.

———. 1996. *The Postmodern Self*. New Haven, CT: Yale University Press.

Schutz, Alfred. 1962. *Collected Papers*, Vol. I, *The Problem of Social Reality*. Ed. with intro. by Maurice Natanson; preface by H. L. Van Breda. The Hague: Martinus Nijhoff.

———. 1964. *Collected papers*, Vol. II, *Studies in Social Theory*. Ed. with intro. by Arvid Brodersen. The Hague: Martinus Nijhoff.

———. 1966. *Collected papers*, Vol. III, *Studies in Social Phenomenological Philosophy*. Ed. Ilse Schutz. The Hague: Martinus Nijhoff.

———. 1967. *The Phenomenology of the Social World*. Trans. George Walsh and Frederick Lehnhert; intro. by George Walsh. Evanston, IL: Northwestern University Press.

———. 1970. *Reflections on the Problem of Relevance*. Ed. Richard M. Zaner. New Haven, CT: Yale University Press.

Schwartz Gary. 1997. "Toni Morrison at the Movies; Theorizing Race through Imitation of Life." In *Existence in Black*, pp. 111–128. (See Gordon 1997a.)

Sekida, Katsuki. 1975. *Zen Training: Methods and Philosophy*. Ed. with an intro. by A. V. Grimsone. New York: Weatherhill.

Sekyi-Otu, Ato. 1996. *Fanon's Dialectic of Experience*. Cambridge, MA: Harvard University Press.

Senghor, Léopold Sedar, ed. 1948. *Anthologie de la nouevelle poésie Nègre et malgache*. Paris: Présence Africaine.

———. 1971. *The Foundations of "Africanité" or "Négritude" and "Arabité."* Paris: Presence Africaine.

———. 1983. *Liberté*. Paris: Éditions du Seuil.

Serequeberhan, Tsenay, ed. 1991. *African Philosophy: The Essential Writings*. New York: Paragon.

———. 1994. *The Hermeneutics of African Philosophy: Horizon and Discourse*. New York and London: Routledge.

———. 1998. "Africanity at the End of the Twentieth Century," *African Philosophy* 11, no. 1: 13–21.

Sharpley-Whiting, T. Denean. 1998. *Frantz Fanon: Conflicts and Feminisms*. Lanham, MD: Rowman & Littlefield.

———. 1999. *Black Venus: Sexualized Sausages, Primal Fears, and Primitive Narratives in French*. Durham, NC: Duke University Press.

———. See also Gordon, 1996a.

Silverman, Hugh. 1987. *Inscriptions Between Phenomenology and Structuralism*. New York: Routledge & Kegan Paul.

Silverstein, Ken, and Alexander Cockburn. 1994. "Racism USA, 1994: For Whom the Bell Curve Tolls." *CounterPunch* 1, no. 19 (November 1): 1–6.

Slaughter, Jr., Thomas. 1983. "Epidermalizing the World: A Basic Mode of Being Black." In *Philosophy Born of Struggle*, pp. 283–287. (See Leonard Harris 1983).

Smith, John E. 1992. *America's Philosophical Vision*. Chicago: University of Chicago Press.

Smitherman, Geneva. 1999. *Talkin' That Talk: Language, Culture, and Education in African America*. New York: Routledge.

Sokolowski, Robert. 1964. *The Formation of Husserl's Concept of Constitution*. The Hague: Martinus Nijhoff.

Sollors, Werner, and Maria Diedrich, eds. 1994. *The Black Columbiad: Defining Moments in African American Literature and Culture*. Cambridge, MA: Harvard University Press.

Solomon, Robert C. 1987. *From Hegel to Existentialism*. New York: Oxford University Press.

Sophocles. 1954. *Sophocles I: "Oedipus the King,"* Translated by David Grene, *"Oedipus at Colonus,"* trans. Robert Fitzgerald; and *"Antigone,"* trans. Elizabeth Wykoff Chicago: University of Chicago Press.

Spivak, Gayatri. 1980. "The Revolutions that as Yet Have No Model." *Diacritics* 10, no. 4: 47–48.

———. 1988. "Can the Subaltern Speak?" In *Marxism and the Interpretation of Culture*. Ed. Cary Nelson and Lawrence Grossberg. Urbana-Champaign: University of Illinois Press.

———. 1996. *The Spivak Reader: Selected Works of Gayatri Chakravorty Spivak*. Ed. Donna Landry and Gerard Maclean. New York: Routledge.

Stone, Robert V. 1985. "Freedom as a Universal Nothing in Sartre's Ethical Theory," *Revue Internationale de Philosophie* 39, nos. 152–153 (1985): 137–148.

Stone, Robert, and Elizabeth A. Bowman. 1986. "Dialectical Ethics: A First Look at Sartre's Unpublished 1964 Rome Lecture Notes." *Social Text*. 13/14 (winter/spring): 195–214.

Strickland, Dorothy, ed. 1982. *Listen Children: An Anthology of Black Literature*. New York: Bantam Books.

Taplin, Oliver. 1993. *Greek Tragedy in Action*. London: Routledge.

Taylor, Charles. 1992. *Multiculturalism and "The Politics of Recognition": An Essay by Charles Taylor*. Ed. Amy Gutman; commentary by Amy Gutmann, Steven Rockefeller, Michael Walzer, and Susan Wolf. Princeton, NJ: Princeton University Press.

———. 1979. *Hegel and Modern Society*. New York: Cambridge University Press.

Tempels, Placide. 1959. *Bantu Philosophy*. Trans. Colin King; foreword by Margaret Read. Paris: Présence Africaine.

Thompson, Robert Farris. 1983. *Flash of the Spirit: African and Afro-American Art and Philosophy*. New York: Random House.

Thornton, Russell. 1987. *American Indian Holocaust and Survival: A Population History since 1492*. Norman: University of Oklahoma Press.

Thoreau, Henry. 1975. *The Portable Thoreau*, ed. by Car Bode. New York: Penguin Books.

Tillich, Paul. 1953. *The Courage to Be*. New Haven, CT: Yale University Press.

———. 1965. *Dynamics of Faith*. New York: Harper & Row.

Todorov, Tzvetan. 1984. *The Conquest of America: The Question of the Other*. Trans. Richard Howard. New York: Vintage.

Ture, Kwame and Charles V. Hamilton. 1992. *Black Power: The Politics of Liberation in America*. New York: Vintage Books.

Turner, Lou, and John Alan. 1986. *Frantz Fanon, Soweto, and American Black Thought*. Chicago: News and Letters.

Turner, V. I. 1967. *The Forest of Symbols*. Ithaca: Cornell University Press.

Twiss, Sumner, and Walter H. Conser Jr., eds. 1992. *Experience of the Sacred: Readings in the Phenomenology of Religion*. Hanover, NH: Brown University Press/University Press of New England.

Walker, Alice. 1983. *In Search of Our Mother's Gardens: Womanist Prose*. New York: Harcourt Brace.

Walker, Margaret. 1988. *Richard Wright: Daemonic Genius*. New York: Warner Books.

Walzer, Michael. 1988. *The Company of Critics: Social Criticism and Political Commitment in the Twentieth Century*. New York: Basic Books.

Weber, Max. 1946. *From Max Weber: Essays in Sociology*. Trans. with an intro. by H. H. Gerth and C. Wright Mills. New York: Oxford University Press.

Weil, Simone. 1977. *The Simone Weil Reader*, ed. by George A. Panichas. Mt. Kisco, NY: Moyer Bell Limited.

West, Cornel. 1977–1978. "Philosophy and the Afro-American Experience," *The Philosophical Forum* IX, nos. 2–3 (Winter–Spring): 117–148.

———. 1982. *Prophesy, Deliverance!: An Afro-American Revolutionary Christianity*. Philadelphia: Westminster Press.

———. 1989. *American Evasion of Philosophy: A Genealogy of Pragmatism*. Madison: University of Wisconsin Press.

———. 1993a. *Race Matters*. Boston: Beacon Press.

——— . 1993b. *Keeping Faith: Philosophy and Race in America*. New York: Routledge.

——— . 1993. *Beyond Eurocentrism and Multiculturalism*. Monroe, ME: Common Courage.

——— . 1998. *The Future of American Progressivism: An Initiative for Political and Economic Reform*. Boston: Beacon Press.

Westley, Robert. 1997. "White Normativity and the Racial Rhetoric of Equal Protection." In *Existence in Black*, pp. 91–98. (See Gordon 1997a.)

White, Renée T. 1999. *Putting Risk into Perspective: Black Teenage Lives in the Era of AIDS*. Lanham, MD: Rowman and Littlefield.

Wideman, Daniel. Forthcoming. "The 'African Origin' of AIDS: De-Constructing Biomedical Discourse." In *Black Texts and Black Textuality*. (See Gordon and White, forthcoming.)

Wideman, Daniel, and Rohan Preston, eds. 1996. *Soulfires: Young Black Men on Love and Violence*. New York: Penguin.

Wild, John. 1963. *Existence and the World of Freedom*. Englewood Cliffs, NJ: Prentice Hall.

Willett, Cynthia. 1995. *Maternal Ethics and Other Slave Moralities*. New York: Routledge.

Williams, Jr., Vernon. 1996. *Rethinking Race: Franz Boas and His Contemporaries*. Lexington: University of Kentucky Press.

Wills, David W. 1997. "The Central Themes of American Religious History: Pluralism, Puritanism, and the Encounter of Black and White." In *African-American Religion*, pp. 7–10. (See Fulop and Raboteau 1997.)

Wilmore, Gayraud S., ed. 1989. *African American Religious Studies: An Interdisciplinary Anthology*. Durham, NC: Duke University Press.

Wilson, R. M. 1967. "Mani and Manichaeism." In *The Encyclopedia of Philosophy*, vol. 5, Paul Edwards, editor in chief. New York: Macmillan and The Free Press.

Winant, Howard. 1994. *Racial Conditions: Politics, Theory, Comparisons*. Minneapolis: University of Minnesota Press.

Woddis, James. 1972. *New Theories of Revolution: A Commentary on the Views of Frantz Fanon, Régis Debray and Herbert Marcuse*. New York: International Publishers.

Wolff, Robert Paul, Barrington Moore Jr., Herbert Marcuse. 1969. *A Critique of Pure Tolerance*. Boston: Beacon Press.

Wright, Richard. 1953. *The Outsider*. New York: Harper & Row.

——— . 1960. *Native Son*. New York: Harper & Row.

——— . 1965. "I Tried to Be a Communist." In *The God That Failed*, ed. Richard Crossman. New York: Harper & Row.

Wynter, Sylvia. 1992a. "Rethinking 'Aesthetics': Notes Towards a Deciphering Practice." In *Ex-Iles: Essays on Caribbean Cinema*, ed. by Mbye B. Cham, 237–279. Trenton, NJ: Africa World Press.

————. 1992b. "Beyond the Categories of the Master Conception: The Cantes doctriene of the Jungian Poieses." In *C. L. R. James's Caribbean*. (See Henry and Buhle 1992.) Pp. 63–91.

————. 1996. "Is 'Development' a Purely Empirical Concept or Also 'Teleological'? A Perspective from 'We the Underdeveloped,'" in *Prospects for Recovery and Sustainable Development in Africa*, ed. by Aguibou Y. Yansané. Westport, CT: Greenwood Press.

X, Malcolm. 1965. *The Autobiography of Malcolm X as Told to Alex Haley*. New York: Ballentine.

Young-Bruehl, Elisabeth. 1982. *Hannah Arendt: For Love of the World*. New Haven, CT: Yale University Press.

Young, III, and Josiah Ulysses. *A Pan-African Theology: Providence and the Legacies of the Ancestors*. Trenton, NJ: Africa World Press, 1992.

————. 1998. *No Difference in the Fare: Dietrich Bonhoeffer and the Problem of Racism*. Grand Rapids, MI: William B. Eerdmans.

Yancy, George. 1997. "Cornel West's Postmodern Historicist Philosophy of Religion: Problems and Implications," *The Journal of Religion* 52, no. 1: 27–44.

Yancy, George, ed. 1998. *African American Philosophers: Seventeen Conversations*. New York: Routledge.

Zack, Naomi. 1993. *Mixed-Race*. Philadelphia: Temple University Press.

————. 1994. "Race and Philosophic Meaning," *American Philosophical Association Newsletter on Philosophy and the Black Experience* 91, no. 1: 14–21.

————, ed. 1995. *American Mixed Race*. Boston: Rowman & Littlefield.

————. 1996a. *Bachelors of Science*. Philadelphia: Temple University Press.

————, ed. 1996b. *Sex/Race: Comparing the Categories*. New York and London: Routledge.

————. 1997. "Race, Life, Death, Identity, Tragedy, and Good Faith." In *Existence in Black*, pp. 99–110. (See Gordon 1997a.)

Zahar, Renate. 1974. *Frantz Fanon: Colonialism and Alienation, Concerning Frantz Fanon's Political Theory*. Trans. Willfried F. Feuser. New York: Monthly Review Press.

Zegeye, Abe, Leonard Harris, and Julia Maxted. 1991. *Exploitation and Exclusion: Race and Class in Contemporary US Society*. London: Hans Zell Publishers.

Zimra, Clarisse. 1990. *Out of the Kumbla: Caribbean Women and Literature*. Trenton, NJ: Africa World Press.

Zuberi, Tukufu. Forthcoming (2000). "Social Statistics and Race: Problems in Population Analysis." *Annals of the American Academy of Social and Political Science*.

CPSIA information can be obtained
at www.ICGtesting.com
Printed in the USA
BVOW06s0233240817
492979BV00006B/12/P